The Sacraments
Francis J. Hall (1857-1932)

Printed by Longmans, Green & Co., New York, 1921
Book-scan by GoogleBooks

 Nashotah House Press

A Nashotah House Press facsimile re-print
2013

Cover photo courtesy of
The Christoph Keller, Jr. Library,
General Theological Seminary

Photograph of Francis Joseph Hall
taken by Rockwood Photography, New York, 1890
held at Portraits of Faculty at the General Theological Seminary,
Special Collections, BV4070 .G475

Book Design by Ben Jefferies

THE SACRAMENTS

THE SACRAMENTS

BY THE
REV. FRANCIS J. HALL, D.D.
PROFESSOR DOGMATIC THEOLOGY IN THE GENERAL THEOLOGICAL
SEMINARY, NEW YORK CITY

LONGMANS, GREEN AND CO.
FOURTH AVENUE & 30TH STREET, NEW YORK
39 PATERNOSTER ROW, LONDON
BOMBAY, CALCUTTA, AND MADRAS
1921

Dedicated
TO THE
BLESSED MEMORY
OF
PETER LOMBARD
WHOSE WORK IT WAS TO CRYSTALLIZE
THE DEFINITION AND ENUMERATION OF
SACRAMENTS IN CATHOLIC THEOLOGY

PREFACE

THIS volume is very closely related to the previous one; for the Church, its ministry and its sacraments make up in interconnected order one appointed working system of the new covenant — based, indeed, upon Christ's redemption, but constituting the immediate machinery of the quickening, saving and sanctifying dispensation of grace through which the benefits of Christ's mediation are conveyed to us. The two volumes really have one subject, *The New Covenant*, constructively treated in relation to the more fundamental mysteries discussed in earlier volumes.

The criticism has been made that proportion has been violated in assigning only two of these ten volumes to this large subject. The writer has expected such criticism; and, if he had been controlled by the relative amount of attention which for various reasons our pastors rightly give to teaching concerning the Church, its ministry and its sacraments, and by the number of controversial questions involved, he would have assigned a larger share of his space to these subjects.

But the purpose of this series is to supply, what has not been produced heretofore in Anglican literature, a large constructive and positive exhibition of the whole range of revealed doctrine in connected order. The constructive aim has dominated; and the

PREFACE

practical need which the writer has had in view has been to promote among Anglican priests a fuller study of the great series of fundamental doctrines which furnish the interpretative background and safeguarding premises of sound sacramental teaching. The lack of serious study of constructive theology among Anglicans is a source of grave danger. It explains much of the shallowness and unconvincing quality of many current sacramental monographs. They lack background.

A patient student will see that threads of ecclesiastical and sacramental teaching run through the whole series, as they should do in a constructive work of this kind. These two volumes, therefore, complete and bring to articulate conclusion much previous discussion. They do not contain all of the writer's treatment of their subject-matters, but are constructively developed as following upon much previous argument. The cross references to preceding volumes will serve to confirm this statement.

The writer is very greatly indebted, in producing these two volumes, to several exceedingly valuable and trustworthy works by Dr. Darwell Stone, which have materially facilitated his labour, and have enabled him to avoid some mistakes in the history of Eucharistic doctrine.

It is hoped, after this series is completed, to prepare a treatise of *Moral Theology*, having the joint authorship of Dr. F. H. Hallock of Seabury Divinity School and the present writer.

CONTENTS

CHAPTER I

BAPTISM

PART I. *Introductory*

		PAGE
§ 1.	New Testament landmarks	1
§ 2.	Ecclesiastical landmarks	4
§ 3.	Antecedent truths	7
§ 4.	The covenant status of the baptized	10

PART II. *Benefits*

§ 5.	Incorporation and adoption	13
§ 6.	Regeneration	15
§ 7.	Remission and justification	19
§ 8.	Character and sacramental capacity	22

PART III. *Incidental Matters*

§ 9.	The operation and gift of the Holy Spirit	24
§ 10.	The necessity of Baptism	28
§ 11.	Infant Baptism	30
§ 12.	Lay Baptism. Membership in the Church	33

CHAPTER II

CONFIRMATION

PART I. *Introductory*

§ 1.	In the New Testament	38
§ 2.	In the ancient Church	41
§ 3.	Sixteenth-century departures	44
§ 4.	Delay in the time of Confirmation. Its cause and results	45

CONTENTS

Part II. *Benefits*

		PAGE
§ 5.	Gift of the Holy Spirit	48
§ 6.	The sevenfold gifts	51
§ 7.	Character	56
§ 8.	Practical value and purpose	57

Part III. *Questions*

§ 9.	Need and obligation	61
§ 10.	Prescribed age	63
§ 11.	Catechetical preparation	65
§ 12.	Religious education at large	66

CHAPTER III

THE HOLY EUCHARIST IN HISTORY

Part I. *Biblical*

§ 1.	In the Old Testament	69
§ 2.	Christ's discourse at Capernaum	72
§ 3.	The institution	75
§ 4.	Apostolic practice and teaching	79

Part II. *Patristic and Mediæval*

§ 5.	The Eucharistic gift in patristic thought	83
§ 6.	Patristic assertions of the Eucharistic sacrifice	88
§ 7.	Mediæval controversies as to the gift	90
§ 8.	The Eucharistic sacrifice in mediæval thought	94
§ 9.	Minor controversies between Easterns and Westerns	97

Part III. *Modern*

§ 10.	Causes of ancient peace and later divergences	101
§ 11.	Sixteenth-century departures	104
§ 12.	Official Anglican doctrine	107
§ 13.	Unofficial Anglican developments	112

CONTENTS

CHAPTER IV

THE EUCHARISTIC GIFT

PART I. *The Mystery of Identification*

		PAGE
§ 1.	The "form of sound words"...............	114
§ 2.	Ascending affirmations of faith...........	117
§ 3.	The Eucharistic state of the Body and Blood.....	120
§ 4.	Their numerical identity.................	123

PART II. *The Mystery of Conversion*

§ 5.	"Become the Body and Blood"............	126
§ 6.	Development and motive of transubstantiation terminology........................	129
§ 7.	How we are to regard this terminology.........	131
§ 8.	Twofold description of the sacrament..........	134

PART III. *The Mystery of Presence*

§ 9.	Christ present personally, but as touching His Body and Blood......................	137
§ 10.	Adjective descriptions of the presence..........	139
§ 11.	Manner of the presence..................	141
§ 12.	The doctrine of concomitance..............	144

CHAPTER V

THE EUCHARISTIC SACRIFICE

PART I. *Arguments*

§ 1.	Religion requires sacrifice................	147
§ 2.	Continuity with the old covenant............	150
§ 3.	New Testament witness.................	152
§ 4.	Ecclesiastical witness...................	156

CONTENTS

Part II. *Its Constructive Place*

		PAGE
§ 5.	In divine dispensations at large	159
§ 6.	In relation to the Cross	162
§ 7.	In relation to the heavenly priesthood	163
§ 8.	One sacrifice in time and space	166

Part III. *Its Description*

§ 9.	Wherein sacrificial	168
§ 10.	Descriptive terms	171
§ 11.	In relation to bloody offerings	174
§ 12.	As primary form and synthesis of worship	176

CHAPTER VI

BENEFITS OF THE EUCHARIST

Part I. *How Received*

§ 1.	Through the *res*, and with each kind	178
§ 2.	Spiritually by faith	180
§ 3.	Three subjective conditions	182
§ 4.	Two Ecclesiastical prerequisites	184

Part II. *Their Nature*

§ 5.	Sacrificial	188
§ 6.	Spiritual nourishment	190
§ 7.	Sanctification and cleansing	192
§ 8.	Communion with God — *via unionis*	194

Part III. *Incidental Privileges*

§ 9.	Communion with the faithful — sacrament of unity	196
§ 10.	Spiritual communion	198
§ 11.	Objective worship	200
§ 12.	Devotions before the reserved sacrament	205

CONTENTS

CHAPTER VII

PENANCE

PART I. *Its History*

	PAGE
§ 1. Definition and biblical development	211
§ 2. Ecclesiastical developments	214
§ 3. Sixteenth-century departures	217
§ 4. Anglican doctrine	219

PART II. *Its Theology*

§ 5. Repentance apart from this sacrament	223
§ 6. Special benefits	226
§ 7. Nature and limits of the power of absolution	229
§ 8. Parts of repentance: satisfaction	232

PART III. *Certain Details*

§ 9. Contrition and attrition	235
§ 10. Confession	238
§ 11. The seal	240
§ 12. Questions	243

CHAPTER VIII

HOLY ORDER

PART I. *Introductory*

§ 1. Definition. Recapitulation as to the Church's ministry	246
§ 2. Ancient and mediæval developments	248
§ 3. Sixteenth-century departures	252
§ 4. Anglican doctrine and Orders	255

CONTENTS

Part II. *Exposition*

		PAGE
§ 5.	Sacramental nature of Holy Order	257
§ 6.	*Gratia gratis data* and character	259
§ 7.	*Gratia gratum faciens*	261
§ 8.	Mission and jurisdiction	263
§ 9.	Habitual and actual, spiritual and coercive jurisdiction	265
§ 10.	The several functions of bishops, priests and deacons	267

CHAPTER IX

HOLY MATRIMONY

Part I. *Introductory*

§ 1.	Marriage and Holy Matrimony defined. Paramount obligations	271
§ 2.	Three stages of Marriage in sacred history	273
§ 3.	Church doctrine and practice	276
§ 4.	Sacramental nature of Holy Matrimony	279

Part II. *Essentials and Obligations*

§ 5.	Lawful union and Baptism of both parties	281
§ 6.	Pre-marital obligations	284
§ 7.	Mutual obligations in Matrimony	286
§ 8.	Parental obligations of the married	290
§ 9.	Religious obligations in Matrimony	292

Part III. *Impediments*

§ 10.	Nullifying impediments	294
§ 11.	Non-nullifying impediments	299
§ 12.	Complex relations involved	300
§ 13.	Divorce	301

CONTENTS

CHAPTER X

UNCTION OF THE SICK

PART I. *Introductory*

		PAGE
§ 1.	In the New Testament	307
§ 2.	In the ancient Church	310
§ 3.	Mediæval developments	312
§ 4.	In the Anglican reformation	313

PART II. *Expository*

§ 5.	Sacramental status	317
§ 6.	Physical benefit	320
§ 7.	Spiritual benefit	324
§ 8.	Occasions and frequency	327
§ 9.	Need of revived use	329

THE SACRAMENTS

CHAPTER I

BAPTISM

I. *Introductory*

§ 1. In commissioning His Apostles our Lord said, "Go ye . . . and make disciples of all the nations, baptizing them into the name of the Father and of the Son and of the Holy Ghost."[1] Elsewhere He had taught that Baptism was to be the necessary condition of entrance into the Kingdom of God and an instrument of new birth of the Spirit. "Except a man be born of water and the Spirit, he cannot

---

[1] St. Matt. xxviii. 19. On the genuineness of the text and of the baptismal commission, see A. Plummer, *in loc*. The requirements for valid Baptism are considered in *The Church and the Sacramental System*, ch. x. § 6.

On Baptism in general, see Darwell Stone, *Holy Baptism* (contains a mine of patristic and later references, pp. 218–292); E. B. Pusey, *Doctrine of Holy Baptism* (formerly *Tracts for the Times*, No. 67); M. F. Sadler, *Second Adam and the New Birth; Sacrament of Responsibility;* and *Church Doctrine, Bible Truth;* A. P. Forbes, E. C. S Gibson, E. H. Browne, E. T. Green and E. J. Bicknell, *Thirty-Nine Arts.*, XXVII; C. S. Grueber, *Sacrament of Regeneration;* The Encyclopedias, *q.vv.;* St. Thomas, *Summa Theol.*, III. lxvi-lxx; Wilhelm and Scannell, *Manual of Cath. Theol.*, vol. II. pp. 379–392; Jos. Pohle, *The Sacraments*, vol. I. pp. 204–275. These works will usually be designated in the refs. of this chapter by their authors' names only.

enter into the Kingdom of God."[1] The Baptism of John the Baptist was not that of the Holy Ghost, not Christian Baptism, but that of repentance.[2] Yet our Lord, who needed no repentance, submitted to it, saying, "Thus it becometh us to fulfil all righteousness."[3] The explanation seems to be that Baptism was to be obligatory in His Kingdom as an element of its righteousness. To these passages should be added the language ascribed to Christ in the supplement of the second Gospel, "He that believeth *and is baptized* shall be saved."[4] Clearly our Lord instituted Baptism to be the necessary initial rite for all who would enter the Kingdom, and the instrument of regeneration by the Spirit. This fact abundantly justifies the emphasis placed upon it in apostolic teaching and in subsequent catholic doctrine.

The contents of apostolic teaching will be indicated in the rest of this chapter. It seems well, however, to give here the principal direct statements and allusions *ad rem*, with the reminder that the large number of passages which declare or imply that Christians — that is, the baptized — are all subjects of grace, saints, elect, members of Christ and so forth,[5] cannot rightly be disregarded in ascertaining the New Testament doctrine of Baptism.

1. Acts ii. 38-39: "Repent ye, and be baptized every one of you in the name of Jesus Christ unto the remission of your

---

[1] St. John iii. 3-8.
[2] St. Matt. iii. 11 and parallels.
[3] St. Matt. iii. 15.
[4] St. Mark xvi. 16.
[5] Cf. § 4, below.

sins; and ye shall receive the gift of the Holy Ghost. For to you is the promise, and to your children," etc.

2. Acts xxii. 16: "And now why tarriest thou? Arise, and be baptized, and wash away thy sins."

3. Rom. vi. 1–4: "Shall we continue in sin that grace may abound? God forbid. We who died to sin, how shall we any longer live therein? Or are ye ignorant that all we who were baptized into Christ Jesus were baptized into His death? We were buried therefore with Him through Baptism into death: that like as Christ was raised from the dead through the glory of the Father, so we also might walk in newness of life," etc.

4. 1 Cor. xii. 12–27: "For as the body is one, and hath many members, and all the members of the body, being many, are one body; so also is Christ. For in one Spirit were we all baptized into one body. . . . Now ye are the body of Christ, and severally members thereof."

5. Gal. iii. 26–27: "For ye are all sons of God, through faith, in Christ Jesus. For as many of you as were baptized into Christ did put on Christ."

6. Ephes. v. 25–26: "Even as Christ also loved the Church and gave Himself up for it; that He might sanctify it, having cleansed it by the washing of water with the word."

7. Col. ii. 12–13: "Having been buried with Him in Baptism, wherein ye also were raised with Him through faith in the working of God. . . . And you being dead through your trespasses and the uncircumcision of your flesh, you, I say, did He quicken together with Him, having forgiven us all our trespasses."

8. Tit. iii. 5–6: "Not by works done in righteousness, which we did ourselves, but according to His mercy He saved us, through the laver of regeneration and renewing of the Holy Ghost . . . that being justified by His grace, we might be heirs according to the hope of eternal life."

9. 1 St. Pet. iii. 21: "Which also" [water] "after a true likeness doth now save you, even Baptism," etc.

BAPTISM

§ 2. The history of baptismal doctrine in the Church [1] shows a catholic consensus from primitive days that Baptism is a true instrument of regenerating and sanctifying grace and of remission of sin, employed by the Holy Spirit, divinely instituted, necessary for entrance into the Church and into the new covenant (as circumcision had been in the old covenant), making its subjects members of Christ and adopted children of God, and alone enabling them to receive the grace of other sacraments. The efficacy and importance of infant Baptism has also been generally maintained. It is true that in early ages there arose a practice in some quarters of putting off the reception of Baptism because of fear of the consequences of post-baptismal sin, but this practice was not generally approved of, and did not signify disbelief in the regenerative effect of infant Baptism.[2]

The first serious baptismal controversy grew out of the denial by St. Cyprian and others of the validity of schismatical Baptism;[3] and a parallel objection

---

[1] On which, see J. F. Bethune-Baker, *Early Hist. of Christian Doctr.*, ch. xx; K. R. Hagenbach, *Hist. of Christ. Doctrines*, §§ 72, 137, 191, 270, 303; J. Tixeront, *Hist. of Dogmas*, vol. I. pp. 366-376; II. pp. 161-168, 306-311, 397-407; III. 358-361; Hastings, *Encyc. of Religion*, s.vv. "Baptism (Early Christian)" and "Baptism (Later Christian)," informing articles but to be read with caution. Valuable collections of patristic passages are given by E. B. Pusey; and Darwell Stone (esp. chh. iv, ix and notes).

[2] See Darwell Stone, pp. 96-99.

[3] St. Cyprian, *Epp.* lxix-lxxv. Tertullian had taken similar ground: *De Bapt.*, xv. See C. J. Hefele, *Hist. of the Christ. Councils*, vol. I. pp. 86-87, 89, 98-116, 188-189, 430-431.

INTRODUCTORY

was made to the validity of heretical Baptism, especially in cases where the heresy vitiated the meaning of the trinitarian form. Within two centuries this and other questions concerning the minister of Baptism were settled, although without ecumenical action, by general sentiment and practice, especially in the West.[1]

It was St. Augustine's discussion of these questions in controversy with the Donatists that quickened this settlement. The Donatists revived the older objections to schismatical and heretical Baptism, and on puritan grounds rejected Baptism by unworthy ministers. Their premise was that nobody can give what he does not have, and they insisted that the ministers to whom they objected had not the Holy Spirit. St. Augustine met this difficulty by enunciating the catholic doctrine that the true minister in every sacrament is Jesus Christ, and that it is because of His agency that when the external requirements are rightly and seriously performed the promised operation of the Spirit is pledged. It is the Saviour's institution and promise, rather than the earthly minister's faith and worthiness, that makes the sacrament valid. This teaching has been determinative, ever since, of catholic thought on the subject.

Incidentally St. Augustine laid down and crystallized the further doctrine that those who receive Bap-

---

[1] The Western Council of Arles, 314 A.D., had decided against St. Cyprian's contention, and the 8th Canon of Nicea accepted the Novatian Baptism.

tism in heresy and schism, although validly baptized and obtaining the baptismal "character," receive the sacrament unworthily, and therefore are not benefited by it, unless and until they repent and submit to the Church. On such reconciliation the benefits of Baptism, previously suspended, are actualized. This is the doctrine of reviviscence, which presupposes that Baptism, or any sacrament conferring character, may not be repeated.

Mediæval development *in re* consisted of constructive and technical exposition of the doctrine of Baptism as St. Augustine had left it, rather than of any enlargement of it. But there gradually came about a general recognition that Baptism is valid when administered by any rational agent, even an unbaptized infidel or a woman, provided the intention of administering the Church's rite is manifested by serious performance of its requirements.[2]

The first formidable departures from the catholic doctrine of Baptism took place among the Protestants and Reformers of the sixteenth century. These departures were due mainly to the Lutheran stress upon justification by faith only, and to the Calvinistic doctrine of secret election. They were made easy by the rejection of catholic authority, and were defended by novel interpretations of New Testament passages on the subject, in which the important difference between

---

[1] Cf. *The Church and the Sacramental System*, ch. x. § 4, *fin*.
[2] Cf. *Idem*, ch. x. § 3; and § 12, below. See Darwell Stone, ch. ix and notes on pp. 261–266.

regeneration and conversion was disregarded. We have no space to describe these departures in detail;[1] but to-day the more orthodox Protestants regard Baptism as a sign and pledge of grace rather than as an instrument, and many treat it as merely a ceremony of dedication, edifying but not really necessary. These lower conceptions have induced much laxity in the method of administering the sacrament, with consequent uncertainty in many instances as to its validity. Fortunately the Anglican reformation left the catholic doctrine and method of Baptism plainly expressed and prescribed in the *Church Catechism* and in the appointed forms of ministration of this sacrament; and the twenty-seventh of the *Articles of Religion* agrees therewith.[2]

§ 3. For an adequate understanding of the place and function of Baptism in the dispensation of Christian grace it is needful to reckon with certain antecedent truths set forth in the New Testament.

(a) The first of these is the doctrine of the second Adam.[3] Men are social beings, and historically this

[1] See K. R. Hagenbach, § 270; Hastings, *Encyc. of Religion*, s.v. "Baptism (Later Christian)," pp. 400–406.

[2] See A. P. Forbes on art. xxvii; Darwell Stone, pp. 58–64. A useful Anglican catena is given in *Tracts for the Times*, No. 76.

[3] On which, see *Passion and Exaltation*, pp. 115–117; Archd. Wilberforce, *Doctr. of the Incarnation*, chh. ii–iii, x–xi; M. F. Sadler, *Second Adam,* ch. ii. The chief N. T. passages are Rom. v. 12–21; 1 Cor. xv. 20–22; Ephes. i. 3–11; Col. i. 12–22. The doctrine of our recapitulation in Christ for redemption and curative grace is seen in St. Irenæus, *c. Hær.*, III. xvi. 6; xviii. 1, 7; xxi. 10; xxii. 2–3; V. xiv. 1–2; and St. Athanasius, *de Incarn.*, 4–9.

appears in the genetic relation of all men to the first Adam. His loss of grace caused him to revert to unassisted nature's moral weakness and mortality, and it was this natural weakness and liability to death which he transmitted to his posterity. All have sinned, and in Him all die.[1] The method by which God saves us from these consequences, and renews our progress towards the destiny for which mankind was created, is in line with our racial solidarity in Adam. That is, a new race has been constituted, one that is bound together in a second Adam, whose redemptive victory over death and fulness of grace redounds to the regeneration, moral renewal and sanctification of His members.[2] In Christ shall all be made alive, for He is our quickening Spirit.[3] This is also incidental to making good the original and eternal purpose of God that Christ should have the preëminence, that in Him all fulness should dwell, and that in His Body He should be our Mediator with God, and the source to us of the grace of eternal life and glory.[4] To this end Christ identified Himself with us by taking our nature, and perfected His Manhood for saving and sanctifying functions by victory over sin, suffering and death, and by enthroning it in the heavens. There it becomes at once a perpetual oblation to the Father for us, and the source to His members of quickening, saving and sanctifying grace.[5]

[1] See *Creation and Man*, pp. 277–279 and ch. ix.
[2] Ephes. iv. 7–16. [3] 1 Cor. xv. 20–21, 45.
[4] Col. i. 18; ii. 9–10; 1 Tim. ii. 5; 1 St. John v. 11–12.
[5] Cf. *Passion and Exaltation*, pp. 105–106.

INTRODUCTORY

(b) The efficient cause of all that the Saviour doeth for us is the Holy Spirit; but the method of the Spirit's operation is conditioned by that of redemption, and is both corporate and sacramental, the entire mystery of redemption and grace being accommodated to human nature. Therefore it is in and from the glorified Manhood of Christ that the Spirit operates.[1]

(c) His initial act in the new dispensation, accordingly, was to bring the Body of Christ within human reach; and He did this once for all on the day of Pentecost, when He descended upon the apostolic Church and vitally united it with this Body. He thereby elevated it to a supernatural level, and made it to be the mystical Body of Christ. As such it is the abiding centre of the Spirit's work among men, and the earthly medium of our union with Christ and participation in His sanctifying grace.[2]

(d) It accords with such a dispensation, and meets the limitations of our composite nature, that the Spirit employs duly appointed human ministrations and sacramental instruments for incorporating individuals into the mystical Body of Christ, and for enabling them to participate in the grace therein afforded.[3] Baptism is the instrument of this incorporation and of bringing about the interior relation to

---

[1] Cf. *Idem*, pp. 292-293.
[2] Cf. *The Church*, ch. i. §§ 6-7, 10; and see Acts ii. 2-4, 33; Rom. v. 5-11; Ephes. ii. 18, 22; iv. 3-4.
[3] Cf. *Idem*, ch. ix. §§ 1-4.

Christ upon which the possibilities of sanctifying grace depend. It is for each soul the true beginning of eternal life.

§ 4. The design and the effects of Baptism are shown in the New Testament not only by the passages that deal directly with the subject, but also by the very numerous descriptions of the distinctive status, advantages and responsibilities of Christians; for it is by Baptism that we put on Christ and this mystery is presupposed in these descriptions.[1]

(a) It is assumed that the baptized, as being members of Christ, by virtue of this identification are Abraham's seed of promise and members of the new and better covenant made therewith in Christ.[2] Accordingly Baptism takes the place in the new covenant which was occupied by circumcision in the old, and in one passage is described as "a circumcision not made with hands."[3] In brief Baptism initiates men into the new covenant, and makes available all its privileges.

[1] That Christians are made so by Baptism seems to be clearly assumed in Acts ii. 37–41; viii. 12–13, 35–38; ix. 18; x. 44–48; Rom. vi. 1–4; 1 Cor. i. 13; Gal. iii. 27; Col. ii. 12; Heb. vi. 1–2; etc. The attempt to distinguish between believers and the Baptized in N. T. usage is modern and futile.

[2] Rom. iv. 9 et seq.; ix. 4–13; Gal. iii. esp. 27–29. Cf. St. Matt. iii. 9.

[3] Col. ii. 11–12. The N. T. writers discern several types of Baptism in the O. T., e.g. the ark wherein souls were saved through water (1 St. Pet. iii. 20–21) and the escape of Israel through the Red Sea (1 Cor. x. 1–2). The use of symbolical washings by the Jews, in particular of Baptism of proselytes, prepared their minds for the baptismal rite of the new covenant.

INTRODUCTORY

(b) The seed of promise constitutes the elect, and the baptized are addressed in apostolic letters as being the elect, chosen in Christ before the foundation of the world.[1] That they can miss the final destiny prepared for the elect is plainly indicated, and is the implied premise of many rebukes and warnings. They have to "work out" their "own salvation with fear and trembling," and to make their calling and election sure.[2] But all of them are designated as the elect. And the notion that by such description the apostolic writers were designating only such recipients of their letters as in fact would persevere to the end and be finally glorified is inconsistent with the warnings against falling away which they repeatedly give them.

(c) Again, the baptized are everywhere addressed as being endowed with saving grace.[3] They are repeatedly rebuked for their sins and backslidings, but nowhere is it either said or implied that their sins prove their not having received sufficient grace. It is abuse of grace or fall therefrom that is condemned; and the notion that they have still to wait for grace as for something not yet bestowed upon them has no

---

[1] Ephes. i. 4-5, 11. See Acts xiii. 48; Rom. i. 6; ix. 29-39 (in which St. Paul plainly treats Christians and the elect as equivalent terms); ix. 23-24; Col. iii. 12; 1 Thess. i. 4; ii. 12; 2 Thess. ii. 13; 2 Tim. i. 9; 1 St. Pet. i. 2. Cf. The English *Church Catechism*, "Who sanctifieth me, and all the elect people of God." Also Geo. S. Faber, *Primitive Doctr. of Election, passim*.

[2] Phil. ii. 12; 2 St. Pet. i. 10; St. John xvii. 12 (in which one of those given to Christ is said to have perished).

[3] E.g. St. John i. 16-17; Rom. vi. 1-7, 14-16; 1 Cor. iii. 16-17; Ephes. iv. 7.

New Testament warrant.[1] If they repent, it is their restoration, rather than their first reception of grace, that is promised.[2]

(d) The baptized are also addressed or described as saints, holy and sanctified,[3] and this in contexts of stern admonition for their wickedness.[4] They are saints as set apart to God and consecrated to a new life, the possibility of which has been afforded to them in Christ. But their sainthood is a vocation of self-assimilation to Christ, one that requires for successful pursuit an endurance of hardness which they are rebuked for shirking. The implication is that Baptism is a sacrament of peculiarly grave responsibility because of the sanctifying grace which it conveys, not less so because this grace is not irresistible.

In general, whatever of grace and privilege is attributed in the New Testament to Christians because they are Christian is to be understood as an effect of Baptism, for it is by Baptism that they become Christian or put on Christ, and enter the Kingdom of God in its earthly dispensation.[5]

[1] Cf. the rebukes given to the Corinthians, who are reminded of their gifts of grace, which they may receive in vain (2 Cor. vi. 1). The Galatians are not told that they have not had grace, but that they are fallen from grace, ch. v. 4. Cf. ch. i. 6.

[2] 2 Cor. vii. Cf. Darwell Stone, pp. 36-38.

[3] Acts ix. 13, 32, 41; Rom. i. 7; xvi. 15; 1 Cor. i. 2; 2 Cor. i. 1; xiii. 13; Ephes. i. 4; iv. 12; Col. i. 12; iii. 12; Heb. iii. 1; x. 10, 14; 1 St. Pet. ii. 9; St. Jude 3; etc.

[4] E.g. 1 Cor. vi. 1-2. On the scriptural meaning of holiness, see *The Church*, ch. v. § 7 and refs. there given.

[5] On the subject of this section, see M. F. Sadler, *Second Adam*, chh. vi-xi, *passim*.

II. *Benefits*

§ 5. Incorporation into Christ through union with His mystical Body, the Church, is the first in causal sequence of the benefits of Baptism, because it is upon the basis of an organic and interior relation to Christ that His grace is imparted to us by the operation of His Holy Spirit. As St. Paul says, our life "is hid with Christ in God," and St. John writes, "He that hath the Son hath the life; and he that hath not the Son of God hath not the life." Christ in us is the hope of glory, and "of His fulness we all received and grace for grace."[1]

That Baptism is the means employed by the Spirit in uniting us with Christ is clearly asserted in the words, "As many of you as were baptized into Christ did put on Christ";[2] and, in view of the biblical usage of treating the name of Christ as symbolical of Himself, the several descriptions of Baptism as "into the name of the Lord Jesus"[3] may be taken to teach the same truth. The baptized are addressed as "in Christ Jesus," as having "through Him" "access in one Spirit unto the Father," and as "builded together" in Him "for a habitation of God in the Spirit."[4] The doctrine of the second Adam already

---

[1] Col. iii. 3; 1 St. John v. 12; Col. i. 27; St. John i. 16. Cf. Darwell Stone, pp. 27–28.

[2] Gal. iii. 27. Cf. Col. iii. 9–10.

[3] Acts viii. 15; xix. 5. Cf. ii. 38; x. 48 where ἐν is used instead of εἰς.

[4] Ephes. ii. 13–22.

defined is of course in line with this. "As in Adam all die so also in Christ shall all be made alive."[1]

St. Paul's doctrine of the mystical Body,[2] prepared for by our Lord's teaching that He is the Vine of which His disciples are branches,[3] explains in a measure how Baptism unites us with Christ. We are "baptized into one Body,"[4] and this is the manner in which we are made members of Christ. For the Church, of which Baptism makes us members, is the Body of Christ.[5] Our growth in the Body and our growth in Christ are the same mystery, for from Christ "all the Body, being supplied and knit together through the joints and bands, increaseth with the increase of God."[6] Our Lord had taught that the unity of the Body enables its participants to share in a sense in the divine unity, and to be perfected.[7]

The identification with Christ which Baptism thus secures for us is so close that we are thereby made to share by grace in His sonship and become adopted sons of God.[8] The result is that the baptized are the seed of promise and joint heirs with Christ of eternal life.[9] We are also mystically identified with

---

[1] 1 Cor. xv. 22. Cf. pp. 7-8, above.
[2] Cf. pp. 9-10, above; *The Church*, ch. iii. §§ 5-8.
[3] St. John xv. 1-7.   [4] 1 Cor. xii. 12-13.
[5] Rom. xii. 5; 1 Cor. xii. 27; Ephes. i. 23, 30; Col. i. 24.
[6] Col. ii. 19. Cf. Ephes. ii. 21-22; iv. 16.
[7] St. John xvii. 21-23.
[8] St. John i. 12-13; Rom. viii. 29; Gal. iii. 26-27; iv. 4-7; Ephes. i. 5; Heb. ii. 11, 13. On adoption, see Hastings, *Dic. of Bible*, q.v.; *Cath. Encyc.* s.v. "Adoption, Supernatural."
[9] Rom. viii. 15-17; Gal. iii. 29; Tit. iii. 5-7; 1 St. Pet. iii. 7.

Christ in His death and resurrection,[1] so that He is our true vicar and representative — not as substitute but as summing us up in Himself and as our Head reconciling us in Himself to God.[2]

§ 6. Regeneration or new birth of the Spirit is the immediate effect of our union with Christ in His lifegiving Body. Our Lord said to Nicodemus, "Except a man be born of water and the Spirit, he cannot enter the Kingdom of God." With this should be compared St. John's statement, "As many as received Him, to them gave He the right to become children of God, even to them that believe on His name; which were born, not of blood, nor of the will of the flesh, nor of the will of man, but of God." And it is in the light of the truth that by Baptism we put on Christ that we should take the teaching that God gave unto us eternal life, and this life is in His Son. He that hath the Son hath the life; He that hath not the Son of God hath not the life." St. Paul says, "According to His mercy He saved us through the laver of regeneration and renewing of the Holy Ghost."[3]

As a factor in salvation from sin, regeneration is closely associated with moral conversion and the new

---

[1] Rom. vi. 3-5; Col. ii. 12-13.
[2] Ephes. i. 10. Cf. *Passion and Exaltation*, pp. 115-118.
[3] St. John iii. 3-8; i. 12-13; 1 St. John v. 11-12; Tit. iii. 5 (R. V. margin). Cf. also descriptions of the baptized as having received life: Col. ii. 13; iii. 3; 1 St. John v. 11-13; Gal. vi. 11. On baptismal regeneration, see *The Church*, ch. i. § 7; Darwell Stone, index, *q.v.*; M. F. Sadler, *Second Adam*, ch. iii and *passim*; *Cath. Encyc.*, *q.v.*; A. J. Mason, *Faith of the Gospel*, ch. ix. § 7.

manner of conduct whereby conversion manifests itself. The conduct of truly converted Christians is the proper fruit of regenerating grace, and affords the most convincing evidence of its reality and transforming power. Consequently regeneration and the sonship which it initiates are described in the New Testament in terms of its moral effects, of conduct. Thus St. John says, "Whosoever is begotten of God doeth no sin, because his seed abideth in him; and he cannot sin, because he is begotten of God. In this the children of God are manifest, and the children of the devil. Whosoever doeth not righteousness is not of God." St. Paul says, "As many as are led by the Spirit of God, these are sons of God."[1]

But these and other passages which are cited to prove that regeneration means conversion of heart and of conduct do not prove it. The difference between them appears in the above quotation from St. John, who clearly distinguishes between the seed which abideth in Christians and the freedom from sin of which it is the cause. Regeneration is the implanting of this seed, and in so far as we bring forth its fruit we cannot sin; although, as St. John bears witness in the same Epistle, "If we say that we have no sin, we deceive ourselves, and the truth is not in us."[2] The obvious explanation is that the fruits of regenerate life are mixed in our conduct with those of our carnal nature. And when St. Paul identifies the

[1] 1 St. John iii. 9-10; Rom. viii. 14 (Cf. vi. 1-7).
[2] 1 St. John i. 8-10.

sons of God by their being led by the Spirit of God, he simply accentuates in a vivid way the fact that such following of the Spirit is the proper manifestation of our being sons of God — not that every son of God acts consistently with his sonship. This interpretation is necessary if St. Paul is consistent with himself, for he is frequently found rebuking the unspiritual conduct of those whom he addresses as participating by grace in Christ's sonship. The determinative reason why we cannot identify regeneration with conversion or moral change of heart is that regeneration is taught in the New Testament to be an effect of Baptism,[1] and it is a patent fact of experience that that sacrament does not of itself normally cause conversion. The baptized are treated as the regenerate both in the New Testament and in the teaching of the Catholic Church of every age.[2]

Using a certain analogy, and appropriating to spiritual things a term of natural science, we may describe regeneration as a "biological" rather than a moral change, one which is brought about by the infusion of a new germ or seed, derived from the life-giving Manhood of Christ and through the operation of the Spirit. This seed supplies the dynamic of the righteousness of converted Christians; but it can

---

[1] St. John iii. 5; Tit. iii. 5.
[2] Darwell Stone, ch. iv and pp. 231–240; E. B. Pusey, *passim*. Cf. the language prescribed in the Anglican Prayer Books to be used by the minister after baptizing, "Seeing now . . . that *this child* is regenerate," etc.

and often does, fail to produce righteousness because of failure of its recipients to coöperate with the enabling grace which it affords. Changing the figure, Baptism makes us branches of the true vine,[1] members of Jesus Christ, and by virtue of this result the life-sap of the vine quickens us, also purging us so that we may be fruitful. But the branches may none the less remain unfruitful, and finally be cast out for burning. It is our grafting in, and our being made channels of the life-giving sap of the vine, that represents our regeneration. Our fruitfulness in a new righteousness is intended to follow, but is not the same thing with regeneration.

In the spiritual "biology" of which we speak, three mysteries stand out in vital sequence. The first of these is the resurrection of our Lord, by which His Manhood was carried successfully through death that it should become the seat and source of human immortality.[2] The second is that of Baptism, by which our Lord's resurrection life is germinated in us by our incorporation into His Body. The third is our own resurrection in that body which in Baptism begins to grow in us, and our participation in the immortality of Christ. St. Paul's mind travels backward and forward in these mysteries,[3] and baptismal regeneration cannot be rightly understood except in

---

[1] St. John xv. 1-6.
[2] 1 Cor. xv. 20-22.
[3] Rom. vi. 1-11; viii. 11; 2 Cor. v. 4; Ephes. ii. 1-6; 2 Tim. i. 10. Cf. 1 St. Pet. i. 3-5, 23.

such a context. Furthermore our regeneration is the nucleus of a larger regeneration of the cosmos in a new heaven and earth, for we are begotten of God in order to be "a kind of firstfruits of His creatures."[1]

§ 7. By consecrating us to God in Christ, and by making us sharers in the purifying life of Christ's Body, Baptism initiates our enjoyment of sanctifying grace, of remission and cleansing and of the whole series of graces which the Church's sacraments afford and which regeneration enables us to receive.

By Baptism itself our sins are remitted,[2] that is, if and when we fulfil the conditions of faith and repentance.[3] This is so because we are baptized into Christ's death, that like as He was raised from the dead, we also might walk in newness of life, our old man being crucified with Him "that the body of sin might be done away, that so we should no longer be in bondage to sin."[4] Baptism is the fountain which Zechariah predicted would be opened for sin and uncleanness in the day of the Messiah.[5] And the fact that it is prescribed by Christ as a means of salva-

[1] St. James i. 18. Cf. St. Matt. xix. 28.
[2] On baptismal remission, see Bishop Pearson, *Apos. Creed*, fol. 368; J. J. Lias, *Nicene Creed*, pp. 306–310; E. C. S. Gibson, art. xxvii. pp. 625–627; St. Thomas, III. lxix. 1; Jos. Pohle, pp. 228–230; *Cath. Encyc.*, s.v. "Baptism," p. 268.
[3] Infants, who offer no barrier of either unbelief or actual sin, are obviously excepted; but when they come to years of discretion their continuance in sanctifying grace is dependent upon these conditions.
[4] Rom. vi. 3–6. Cf. Col. ii. 11–13.
[5] Zech. xiii. 1. Cf. Ezek. xxxvi. 25.

tion,¹ which can mean nothing else than salvation from sin, implies that it is a means of remission.

The direct teaching of the New Testament on this point is clear. St. Peter exhorted his listeners on the day of Pentecost to be baptized unto the remission of their sins; and Ananias said to the converted persecutor, Saul, "Arise, and be baptized, and wash away thy sins."² St. Paul himself tells the baptized Corinthians, "And such" [sinners] "were some of you: but ye were washed, but ye were sanctified, but ye were justified in the name of the Lord Jesus Christ, and in the Spirit of our God."³ In whatever sense we inherit Adam's guilt, and are by nature children of wrath,⁴ in this same sense original as well as actual sin is necessarily remitted; for God, "even when we were dead through our trespasses, quickened us in Christ (by grace have ye been saved) and raised us up with Him."⁵

In a passage quoted a few lines above,⁶ St. Paul couples justification with baptismal washing and sanctification, as involved in them; and Baptism is described in catholic theology as the instrumental cause of justification.⁷ This is not at all inconsistent

---

[1] St. Mark xvi. 16. Cf. Acts ii. 40–41, 47; xvi. 30, 33; Tit. iii. 5; 1 St. Pet. iii. 21.

[2] Acts ii. 38; xxii. 16.   [3] 1 Cor. vi. 11.

[4] The sense is symbolical, borrowed from the fact that by reason of Adam's loss of grace we are naturally prone to sin, which incurs God's wrath. See *Creation and Man*, pp. 277–279, 295–297, 310 (b).

[5] Ephes. ii. 3–6.

[6] 1 Cor. vi. 11. Cf. Rom. v. 18–21; viii. 1, 29–30; Tit. iii. 5–7.

[7] Cf. *Passion and Exaltation*, pp. 257–258; *The Church*, p. 263.

with our being justified by faith, for in any case it is by the grace of life, and a faith which does not involve Baptism is not the faith which St. Paul declares to be justifying. Baptism is the sacrament of faith. By Baptism we become children of God, and it is as children of grace that we are reckoned as righteous.[1] That is, Baptism affords the grace which makes justifying faith the inception of growth in righteousness. And God estimates us morally and spiritually at the value of the Christlike man which begins to grow in us when we are born anew of water and the Spirit. We are given a new footing. And that which our regeneration makes potential and incipient in us is reckoned from the outset, and as long as we continue in grace, as if fully actualized; for it will be thus actualized when our growth in grace is completed. The child is reckoned at the value of the man that is to be.[2]

Our regeneration is accomplished by Baptism *ex opere operato*,[3] and the character of sons of God thereby obtained is indelible. Accordingly, if we fall from grace, our repentance and restoration neither requires nor permits this sacrament to be repeated. But the moral benefits of Baptism which we are considering in this section depend upon subjective conditions of faith and repentance in all who have attained the

---

[1] Rom. iii. 24; iv. 16; v. 1-2; vi. 1-7; Gal. v. 4; Tit. iii. 7.
[2] Cf. *Creation and Man*, ch. x. §§ 9-10; *The Church*, ch. viii. §§ 6-8.
[3] On which phrase, see *The Church*, pp. 321-323.

years of moral discretion. In other words, like other sacraments, Baptism is a moral instrument; and its remissive, justifying and morally enabling benefits are morally conditioned — conditioned by our dutiful response to grace and coöperation with it. If this response is sinfully interrupted, these benefits are suspended. We are fallen from grace, or, when Baptism is unworthily received, we cannot begin to enjoy its benefits until we repent. Baptism is a "sacrament of responsibility" for the proper reception of, and persevering coöperation with, the grace which it conveys.

Many of St. Paul's admonitions to sinful Christians bear witness to their having fallen from grace; and the fact that they once had it, and that it is restored after repentance, is clearly implied.[1] This renewal of the beneficial operation of baptismal grace is called "reviviscence" in catholic theology. And the law of grace involved applies to the other sacraments which convey permanent character — Confirmation and Holy Order. It applies also to Holy Matrimony, which cannot be repeated between the same parties.[2]

§ 8. Baptismal "character" is an indelible seal[3] or

---

[1] On all which, see Acts viii. 13, 18–23; 1 Cor. iii. 16–17; v. 3–5; vi. 11–20; ix. 26–27; Gal. v. 2, 4, 19–21.

[2] On reviviscence, see *The Church*, p. 321 and refs. there given.

[3] 2 Cor. i. 21–22; Ephes. i. 13–14; iv. 30. Cf. 2 Tim. ii. 19; Revel. ix. 4. Although implicitly taught by earlier writers, the doctrine of sacramental character or *sphragis* was first clearly set forth by St. Augustine in connection with the teaching that to repeat Baptism

spiritual mark, which evermore differentiates the regenerate from the unregenerate. Because of it Baptism neither needs nor ought to be repeated; and when the validity of previous Baptism is in doubt, the hypothetical form is prescribed, for the avoidance of sacrilege. But, of course, even when such form is not resorted to — no hypothetical forms are provided for Confirmation and Holy Order, which also impress character — the intention not to repeat the sacrament is implicit in all normal ministrations of the Church. This consideration is to be borne in mind in estimating cases of unintentional re-baptizing.

The abiding nature of the baptismal seal carries with it a solemn warning. For, if the mark of regenerate sonship glorifies those who are faithful to baptismal responsibilities, it increases the dishonour and shame of those who fall from grace and are lost. A withered branch of the vine is still visibly a branch and this fact accentuates the significance of its withered state, even when it is cut off.

The possession of baptismal character is the sign of sacramental capacity — of capacity to receive the sanctifying grace of other sacraments that are provided for the equipment and nourishment of God's children and for the other ends for which the sacra-

---

is sacrilegious. *Epis.* clxxiii. 3; clxxxv. 23; *Contr. Epis. Parmen.*, ii. 29. On character, see P. Pourrat, *Theol. of the Sacraments*, pp. 215–255 *et passim* (patristic and mediæval developments); St. Thomas, III. lxiii, lxvi. 9; Darwell Stone, pp. 93–95; *Cath. Encyc.*, *q.v.*; *Concil. Trid.*, Sess. VII. can. 9; Jos. Pohle, pp. 89–95.

ments have been instituted. All sanctifying grace is derived by us from the Body of Christ. Accordingly, the antecedent condition of our enjoyment of such grace is our incorporation into the Body, which is accomplished by Baptism. Sanctifying grace is applicable only to one who has become the child of God by adoption and grace. Just as one must first be born in order to receive natural gifts, so one must be born anew of water and the Spirit in order to receive supernatural gifts. Entrance into the order of life which is involved is the presupposition of receptivity of any advantages that pertain thereto. So it is that whatever other conditions may be imposed upon those who would receive particular sacraments, in every case, and in every part of the Catholic Church, Baptism is required as the enabling antecedent.

III. *Incidental Matters*

§ 9. The part of the Holy Spirit in Baptism has to be reckoned with. As is the case with other sacraments, the effects of its ministration cannot be explained by the natural efficacy of the visible instrument employed. Washing with water is indeed a fitting symbol of cleansing from sin, but no physical washing can of itself do duty for such cleansing, which is distinctly supernatural. And because it is this, its achievement exceeds the personal power of any human agent in the mystery. This disparity between the visible agency and sign employed and the effects brought to pass compels us, if we accept the New Testament and catholic doctrine that Baptism "effects what it figures," to receive the further teaching that the Holy Spirit operates in Baptism. To His operation is due the efficacy of this and of every Christian sacrament; and the fact that He operates sacramentally, with the use of appointed outward signs and ministerial agents, is part of God's merciful accommodation of the dispensation of grace to human nature and to our limitations.[1]

Christian Baptism is distinguished from the Baptism unto repentance of the Baptist as being of the Holy Spirit, and this description is reënforced in various ways. The Baptist himself said, "I indeed baptize you with water unto repentance; but He that cometh after me ... He shall baptize you with the Holy Ghost and with fire."[2] There is, of course, an allusion here to the pentecostal descent of the Spirit;[3] but neither Christ nor His Apostles confined the idea of Baptism of the Spirit to this event. Our Lord declared that "Except a man be born of water and the Spirit, he cannot enter into the Kingdom of God." St. Peter applied the Baptist's prophecy to the case of Cornelius, and promised "the gift of the Holy Ghost" to all who should be baptized. St. Paul teaches also that "in one Spirit were we all baptized into one body ... and were all made to drink of

[1] Cf. *The Church*, ch. ix. §§ 1-4.
[2] St. Matt. iii. 11. Cf. St. Mark i. 8; St. Luke iii. 16; St. John i. 33.
[3] Cf. Acts i. 5.

one Spirit."[1] In these and other New Testament passages two particulars appear: the Spirit's efficient operation, and some kind of reception of the Spirit by those who are baptized.

(a) The Spirit is the giver of life,[2] and His method of life-giving is to incorporate us by Baptism into the Body of Christ,[3] wherein the vital seed that is in Christ germinates in us and produces the various effects of sanctifying grace that have been indicated in previous sections. Baptismal regeneration and washing is therefore described as the "renewing of the Holy Ghost," and it is in the Spirit that our incorporation is our being "builded together for a habitation of God."[4] In this building by the Spirit we are washed, sanctified and justified; and are "sealed with the Holy Spirit of promise."[5]

(b) We also become "a temple of God" in whom the Spirit "dwelleth."[6] That is, in some sense the Spirit is given to us in Baptism. The most obvious interpretation of St. Peter's promise that those who were baptized should "receive the gift of the Holy Ghost"[7] connects the gift with Baptism, although the reference may be to the laying-on-of-hands, which in apostolic days was performed immediately after Baptism. But even if we suppose St. Peter to

---

[1] St. John iii. 5; Acts xi. 16; ii. 38; 1 Cor. xii. 13.
[2] Rom. viii. 2.   [3] Cf. § 5, above.
[4] Tit. iii. 5; Ephes. ii. 22.
[5] 1 Cor. vi. 11 (Cf. 2 Thess. ii. 13); Ephes. i. 13 (Cf. iv. 30; 2 Cor. i. 22).
[6] 1 Cor. iii. 16; vi. 19.   [7] Acts ii. 38.

refer to Confirmation, it is practically impossible, in view of the general effects of Baptism as described in the New Testament, to suppose that the Spirit is in no sense bestowed in Baptism. By that sacrament we put on Christ and become members of the Body in which the Spirit dwells. We thus come to be in the Spirit and are His temple.

Yet we are distinctly told that certain who had been baptized had not previously to their Confirmation received the Holy Ghost.[1] Such teaching cannot reasonably be interpreted in terms of quantity, as if the Holy Spirit were given to some extent in Baptism and more abundantly in Confirmation. If the Spirit Himself is given at all, He must surely be given entirely. There is no more or less in His Person. The difference must lie in the sense in which, or the purpose for which, the Spirit is given in each case. Scripture does not afford definite teaching on this point, but we may gather from its various allusions, and from the analogy of the Spirit's bestowal upon Christ's own Manhood, that, while we receive the Spirit in Baptism in so far as we are thereby *brought into Him* and become subjects of His sanctifying operations, we do not until Confirmation receive Him as a *formal and objective gift*, and for our ordination to the common Christian priesthood.[2]

[1] Acts viii. 14–17. Cf. xix. 1–6.

[2] See ch. ii. § 5, below. For the view that the Spirit is given in Baptism, see Darwell Stone, ch. v; A. T. Wirgman, *Doctr. of Confirmation*, Prefatory Note *et passim;* W. H. Hutchings, *Person and Work of the Holy Ghost*, pp. 180–182. For the other view, see A. C.

§ 10. That Baptism is necessary for salvation [1] is clearly apparent when we consider the benefits which depend upon the reception of this sacrament.

In previous sections it has been shown from the New Testament that without Baptism one cannot be brought within the Kingdom and covenant of God, that he cannot be incorporated into Christ and share in His sonship by adoption and grace, that he cannot be born anew of the Spirit and become an heir of eternal life, that he cannot be cleansed from sin and justified, and that he cannot be enabled to receive the various forms of sanctifying grace which are made available to the subjects of salvation in the Church. To say that salvation can be separated from these benefits is to speak foolishly; and a sacrament which is necessary for their enjoyment is plainly necessary for salvation.

And this conclusion is clearly taught by Christ when He says, "He that believeth and is baptized shall be saved; but he that disbelieveth shall be condemned." [2] St. Paul says, "According to His mercy He saved us, through the laver of regeneration and renewing of the Holy Ghost." And St. Peter declares, "Eight souls were saved through water, which also after a

---

A. Hall, *Confirmation*, ch. v; F. W. Puller, *What is the Distinctive Grace of Confirmation?* A. J. Mason, *The Relation of Confirmation to Baptism*, passim.

[1] On its necessity, see Darwell Stone, ch. viii; Jos. Pohle, pp. 238–253; A. J. Mason, Faith of the Gospel, ch. ix. §§ 5–7; *Cath. Encyc.*, s.v. "Baptism," IX–XI. Cf. *Church Catechism*.

[2] St. Mark xvi. 16. Cf. St. John iii. 5; St. Matt. xxviii. 19.

true likeness doth now save you, even Baptism." It is clearly taught by the same Apostle that every one who would be saved must "repent and be baptized . . . unto the remission of sins."[1]

The sum of the matter is that Baptism is necessary in two ways: (a) *necessitate medii,* as the means of entrance into the state of salvation; and (b) *necessitate præcepti,* by reason of Christ's command.

Is there then no hope of salvation for those who are given no real chance to be baptized? Such an inference is rash. The laws of the covenant bind us, and if we wilfully and carelessly disregard them, we cannot rightly expect to escape the consequences. But they do not set a limit to the resources of divine mercy; and God may find other than covenant means of saving those whose failure to be baptized is not wilful, without thereby undermining the laws of His Kingdom. Whatever is right to do for these unfortunates we believe that God will do.[2] Beyond this we cannot make assertions without presumption. But the doctrine that all the unbaptized will be eternally lost is neither declared in Scripture nor in accordance with enlightened Christian judgment.[3]

Two classes at least of the unbaptized — of those who have endured martyrdom for Christ's sake, and of those who have wished to be baptized but have

---

[1] Tit. iii. 5; 1 St. Pet. iii. 20–21; Acts ii. 38.
[2] Cf. 1 Tim. ii. 4.
[3] *Creation and Man,* pp. 352–353; *Passion and Exaltation,* pp. 158–163.

had no real chance — have been generally reckoned by Christian writers as among the saved. They are rhetorically described as having received a Baptism either of blood or of desire.[1]

We should not infer from the saving function of Baptism either that this sacrament completes the process of salvation or that no one can be lost who has been baptized. The New Testament teaches clearly that the baptized have to work out their salvation "with fear and trembling," and that they may fall from grace and be lost. By Baptism we are put in a state of being saved, but the condition of our coöperation with grace has still to be fulfilled. Baptism is the sacrament of responsibility; and post-baptismal sin is necessarily fatal, unless we repent and bring forth fruits worthy of repentance. In brief, Baptism is the inception, not the completion, of salvation.[2]

§ 11. The necessity of Baptism for salvation, coupled with God's will that all shall be saved, has made infant Baptism when practicable and prudent a matter of precept and the normal practice of every part of the Catholic Church from the earliest age.[3]

---

[1] *Cath. Encyc.*, vol. II. p. 266; D. Stone, pp. 112-113 and notes 2-4, pp. 258-260; St. Thomas, III. lxviii. 2 (cf. lxvi. 11-12).

[2] Cf. pp. 21-22, above. See Darwell Stone, pp. 206-208; M. F. Sadler, *Church Doctrine*, pp. 68-77.

[3] On infant Baptism, Wm. Wall, *Hist. of Infant Baptism;* D. Stone, ch. vii and pp. 254-258; M. F. Sadler, *Second Adam*, ch. iv; *Church Doctrine*, ch. iii. § 4; St. Thomas, III. lxviii. 9-11; Jos. Pohle, pp. 268-275.

It is true that no absolute proof exists that the Apostles baptized infants, although their baptizing entire households [1] affords strong presumptive evidence that infants were included. The fact that they are not mentioned is nonsignificant in view of the limitations of New Testament narratives.

These narratives are concerned with the preaching of the Gospel to adults, and the apostolic teaching that faith and repentance should precede Baptism ought to be understood in the light of this fact. These conditions are required in case of adult Baptism for the obvious reason that disbelief and actual sin not repented of offer moral barriers to the beneficial operation of baptismal grace, especially to remission of sins. But infants can offer no such barriers; and, unless some other obstacle exists in their case, no reason remains for excluding them from Baptism. None the less, the Church provides by the appointment of sponsors for the proper upbringing of baptized infants in the true faith and in readiness to repent of such sins as they may commit when they reach the years of discretion.

No other obstacle is known to exist. If infants can be born into the order of nature without exercising any conscious or volitional part in the matter, we may well believe that by the power of God they can also be born anew into the order of grace. And if they can incur the spiritual handicap of original sin previous to any moral experience of their own, they

[1] Acts xvi. 15, 33; 1 Cor. i. 16.

surely ought to be susceptible of deliverance therefrom at this stage of their existence. If the new birth meant their being converted, a change which presupposes conscious moral experience and volition, the case would be different. But, as has been shown,[1] regeneration has no such meaning. It is a mystery of spiritual biology, rather than of moral turning about; and its achievement does not depend upon conscious conditions in its beneficiaries. Moral conditions have to be supplied, indeed, when the baptized grow up, if they are to continue in grace; but the same is true of those who are baptized in adult years. Baptism is a sacrament of responsibility in any case for all who possess moral discretion, whether the age of such discretion is reached before or after Baptism.

Baptism is the rite by which we are admitted to the new covenant, filling the place which was occupied by Circumcision in the old covenant.[2] The fact, therefore, that Circumcision was by divine requirement administered to the infants of Jewish households[3] affords strong presumption that Baptism was divinely intended to be administered to the infants of Christian households. In the absence of contrary New Testament teaching, this presumption amounts to moral certainty.

And this conclusion is confirmed by the fact that Christ rebuked those who discouraged the bringing of little children to Him, declaring with emphasis

---

[1] In § 6, above.   [2] Cf. § 4 (a), above.
[3] Gen. xvii. 12; Levit. xii. 3.

that of such is the Kingdom of Heaven.[1] Indeed the Kingdom would seem to suffer impoverishment by their exclusion, and Christ expressly teaches the necessity of Baptism for entrance into it.

The rejection of infant Baptism, with nonpertinent exceptions, is comparatively modern. It is historically due to the rise of erroneous ideas, especially to the confusion of regeneration with conversion and the consequent misapprehension of the place and function of Baptism in the Christian covenant. If this error had not arisen, the modern rejection of infant Baptism by certain denominations would in all probability not have occurred.

The only circumstances under which Baptism can rightly be withheld from infants are two. In the first place, if the parents refuse consent, their authority cannot lawfully be overruled, and the responsibility rests upon them. In the second place, when no reasonable provision can be made for subsequent Christian upbringing, Baptism should be deferred; for under such circumstances the infant is more likely to be injured than to be benefited by baptismal regeneration. This condition does not apply, however, to the dying.[2]

§ 12. Two important questions remain to be considered.

(a) The first is concerned with lay Baptism, the

---

[1] St. Mark x. 13–16 and parallels. Cf. St. Matt. xviii. 1–10 and parallels; and Acts ii. 39.
[2] Cf. *The Church*, p. 327.

validity of which, as distinguished from its regularity, has been very generally accepted in the Church.[1] How can such acceptance be reconciled with the catholic doctrine that the Eucharistic sacrament cannot be validly consecrated except by a priest? Our first answer is this, that the judgment of the Church must determine our conclusion, whether we can fully understand its reasons or not; for ecclesiastical authority in a matter of this kind is the highest on earth, and no private judgment can avail against it.

But there are considerations which appear to confirm the judgment of the Church in this matter. Baptism is the Christian substitute for Circumcision, and the Holy Eucharist takes the place in the new covenant of the sacrificial rites of the old covenant. But Circumcision could be administered by any one, whereas the sacrifices had to be performed by duly appointed priests. Argument from analogy creates a presumption that a parallel difference will be found in Christian requirements for Baptism and the Holy Eucharist, and such is the fact.

Moreover, the analogy is not a superficial one. Circumcision and Baptism resemble each other in being the means of incorporation of individuals into the Church, and such incorporation is a private rather than a public function. It need not necessarily enlist action on the part of a corporate official of the Church. The point may be illustrated by a furthur analogy. Men become members of a nation by natural birth,

[1] *Idem*, pp. 325-326.

brought about by private action; but they cannot take part in the nation's corporate functions except by enlisting the action of civil officials having corporate and representative status. Similarly, men become members of the Church by spiritual birth, and the Church acknowledges the possibility of this being accomplished by private or lay Baptism; but they take part in the Church's corporate Eucharist only by making use of its official agents, its ministerial priests.

These analogies are only partial, of course, although they seem helpful; and they are *ex post facto*, depending in extent upon conditions that have deeper foundations in the will of God, as declared by the judgment of His Church. They do not, for instance, justify the resort to lay Baptism when an official minister of the Church can be had, for such Baptism is declared by the Church to be irregular, and only to be justified on the plea of necessity. But just as illicit natural birth is not less real birth because illegitimate, so the Church acknowledges lay Baptism to result in real spiritual birth in spite of its irregularity.

(*b*) The second question is this: Is it not precarious to say that every baptized person is a member of the Catholic Church, if we include among the validly baptized the adherents of religious bodies which have been organized in opposition to the Church? Making use of the political analogy, and admitting that the subjects of foreign nations include individuals who have been born of American stock, these individuals cannot be regarded as members or subjects of the American nation.[1]

The answer depends upon what we mean by membership of the Church. Every valid Baptism causes spiritual birth into the mystical Body of Christ,[2] and such birth cannot be undone by human action. Accordingly the fact that the person baptized renders no allegiance to the Catholic Church does not nullify his being a member — a dissentient one, no doubt — of the Body of Christ, which the Catholic Church is taught in Holy Scripture to be. The subject of a foreign nation who has been born of American stock is, and always continues to be, a member of the American *race*, in spite of his not being a subject of the American *nation*. It is not in his power to de-Americanize his racial status. Similarly one born into the race of the children of grace, the race which makes up the membership of the Body of Christ, belongs to that race whatever he may think or do to the contrary.

In the externally organized sense he may indeed be an alien, and be outside of the *ecclesia* called the Catholic Church. As in the case of one of American blood who is the subject of a foreign nation, his external relations may fail to coincide with his race. A schismatic baptized person is, and must continue to be, a Catholic by spiritual birth, although not a Catholic by allegiance and forensic status.

[1] On this question, see Darwell Stone, pp. 127-128, 264-266. He quotes St. Augustine, *De. Bapt. c. Don.*, i. 14.
[2] Cf. p. 14, above.

What is to be said of such cases? Surely this is to be said. The spiritual jurisdiction of the Church over all the baptized is part of God's revealed will, and disregard of catholic obedience is plainly contrary thereto.[1] An American can become the subject of a foreign nation without wrongdoing. But a baptized Christian cannot reject the catholic allegiance and be true to the responsibilities which his spiritual birth imposes upon him. He is a Catholic by new birth, and it is his duty to be a Catholic by full and dutiful obedience. God is merciful to the invincibly ignorant. But this in no wise alters the fact that schism from the Catholic Church is contrary to the will of Christ, and calls aloud for remedy.

[1] Cf. *The Church*, pp. 210-211.

CHAPTER II

CONFIRMATION

I. *Introductory*

§ 1. Confirmation[1] is the sacrament by which the sevenfold gifts of the Holy Spirit are conferred, consisting of the laying on of hands with prayer, and closely connected with Baptism, of which it is the complement.

The Gospels afford no evidence that the outward sign of this sacrament was instituted by Christ. But the gift of the Holy Spirit which in apostolic usage was conferred by the laying on of hands was clearly promised by Him.[2] Accordingly, in technical Western

---

[1] On Confirmation, see *The Church*, ch. ix. § 11 (constructive survey) and ch. x. § 7 (external requirements); Michael O'Dwyer, *Confirmation;* A. T. Wirgman, *Doctrine of Confirmation;* F. H. Chase, *Confirmation in the Apostolic Age;* P. Pourrat, *Theology of the Sacraments, passim;* Wm. Jackson, *Hist. of Confirmation* (these five are historical); A. C. A. Hall, *Confirmation* (the best comprehensive manual in English); C. S. Grueber, *Rite of Confirmation;* F. W. Puller, *What is the Distinctive Grace of Confirmation?* A. J. Mason, *The Relation of Confirmation to Baptism;* St. Thomas, III. lxxii; Jos. Pohle, *The Sacraments*, vol. I; The various Encyclopædias, *q.vv.* These works will usually be designated in this chapter by the author's names only.

[2] St. John vii. 37-39; xiv. 16, etc.; St. Luke xxiv. 49. Cf. the prophecies of outpouring of the Spirit upon all in the messianic

theology Christ is said to have instituted Confirmation *in genere* rather than *in specie*.[1] The descent of the Spirit upon Him after His Baptism in the form of a dove apparently foreshowed the gift of the Spirit to His members in Confirmation after their Baptism,[2] although it also constituted His ordination for His earthly ministry.

The actions and teachings of the Apostles in this matter seem to indicate that, either by express intimation from Christ or by definite prompting of the Spirit, they had previous warrant for treating the laying on of hands with prayer as the appointed means of eliciting the gift of the Spirit, and as intended to be the normal complement of Baptism. At all events, their belief in its divine sanction and efficacy was vindicated by the miraculous signs which at first followed upon its administration.[3] These signs gradually ceased when their evidential purpose had been achieved; and the cessation of extraordinary gifts was not treated as a reason either for abolishing the rite or for supposing that the gift of the Holy Spirit was no longer conferred by its means. On the

---

Kingdom; Isa. xliv. 3; lix. 21; Ezek. xi. 19; xxxvi. 25-27; espec. Joel. ii. 28-29. St. Peter cites Joel's prophecy and applies it to all: Acts ii. 16-18, 38-39.

[1] This distinction is explained by P. Pourrat, pp. 299-302. He prefers the terms "explicit" and "implicit."

[2] St. Mark i. 10-11 and parallels. See A. T. Wirgman, pp. 41-43, 49-53.

[3] Acts xix. 6. Cf. x. 44-46. That such gifts always followed is not clearly indicated. Cf. Acts viii. 17; ix. 17, where miraculous gifts are not mentioned. See A. C. A. Hall, pp. 15-21.

contrary the laying on of hands is reckoned, along with Baptism, as a "foundation," belonging to the "first principles" of the Christian system.[1]

In St. Peter's pentecostal preaching the gift of the Holy Spirit was treated as the immediate sequel of Baptism,[2] and Confirmation was in apostolic teaching and practice held to be the means for the reception of this gift. Therefore the Apostles habitually administered the laying on of hands as soon as practicable after Baptism.[3] Thus we have New Testament warrant for the catholic doctrine that Confirmation is the proper and normal complement of Baptism. But the Apostles clearly distinguished between the two rites, both in time and in their respective benefits; and the fact that individuals had not received the laying on of hands did not of itself prove that they had not been duly baptized.[4] The complementary relation of Confirmation to Baptism, however, appears in the fact that the Confirmed are described in the New Testament as sealed, a figure suggestive of completion of a previous mystery.[5]

In the outward sign employed by the Apostles Confirmation closely resembles the laying on of hands with prayer in the ordination of ministers; and the language of Christ in ordaining His Apostles teaches

[1] Heb. vi. 1-2.
[2] Acts ii. 38.
[3] Acts viii. 17-18; xvii. 17; xix. 6.
[4] Acts viii. 15-17. Cf. A. J. Mason, pp. 18-34.
[5] 2 Cor. i. 22; Ephes. i. 13. Cf. § 7, below. In Tit. iii. 5; 1 Cor. iii. 16, the two mysteries appear to be coupled together.

that the Holy Spirit is given in ordination.[1] It would appear, therefore, that Confirmation was treated by the Apostles as a kind of lay ordination, not confused at all with ministerial ordination, but somewhat analogous to it. And St. Peter's description of Christians in general as constituting a "royal priesthood" may reasonably be understood as presupposing their reception of Confirmation.[2]

§ 2. The question as to whether the Holy Spirit is first given in Confirmation or whether His indwelling is previously bestowed in Baptism [3] was not faced in the patristic period. In fact the precise distinction in this particular between the grace of Baptism and that of Confirmation has never obtained authoritative definition. The reason for patristic failure to determine the question was the fact that, in accordance with apostolic precedents, the two sacraments were administered together,[4] and the complementary relation of Confirmation to Baptism was more apt to be considered than its distinct nature and effect. The two rites were not, however, regarded as constituting one sacrament, for Baptism continued to be adminis-

---

[1] This indicates successive gifts of the Holy Spirit — not that the earlier gift in Confirmation is either unreal or in need of renewal, but that the Spirit is given in a new sense and for a ministerial office.

[2] 1 St. Pet. ii. 9. Cf. *The Church*, pp. 53-55, 59-63.

[3] Discussed in ch. i. § 9, above. On the ecclesiastical history of Confirmation, see M. O'Dwyer; A. T. Wirgman; P. Pourrat, *passim*; Wm. Jackson; Hastings, *Encyc. of Relig.*; A. Vacant, *Dic. Theol. Catholique* (arts. II-X), and *Cath. Encyc.* (II-V), *q.w.*

[4] E.g., Acts xix. 5-6.

tered separately when a proper minister of Confirmation was unavailable,[1] and the full validity of such Baptisms was acknowledged by all, for they were not repeated.

But there is abundant evidence that from the earliest period it was generally held and taught that Confirmation is a divinely appointed means of grace,[2] and that by it the Holy Spirit is bestowed for the full equipment and sealing of the baptized, the normal prerequisite of enjoyment of full Christian privileges. In no century of Christian history, and in no true part of the Catholic Church, has a denial of this doctrine been treated as consistent with an orthodox faith. The modern idea of Confirmation, as being merely a solemn form of acceptance of Christian obligations and of official reception into full standing in the congregation, would have been generally regarded in any previous age as heretical.

The technical phrase "generally necessary for salvation," has usually been applied only to Baptism and the Holy Communion. But the doctrine that Confirmation is a Christian "foundation,"[3] and that every baptized Christian is under covenant obligation to receive it when practicable, as needed for completion of his appointed equipment of grace, undoubtedly stands the test of the Vincentian rule. It

---

[1] As in New Test. days: Acts viii. 14-20.

[2] For patristic witnesses, see Wm. Jackson, ch. ii; A. T. Wirgman, chh. ii-iv.

[3] Heb. vi. 1-2.

has been held everywhere and always in the Catholic Church, with the general consent of the faithful. A rejection of Confirmation has ever been regarded as involving forfeiture of Eucharistic and other Christian privileges.[1]

The use of unction in Confirmation began very early indeed,[2] although some uncertainty exists as to whether in certain recorded instances it is connected with this sacrament or with Baptism only. So early is its use, and so obvious is its congruity with certain apostolic allusions to Confirmation, that some writers maintain its apostolic origin.[3] This seems very doubtful, however, in view of the silence as to its employment in every direct description of Confirmation in the New Testament. But the obvious symbolism of anointing with oil[4] secured its general and permanent adoption both East and West; and the imposition of hands gradually came to be a minor adjunct, theoretically preserved in the ritual of anointing, but widely reduced in fact to such imposition as may be supposed to be involved in anointing the forehead.[5] This development, in view of the extent of its eccle-

[1] Cf. §§ 4, 9, below, on the practice of admission to Communion before Confirmation.

[2] On the use of the chrism in Confirmation, see M. O'Dwyer, ch. iv *et passim;* Wm. Jackson, ch. iii. § II.

[3] So F. H. Chase, pp. 53–60. Cf. H. B. Swete, *Holy Spirit in the N. T.*, pp. 385–386. The N. T. passages used to support this view are 2 Cor. i. 21–22; 1 St. John ii. 20, 27.

[4] F. H. Chase, pp. 67–69.

[5] The different modern Roman views on the "matter" are given by M. O'Dwyer, pp. 148–161.

siastical sanction, may not be regarded as a nullifying change in the matter of Confirmation.[1] But for closer conformity to apostolic usage, the Anglican Churches since the reformation have abandoned unction in Confirmation [2] and have restored the full laying on of hands.

§ 3. The teaching of the Church as to Confirmation was assailed by Wycliffe and the Bohemians. The latter created a modified rite similar to that subsequently adopted by the Lutherans, which is merely a form of profession of faith and reception by laying on of hands into full privileges of Communion. The Reformers ultimately abandoned Confirmation altogether, although they still examine those who have been baptized in infancy when they come to years of discretion, and on their public profession of faith admit them to Communion. Both Reformers and Lutherans reject the catholic doctrine that Confirmation is a sacrament by which the Holy Spirit is imparted. They have also rejected the ministry through which alone, according to catholic doctrine, Confirmation can be validly administered, for they retain neither bishops nor priests in the catholic sense of these titles.

The Anglican Church carefully preserved Confirmation at the reformation, although with simplification of its ceremonial. The form adopted clearly

---

[1] Only such sacramental signs as have been expressly fixed by our Lord are immutable. See *The Church*, pp. 317–318.

[2] That is in its prescribed ritual. As a voluntarily employed ceremonial adjunct, it has not been forbidden.

implies a sacramental bestowal of the gift of the Holy Spirit. Evangelical influence, however, has led many Churchmen to cherish the Lutheran conception of Confirmation and to disregard the plainly implied sacramental teaching of the Prayer Book Order of Confirmation. This lower conception, tolerated though it be, has, of course, no authority. The name Confirmation signifies in the Church's Order not the confirmation of baptismal vows by the candidates which for edification is now added, but the laying on of hands administered, after apostolic ordinance, by the bishop, with prayer for the sevenfold gifts of the Holy Spirit. In brief, Confirmation means, according to the Prayer Book, an administration of fortifying and sealing grace.[1]

§ 4. In the ancient Church it was usually practicable to have those who were baptized confirmed at once by a bishop. But as the Church grew and episcopal jurisdictions enlarged this became increasingly difficult.[2] The problem was met in the East by delegating the administration of Confirmation to presbyters, with the provision that the oil employed should have been blessed for the purpose by a bishop. This custom had become fully established in the ninth century, and had begun in several regions much earlier.[3]

[1] See F. H. Chase, pp. 10–13; A. C. A. Hall, pp. 4–10. Many Church tracts combat the mistake in question.

[2] For the history of this subject, see Wm. Jackson, ch. iv; M. O'Dwyer, ch. viii.

[3] *The Apostolic Constitutions*, VII. 28, permit presbyters to confirm. See O'Dwyer, pp. 168–169.

In the West the Spanish Council of Toledo, 400 A.D., allowed presbyters to confirm, in the absence of a bishop, a concession which appears to have been withdrawn in the seventh century. St. Gregory the Great, after forbidding presbyters to anoint with the sacred chrism of Confirmation, reversed his prohibition for certain localities. In some instances presbyters were allowed to anoint but not to lay on hands. Pope Innocent III altogether forbade priests to confirm, and from this time a papal license, rarely given, has been necessary in the Roman obedience for presbyterial Confirmation. It can be seen, however, that the sacramental validity of Confirmation by a priest, when authorized to act by competent authority, is recognized. It was conceded by Pope Eugenius IV, at the Council of Florence, A.D. 1439, in his *Decree for the Armenians*, that for urgent reasons and by papal dispensation priests might administer the chrism of Confirmation.[1] But the Council of Trent reiterated the doctrine that a bishop is the sole "ordinary" minister of Confirmation.[2]

The result of this Western retaining of Confirmation in episcopal hands was to bring about an unavoidable separation in time between Baptism and Confirmation; and before the reformation it had become widely customary to confirm the baptized children at the age of seven. This separation was not willingly acquiesced in by ecclesiastical authority,

---

[1] H. Denzinger, *Enchirid. Symbolorum*, 592.
[2] *Idem*, 754, citing *Concil. Trid.* Sess. VII, *De Conf.*, can. 3.

INTRODUCTORY 47

and the practice of confirming infants was probably maintained in many portions of the West until the tenth century. The Easterns have continued the practice to the present time.

It has been a catholic custom to administer Communion to children immediately after their Baptism and Confirmation, and when Confirmation came to be delayed, in some cases apparently the Communion continued to be given immediately after Baptism without waiting for the delayed Confirmation.[1] In view of the catholic doctrine that Confirmation is the complement of Baptism, and therefore is an important part of full spiritual qualification for profitable reception of the Lord's body and blood, this was regarded as an abuse. Archbishop Peckham, of Canterbury, in his *Constitutions* of 1281 A.D., decreed that "No one who is not in peril of death shall be admitted to the Sacrament of the Body and Blood of the Lord unless he be confirmed or has been reasonably hindered from being confirmed."[2] This was subsequently made a rubric in the Baptismal Rite of the Sarum Manual, and the existing Prayer Book rubric is borrowed from it, "And there shall none be admitted to the Holy Communion, until such time as he be confirmed, or be ready and desirous to be confirmed."[3] The abuse in question has for a century and more become widespread in the Roman

---

[1] Because the children were "ready and desirous to be confirmed."
[2] W. Lyndewode, *Constitutiones*, etc., I. tit. 6.
[3] F. Procter, *New Hist. of the Book of Common Prayer* (revised by W. H. Frere), p. 606, n. 2.

Communion. But that it is even there regarded by authority as an abuse is clearly shown by its condemnation in 1897 by Pope Leo XIII, as "not in accordance either with the ancient and constant institution of the Church, or with the good of the faithful." [1]

Our modern Order of Confirmation,[2] which received its present expanded form in 1661, is adjusted to the established rule of postponing Confirmation to the time when the candidate "can say the Creed, the Lord's Prayer, and the Ten Commandments, and is sufficiently instructed in the other parts of the Church-Catechism set forth for that purpose," otherwise expressed as to "the years of discretion." The candidates are called upon in it to "renew the solemn promise and vow that ye made, or that was made in your name, at your Baptism." The purpose for which the Catechism is required to be learned before Confirmation is said to be "to the more edifying of such as shall receive it." And the ratification of baptismal vows is presumably designed to reëmphasize the complementary relation of Confirmation to Baptism, which has been obscured by the mutual separation in time of these sacred rites.

II. *Benefits*

§ 5. In the previous chapter the conclusions have been adopted (*a*) that is some sense the Holy Spirit

---

[1] A. C. A. Hall, pp. 94-95 (quoting from *The Guardian*, August 18, 1897, p. 1270).

[2] Its history is given by Procter and Frere, *op. cit.*, pp. 602-607.

is received in Baptism, inasmuch as by that sacrament we are incorporated into the Body of Christ wherein He operates, and become temples wherein He dwelleth; (b) that the formal and objective gift of the Holy Spirit is none the less to be connected with Confirmation rather than with Baptism; and (c) that this difference is not one of quantity of the gift, but of the sense in which the Spirit is given and of the purpose or effect of the gift.[1]

That the Holy Spirit is the proper gift of Confirmation is clearly indicated in the description of the Baptism and Confirmation of the first Samaritan converts. "Now when the Apostles which were at Jerusalem heard that Samaria had received the word of God, they sent unto them Peter and John: who, when they were come down, prayed for them, that they might receive the Holy Ghost: for as yet He was fallen upon none of them: only they had been baptized into the name of the Lord Jesus. Then laid they their hands on them, and they received the Holy Ghost." The same teaching is contained in the narrative of the Christian Baptism and subsequent Confirmation of certain disciples at Ephesus who had previously received only St. John the Baptist's Baptism of repentance.[2]

It has been shown that we ought not to confuse the gift of the Spirit with the miraculous gifts by which,

---

[1] In § 9, where refs. are given on p. 27, n. 2. They also cover the general subject of this section.
[2] Acts viii. 14–17; xix. 1–6.

for evidential reasons, it was often accompanied in the apostolic age. These demonstrations apparently were not always afforded even then; and their cessation was not regarded as bringing to an end the need and spiritual efficacy of the laying on of hands, which continued to be reckoned among the fundamentals of the Christian dispensation.[1]

In what sense is the Holy Spirit said to be given? Such language does not mean that the Spirit comes to be where He has previously been absent, nor that His effective energy gains entrance where it has previously been excluded. Neither the presence nor the operative power of the divine Spirit can be escaped from at any moment by any creature. He pervades all, and is everywhere continuously operative as efficient and perfecting cause of all that God doeth.[2] Even the wicked are subjects of His overruling power. And as the sunlight is not altered in glory and intrinsic virtue by the foulness of the things upon which it shines, so the Holy Spirit cannot be reduced in power and penetrative operation by the depravity of men. He is in everything, in each soul, because He is divine; and wherever He is He is unceasingly active and almighty.

For the Spirit to be given means His conferring upon those to whom He is said to be imparted a new and personally possessive relation to Himself, a relation carrying with it certain personal endowments of super-

---
[1] Heb. vi. 1–2. Cf. pp. 39–40, above.
[2] Psa. cxxxix. 7–12. Cf. *Creation and Man*, pp. 64–65, 68.

natural grace. The Christian is enabled by the gift of the Spirit to regard Him as in a real sense his personal property — that is, within the limits of the divinely intended purpose and benefit of the gift. This gift was bestowed upon our first parents in their original state of innocency, and was lost through sin; although the Spirit continued to operate within the souls both of them and of their posterity in the changed manners which the presence of sin required.[1] By means of Confirmation the restoration of the primitive gift is completed and sealed; the gift being restored under new conditions and upon the new basis of redemption, of Christ's priesthood in the heavens, of the mystical Body of Christ and of the fresh start which the catholic doctrine of justification describes.

To recapitulate: in Baptism, if there is a "gift" of the Holy Spirit, He is given for regeneration, remission, justification and sanctification. In Confirmation He is given for equipment and strength in the journey Godward, the gift exhibiting itself on sevenfold lines of endowment in relation to the several faculties or functions of the soul. The grace of Confirmation is complementary to that of Baptism.

§ 6. In prophecy it was said of the Messiah, "The Spirit of the Lord shall rest upon Him, the spirit of Wisdom and understanding, the spirit of counsel and might, the spirit of knowledge and of the fear of the

[1] *Creation and Man*, pp. 263-264, 281-282, 328-329; W. H. Hutchings *Person and Work of the Holy Ghost*, ch. ii.

Lord."[1] Citing another and related prophecy, our Lord claimed that the Spirit of the Lord was upon Him, because He anointed Him to preach the Gospel.[2] In several passages of the Apocalypse our Lord is represented as having the seven Spirits of God, a distributive personification of His spiritual equipment.[3] The reference plainly appears to be to the predicted endowments of our Lord's Manhood; for it is in the Manhood that He became the Messiah and by His humiliation unto death obtained the mediatorial glory of His heavenly rule and priesthood.

The formal bestowal of these gifts upon Christ, or His anointing, took place after His Baptism, when the Spirit descended upon Him under the form of a dove.[4] But He received them not merely for His own human perfecting and work, but also in order that His Manhood might become the medium and source of grace for the future members of His Body. From the mystical Body His grace flows into our souls in duly appointed ways. "Of His fulness we all received, and grace for grace."[5]

In this dispensation Confirmation is for us what the descent of the Spirit referred to was for Christ; and the gift thereby bestowed is rightly described by the Church in the sevenfold terms of its prophetic de-

[1] Isa. xi. 2. In the Septuagint and Vulgate a seventh item is given, the spirit of true godliness.
[2] Isa. lxi. 1; St. Luke iv. 17-21.   [3] Revel. i. 4; iv. 5; v. 6.
[4] St. Matt. iii. 16 and parallels. Cf. *Incarnation*, pp. 339-340 and refs. there given.
[5] St. John i. 16.

scription in the Book of Isaiah, as "the Spirit of wisdom and understanding, the spirit of counsel and ghostly strength, the spirit of knowledge and true godliness, and . . . the spirit of Thy holy fear."[1] As thus described, these gifts are clearly designed for the enlightening, strengthening and regulating of the several functional capacities of the soul, and for developing in us the virtues which pertain to Christian perfection, patterned after God in Christ.[2] We take them in what appears to be the logical order, psychologically regarded. Four of them are intellectual and the other three pertain to the will and the affections.[3]

(a) *Understanding* enables us to discern in a penetrating way the mysteries of the faith, or the truths which have been supernaturally revealed and which have to be spiritually examined. This and all the gifts of the Spirit are distributed in diverse proportions to individual Christians.[4]

(b) *Wisdom* also pertains to revealed truth, but has to do with its value as distinguished from its nature or precise content. This gift helps us to judge rightly as from the divine standpoint, and to discriminate by

[1] Isa. xi. 2-3, Septuagint and Vulgate. Cf. The Order of Confirmation in *The Book of Common Prayer*.

[2] Cf. Ephes. v. 1-2; St. Matt. v. 48; and see *Incarnation*, pp. 263-265 and refs. there given.

[3] On the sevenfold gifts, see *The Church*, p. 32; St. Thomas, I. II. lxviii; F. C. Ewer, *Operation of the Holy Spirit*, conf. iv (a very helpful popular expansion of St. Thomas); A. C. A. Hall, ch. x; W. H. Hutchings, *Person and Work of the Holy Ghost*, pp. 192-206, 244-247, 265-272.

[4] 1 Cor. xii. 4-11.

a kind of spiritual taste and qualitative estimate between truth and error. In particular it helps us to estimate the value of Christian evidence.

(*c*) The next two gifts are analogous to those of understanding and wisdom, but pertain to conduct and to the principles by which it should be governed. Thus *knowledge* is analogous to understanding, as helping to penetrative discernment, but to discernment of the moral bearings and applications of truth rather than to perception of truth in the abstract. It tells us, in short, how we ought to live in view of truth, treating the faith as a light which reveals our pathway, and discovering the principles and rules of the righteous and holy life in grace.

(*d*) *Counsel* is obviously the gift of a competent adviser. Like wisdom it pertains to judgment of spiritual values, but of moral rather than of theoretical values. It enables us to grapple successfully with the problems of daily life, and to determine correctly which of practical alternatives confronting us ought to be adopted, if we are faithfully to pursue our chief end in the light of truth and of the principles and laws of Christian love and duty.

So much for the intellectual gifts. By them the virtue of faith is developed and every faculty of cognition and judgment is perfected. The remaining gifts pertain to our other faculties — that of ghostly strength to the will, and those of true godliness and holy fear to the affections.

(*e*) *Ghostly strength* or spiritual fortitude pertains to

power of will and purpose in the battle of life. By it temptations are successfully resisted, and by it the principles and laws of the life in grace are faithfully and perseveringly adhered to amid the snares and difficulties of our earthly pilgrimage. It develops the supernatural virtue of hope, which is a habitual control of desire and purpose for the attainment of our chief end.

(*f*) *True godliness*, more clearly described as holy piety, quickens and develops love for our heavenly Father, and therefore for everything divine and sacred. It helps us to practice true religion with careful reverence, as drawing us near to God. But it also pertains indirectly to brotherly love, relating such love to the love of God, and thus converting the service which we owe to our fellow men into a higher, truer and more abidingly fruitful service. It enables us to perceive, with reasons which a Spirit-filled heart alone apprehends, that our highest and only perfect service to our fellows is to bring them to God. And this makes clear to us the determinative quality of Christian service in general and the openly Godward motive with which every beneficent work should be fulfilled.

(*g*) Finally, *holy fear* elicits and enhances loving anxiety to please God. It is fear, in that it consists of anxiety in apprehending the possibilities of failure. But the failure that is dreaded pertains to the task of pleasing God; and this dread is due to love for Him, which by the help of this gift becomes the ruling motive of all our conduct. Thus holy fear is not servile fear, or dread of hell torment; nor mundane fear, or dread of the world's judgment and treatment; nor even initial fear, or the dread of losing Heaven. It is an aspect of love, entirely unselfish and having reference to pleasing God.

These definitions of the sevenfold gifts, especially of the intellectual ones, are obviously more precise and restrictive than our experience of them justifies. But they bring into bold relief those aspects of them which afford determinative starting points for fuller study. In practice the gifts of the Spirit are not distributed into mutually exclusive compartments, but overlap. And the faculties which they elevate are not mutually separate, except in our description of them. But, in whatever way we may view the gifts in question, whether in complex and united working or in differentiating aspects, they plainly serve for the enhancement of our natural faculties in the pursuit of our supernatural chief end. Their subjective effect is to develop Christian souls in virtue, transforming their natural virtues by developing the theological virtues of faith, hope and love, and filling out the spiritual equipment of Christians for their Godward journey.

§ 7. Like Baptism Confirmation confers character;[1] that is, it affords to its recipient an abiding

---

[1] On character, see ch. i. § 8, above, where refs. are given. On the character of Confirmation, see St. Thomas, III. lxxii. 5; W. H. Hutchings, *op. cit.*, p. 253; Darwell Stone, *Outlines of Christ. Dogma*,

status and functional relation in the Body of Christ, and stamps the soul with an indelible seal agreeing therewith. We should not confuse this character with the sanctifying grace of Confirmation; for, unlike such grace, it remains in the wicked, who continue to be possessed of the spiritual mark and functional order which differentiates the confirmed from the unconfirmed, even when deprived of sanctifying grace because of sin. This deprivation continues until repentance affords the condition of that renewed action of grace which is called reviviscence.[1]

The character conferred in Confirmation is complementary to that imparted in Baptism. This does not mean that the two are not distinct, or that the sacramental character of an unconfirmed baptized Christian is lacking in determinateness and permanency. It means that without Confirmation the baptized child of grace cannot enter upon Christian manhood; and therefore that he does not attain the full status and functional power of a citizen of the Kingdom and of a member of the royal priesthood and of the faithful. The significance of this will be more fully indicated in the next section.

§ 8. We have seen that Confirmation is to be regarded as a divinely appointed means of sanctifying grace, complementary to Baptism, and intended to be administered to all the faithful as the preliminary

---

pp. 165–166; Jos. Pohle, pp. 302–303. The relevant texts are 2 Cor. i. 21–22; Ephes. i. 13; iv. 30.

[1] On which, see *The Church*, p. 321, n. 2, and the refs. there given.

of their full enjoyment of the status and privileges of members of the mystical Body of Christ. What are the practical values of this sacrament and the particular purposes fulfilled by it in the lives of individual Christians?

(*a*) Its first and most obvious value is that it completes the spiritual equipment which each Christian needs for his advance in the pathway that was marked out for him when he was born anew. Baptism elevates its recipient to the supernatural order, imparting to him potentialities in grace which other sacraments help him to actualize and develop. But if the child of grace is to mature in the sphere into which he has been brought, he must be endowed with the grace of maturity, with the sevenfold gifts of the Holy Spirit. That is, he must be confirmed.

(*b*) By the grace of Confirmation, as the name indicates, the baptized Christian is confirmed in grace, and is fortified for the protracted struggle against temptation which he has to face during his earthly pilgrimage and from the time of his attainment of moral and spiritual discretion. So soon as temptation begins to be felt he has need of all the equipment which God provides for him.

(*c*) The gifts conferred by Confirmation are designed effectually to elicit and develop into actualized forms the heavenly virtues, the potential germs of which have been imparted to the soul by baptismal regeneration — the virtues of faith, hope and love. In those who responsively exercise the sevenfold gifts these virtues grow; and in their growth they elevate and transfigure all natural virtues by giving them a supernatural and Godward end and organizing principle. As a result, the Christian develops towards perfection according to the pattern of Christ, and brings forth the fruits of the Spirit. These are love, joy, peace, long-suffering, kindness, goodness, faithfulness, meekness, patience, modesty, temperance and chastity.[1]

The chief immediate purposes fulfilled by the Confirmation gifts are three.

(a) They serve to fortify the soul against the dangers attendant upon adolescence — the fires of youth, and the mental and spiritual unsettlement which is apt to attend the transition from childhood to maturity. It is true that the unconverted are often brought to Christ at this period, which is favourable to moral change. But this liability to change is a source of danger as well as of sensitiveness to religious appeal. The question as to whether good or evil influences are likely to prevail at this period is determined to an important degree by conditions existing previously to the age of puberty. Among desirable previous conditions is the child's endowment with grace, accompanied by training in true religion. Confirma-

---

[1] They are designated by St. Paul in Gal. v. 22–23, according to the fuller reading of certain ancient manuscripts, which best harmonizes with Revel. xxii. 2. The A. V. and R. V., however, mention only nine fruits. These fruits describe activities in which a virtuous Christian is disposed to engage, rather than virtues themselves. Cf. *The Church*, p. 36 (*e*); *Cath. Encyc.*, s.v. "Holy Ghost," VII.

tion should therefore be administered *before* the age of puberty arrives, unless there exists adequate contrary reasons, growing out of peculiar circumstances in individual cases.

(*b*) Confirmation is the appointed instrument of lay ordination, of admission to the royal priesthood in which every Christian is designed to have part, for example in offering the Eucharistic Sacrifice. It is true that not all have the same office in the priesthood, and further ordination is required before the ministerial and representative functions in priesthood can be performed. But the laymen's part is not less real than that of the ministerial priest, although confined to unofficial participation;[1] and Confirmation is his ordination and the means of his equipment for priestly action.

(*c*) Finally, Confirmation not only ordains the Christian for his part in offering the Eucharistic Sacrifice, but affords needed grace for his worthy reception of the wonderful gift of the body and blood of Christ in that sacrament. This explains the catholic principle that Confirmation should ordinarily be received before admission to Holy Communion.[2]

[1] *The Church*, ch. ii. § 7; A. T. Wirgman, pp. 409–415.

[2] Cf. pp. 47–48, above. The fact that English Churchmen in America before the revolutionary war were admitted to Communion without previous Confirmation is obviously a nonsignificant exception. These communicants had not rejected Confirmation, but had simply been unable to be confirmed because of the lack of bishops in America.

III. *Questions*

§ 9. A sacrament may be generally necessary in either or both of two senses: intrinsically and by divine precept. In either case its reception is obligatory. Intrinsically Confirmation is necessary for reception of the sevenfold gifts of the Holy Spirit and for the full equipment of a member of Christ's mystical Body. Furthermore, it is the appointed means by which Christians are prepared fittingly and worthily to exercise the lay priesthood and receive the Blessed Sacrament. Yet it is not described as "generally necessary for salvation," for the baptismal grace of life is previously received in any case, and those who are subsequently hindered by reasonable causes from being confirmed are permitted to take part in the Eucharistic Sacrifice and receive the body and blood of Christ.

But Confirmation is clearly necessary for all baptized Christians with the necessity of precept, both divine and ecclesiastical.[1] In the New Testament it is reckoned among the foundations of the doctrine of Christ, and its reception was plainly treated by the Apostles as the obligatory sequel and needed complement of Baptism. Its value was unmistakably demonstrated from above by miraculous attestation; and there is at least a presumption that our Lord not only promised the gift which it conveys, but also in-

[1] On the general obligation to be confirmed, see A. C. A. Hall, ch. vi; C. S. Grueber, pp. 59–61; Jos. Pohle, pp. 304–306.

structed His Apostles as to its administration before He left them. This certainly is a plausible explanation of their administering it from the start.

Of the catholic precept in this matter there can be no question. Confirmation has always and everywhere constituted the normal sequel of Baptism, and never have the baptized been dispensed from receiving it when it could be obtained. Rejection of it has in all catholic Communions been followed by exclusion from Holy Communion. It has to be remembered in this connection that the Catholic Church regards all the baptized as properly subject to catholic discipline, and cannot consistently exempt Nonconformists because of their independent organization from the conditions which are imposed upon those who would enjoy catholic privileges. To do so would not only encourage Nonconformists in their nonconformity, but would be prejudicial to maintenance of discipline within. The Prayer Book rubric requiring Confirmation or readiness and desire to be confirmed before admission to Holy Communion [1] is clearly de-

---

[1] At the end of the Order of Confirmation: "And there shall none be admitted to the Holy Communion, until such time as he be confirmed, or be ready and desirous to be confirmed."

The closing exhortation of the Baptismal Office for Infants reads, "Ye are to take care that this child be brought to the Bishop to be confirmed by him, so soon as he can say the Creed, the Lord's Prayer, and the Ten Commandments," etc. A rubric at the close of the Office of Baptism of those of Riper Years says, "It is expedient that every person, thus baptized, should be confirmed by the Bishop, so soon after his Baptism as conveniently may be; that so he may be admitted to the Holy Communion."

signed to be applied without exception to all Christians who would fulfil their "bounden duty and service" of receiving the body and blood of Christ and of participating in the Eucharistic Sacrifice. The intrenchment of nonconformity in novel organizations designedly and persistently opposed to catholic authority obviously cannot annul for Nonconformists the principle that obedience to catholic precepts is the only lawful basis of admission to catholic privileges. And to reject Confirmation is to disobey a precept having New Testament as well as catholic sanction.

§ 10. The Anglican Prayer Book prescribes the time for Confirmation on the basis of the established Western practice of separating its administration by several years from that of infant Baptism; and it plainly presupposes the necessity that those who have reached the age of conscious responsibility should be rightly prepared both mentally and morally for the reception of sacramental means of grace. To all such faith and repentance are indispensable conditions of beneficial reception.[1] Accordingly, the Prayer Book defines the time of Confirmation as "so soon as he can say the Creed, the Lord's Prayer, and the Ten Commandments, and is sufficiently instructed in the other parts of the Church-Catechism set forth for that purpose." The need of a right moral disposition is provided for by requiring a ratification of bap-

---

[1] Cf. *The Church*, pp. 320–323.

tismal vows in the Order of Confirmation.[1] In this same Order the time is further defined as "the years of discretion." In cases of adult Baptism, the time is defined as "so soon after his Baptism as conveniently may be."

Common experience establishes the generalization that a normal child can be prepared for Confirmation in the manner thus prescribed by the Church at an age varying from seven to twelve years. And "years of discretion," that is, of personal responsibility for choosing what is true and right, have then been attained. The Church's phrase "so soon as" definitely implies that no delay beyond this age may normally be allowed; and the practical need of reception of the grace of Confirmation before the age of puberty has already been shown. Unhappily there is much ignorance as to this need, and the dangerous error that children should be left uninfluenced by their parents and sponsors in the matter of Confirmation for fear of hampering their full freedom of choice is somewhat widespread. Parents who will use every influence possible to prevent their children from violating public sentiment in morals, leave these same children to the undisturbed influence of irreligion and of organized nonconformity. It is as if they allowed them, when most open to adverse influence, to be

---

[1] The Anglican Churches do not require resort to the sacrament of Penance before Confirmation, and pastors may not in practice assume that they do. But the advantage of sacramental confession and absolution at such a crisis is too clear to be wholly ignored in the pastor's counsels to his individual candidates.

ensnared of the devil in things pertaining to God, with the illusory hope that after the devil had ensnared them they would still be in a position freely and firmly to renounce him. It is very sad; and the failure of many of our clergy to give adequate and clear instruction in this matter is highly culpable.[1]

§ 11. The Church prescribes that candidates for Confirmation shall be "sufficiently instructed" in the Church-Catechism. This means that they shall be given to understand according to their mental capacity what it means to be "a member of Christ, the child of God, and an inheritor of the kingdom of heaven"; also what it means in practice to "renounce the devil and all his works, the pomps and vanities of this wicked world, and all the sinful lusts of the flesh"; to "believe all the Articles of the Christian Faith"; and to "keep God's holy will and commandments . . . all the days of [his] life."[2]

The rest of the Catechism is a partial[3] expansion

[1] When the child is surrounded by adverse home conditions that seem likely to prevent his perseverance in grace, prudence will dictate postponement by the pastor until an age of greater independence of such influences. Parental prohibition in the case of a minor, and moral unreadiness of the child himself, also dictate delay, in the first case until the age of majority and in the other case until conversion. On the proper age for the Confirmation of those who under Western usage are not confirmed (as in the East) in infancy, see A. C. A. Hall, ch. vii; C. S. Grueber, pp. 47-53; A. T. Wirgman, pp. 385-391; Wm. Jackson, pp. 116-118.

[2] On preparation for Confirmation, see A. C. A. Hall, ch. viii. There are many tracts *in re*.

[3] It does not deal with the Church and the minor sacraments. The original plan, never carried out, was to provide a fuller catechism

and explanation of the answers which we have quoted. Whatever criticisms may be made of it — it is obviously susceptible of improvement — the Church-Catechism has the double value of embodying officially expressed teaching, and of containing language which, once effectually memorized, will grow in meaning with the increase of the learner's years and experience. A child should be required to store in his memory such religious terms only as will permanently retain their value. It is quite true that he cannot fully understand the Church Catechism, but he can understand it sufficiently for immediate purposes; and by storing its classic phrases in his memory he obtains abiding premises of future development in religious knowledge. Catechisms that are designed to simplify its lessons do not as a rule succeed in their aim; and the majority of them load the memory with phrases that are quickly outgrown. And when they are outgrown, the lessons embodied in them are apt to be dismissed and forgotten.

§ 12. The Church intends that those who are brought to Confirmation shall have elementary knowledge of the "things which a Christian ought to know and believe to his soul's health." But the mental preparation thus prescribed is only the beginning of a Christian layman's religious education, which should be continued under competent and orthodox teachers, *pari passu*, and in intelligible connection, with his

for the further instruction of Churchmen. See Procter and Frere, *op. cit.*, pp. 601–602.

secular education. The reasons for this are threefold. In the first place, one cannot cease to advance in religious knowledge without gradually losing vital hold upon what he has previously learned — a law observable in every sphere of education. Secondly, an absorbing and exclusive pursuit of secular studies during the freshest and most formative period of one's life tends to drive the truths of religion into the background and to lower the comparative value ascribed to them. Habitually to stress secular education alone involves the tendency to disparage religious knowledge. Thirdly, with advancing years and widening experience many religious problems come to the fore, both theoretical and practical, which require for successful handling a more mature religious education than can be received during the years of childhood. Many instances of falling away from true religion are due to the fact that religious knowledge is so generally neglected by professed Christians. Because of this neglect they are quite unable to discern the obvious fallacies of the anti-Christian and anti-catholic arguments which eager controversialists thrust upon their attention. They readily become victims of secular and critical propaganda, and are lost to the Church of God.

It is neither necessary nor practicable that ordinary laymen should become scientific theologians. Such a consummation is no more to be expected than that average citizens should become expert statesmen. Yet a citizen of general intelligence who knows practically nothing of the constitution and principles of government under which he lives is an anomaly. But he is no more so than the "liberally educated" Christian who can answer correctly hardly a single question concerning the religion upon which he professes to base his eternal welfare.

To be an intelligent Christian one must have learned why he is a Christian and Churchman. He must know what his churchmanship involves in faith and practice, and must be familiar with the whole *Book of Common Prayer*. He must have some acquaintance with the causes of the rise of modern sectarianism. He must be able to give reasons for the hope that is in him, and to detect the falsity of the various specious substitutes for Christianity and for catholic doctrine and practice. He ought, of course, to be habituated to a devout reading of the Holy Scripture, remembering that the purpose for which it is given by God is our upbuilding in the faith which is in Christ Jesus and which the Church is set to teach and define.[1] In all these things he should be informed to a degree proportionate to his general education and experience. This is so because those who are trained to think for themselves in general are likely to do so in religion, whether sufficiently acquainted with its principles or not. It is indisputable, therefore, that a lack of religious education in their case will have serious results.

[1] *Authority*, pp. 241-257.

CHAPTER III

THE HOLY EUCHARIST IN HISTORY

I. *Biblical*

§ 1. The Holy Eucharist [1] is the working centre of

[1] On the Eucharist, the most full and reliable storehouse of historical, definitive and bibliographical material is Darwell Stone's *Hist. of the Doctrine of the Holy Eucharist*, 2 vols. (designated in the following notes by "S. *Hist.*") The following works are also helpful:—

HISTORICAL: Philip Freeman, *Principles of Divine Service*, II. pp. 1-140; W. B. Frankland, *The Early Eucharist* (A.D. 30-180); B. J. Kidd, *Later Mediæval Doctr. of the Euch. Sacrifice;* Hastings, *Encyc. of Relig.*, s.v. "Eucharist"; E. B. Pusey, *Doctr. of the Real Presence . . . in the Fathers;* L. Waterman, *Primitive Tradition of the Eucharistic Body and Blood;* and the Histories of Doctrine.

BIBLICAL: S. *Hist.*, ch. i; Hastings, *Dic. of Bible* (Plummer) and *Dic. of Christ* (D. Stone); W. B. Frankland, *op. cit.;* W. J. Gold, *Sacrificial Worship;* E. H. Archer-Shepherd, *Ritual of the Tabernacle;* W. B. Trevelyan, *Food of Immortality.*

ANGLICAN: Darwell Stone, *Holy Communion* (designated by D. Stone, *H.C.*); and *The Euch. Sacrifice* (popular); Archd. Wilberforce, *Doctr. of the Holy Euch.;* A. P. Forbes, *Thirty-Nine Arts.* XXVIII-XXXI; and *Theol. Defence;* E. T. Green, *The Eucharist;* James DeKoven, *Theol. Defence;* J. G. H. Barry, *The Holy Eucharist;* J. R. Milne, *Doctr. and Practice of the Eucharist;* W. C. E. Newbolt, *Sacrament of the Altar;* P. N. Waggett, *The Holy Eucharist;* Chas. Gore, *Body of Christ;* Henry Wace (editor), *The Doctr. of Holy Communion*, etc. (Fulham Conference Report, 1900); M. F. Sadler, *One Offering.* Cf. S. *Hist.*, chh. x-xiii, xv-xvi.

ROMAN AND EASTERN: St. Thomas, *Summa Theol.*, III. lxxiii-lxxxiii; J. B. Franzelin, *De SS. Eucharistiæ;* J. C. Hedley, *The*

the Christian dispensation, and in it are focussed various vital aspects of truth and grace and worship. It is therefore a complex mystery, requiring a larger treatment than any other sacrament; and its great importance justifies such treatment. To this has to be added the mournful consideration that the flames of controversy have burned fiercely around it for many centuries. Four chapters, however, are all that can be given to the subject, and to write satisfactorily under such limitations, and without serious omissions, is very difficult. Constructive clearness rather than complete exhibition of details will be kept in view.

The Old Testament may not be disregarded in any proper historical introduction to our subject;[1] for, as in other subjects, our Lord gave His Eucharistic teaching from the background of the old covenant, appropriating its incidents, forms and terms in describing and instituting the sacrament. The old

---

Holy Eucharist; Jos. Pohle, *The Sacraments*, vol. II. Cf. S. *Hist.*, chh. ix, xiv. Peter Mogila, *Orthodox Confession* (Transl. Edited by J. J. Overbeck), qq. 106–107; *Acts and Decrees of the Synod of Jerusalem . . . 1672* (Transl. with Notes by J. N. W. B. Robertson), Decree xvii; Macaire, *Théologie Dogmatique Orthodoxe.* Cf. S. *Hist.*, ch. iv.

PROTESTANT: *Schaff-Herzog Encyc.*, s.v. "Lord's Supper" and works there given.

EIRENIC: G. F. Cobb, *Kiss of Peace;* W. R. Carson, *Eucharistic Eirenicon.*

[1] On Old Test. anticipations, see E. H. Archer-Shepherd, esp. pp. 44–52, 71–84; Hastings, *Dic. of Bible*, s.v. "Lord's Supper," II–III; W. J. Gold, Lec. iii; D. Stone, *H.C.*, pp. 10–13; W. S. Moule, *The Offerings Made Like unto the Son of God, passim.*

BIBLICAL 71

covenant was indeed preparatory for, and prefigurative of, the new.

In particular, its sacrificial rites, which were fulfilled on the Cross, also pointed on to the pure offering of the new covenant. The Eucharist is this offering, and in it what the older ritual prefigured comes to be truly represented and effectively applied upon the basis of Christ's sufficient sacrifice for sin — a sacrifice once for all accomplished, but living on both in Christ's heavenly intercession and in the earthly and Eucharistic memorial. In its institution the Eucharist is immediately associated with the Paschal sacrifice; but because it is the memorial of Christ's death, in which all previous sacrifices are recapitulated, and because it completely fills the place in the new covenant which these sacrifices occupied in the old, it likewise recapitulates in a representative and applicatory way the various mysteries which the sacrifices of Israel foreshadowed. As this recapitulatory aspect of the Eucharist will have to be exhibited later,[1] it is enough here to call attention to the fact that the prophets, while anticipating great changes in the messianic Kingdom, distinctly predicted a continuance of sacrificial oblations in it, oblations in which the Gentiles were to have part. "In every place incense shall be offered unto my name, and a pure offering: for My name shall be great among the Gentiles, saith the Lord of hosts."[2]

[1] Cf. ch. v. §§ 2, 5, below.
[2] Mal. i. 11. Cf. Isa. lvi. 7; lxvi. 20–23.

The manna with which the Israelites were miraculously fed during their forty years of wandering affords the starting point of our Lord's discourse on the bread from heaven which He was to give;[1] and, along with the water that poured from the rock at Moses' bidding, is treated as typical of the Eucharist by St. Paul.[2] Various Old Testament incidents have been recognized as types of the same mystery. Melchizedech's bringing forth bread and wine for Abraham when he blessed him, the burning bush of God's presence that was not consumed, and the story of Elijah, his triumphant sacrifice and the supernatural sustenance which brought him safely to the mount of God, are examples.[3] In view of the central importance of the Eucharist in the messianic dispensation to which the prophets looked forward, such mystical interpretations ought not to be regarded as fanciful.

§ 2. Our Lord's Eucharistic teaching is contained in a discourse given at Capernaum, and in His institution of the sacrament. The discourse referred to [4] appears to have been prepared for by the miraculous feeding of the five thousand in the mountain and by the equally miraculous method which He employed

---

[1] Exod. xvi. 14–15, 31–35; Josh. v. 12; St. John vi. 31, 49, 58. Cf. Rev. ii. 17.

[2] 1 Cor. x. 3–4.

[3] Gen. xiv. 18–20; Exod. iii. 1–6; 1 Kings xviii. 18–39; xix. 4–8.

[4] St. John vi. On which, see Archd. Wilberforce, ch. vii; M. F. Sadler and B. F. Westcott, *in loc.;* T. B. Strong, *Doctr. of the Real Presence*, pp. 21–31.

in becoming present in Capernaum. We are also told by the writer that, as was the case with the subsequent institution of the Eucharist, the Passover was at hand. These incidents and connections do not appear to be accidental. They obviously accentuate the teaching which He proceeded to give.

Seizing upon His listeners' reference to the giving of manna from heaven in the wilderness, He tells them that the Father giveth the true bread, "the bread of God that cometh down from heaven and giveth life unto the world," and claims Himself to be this bread of life, in which all must believe who would have eternal life and be raised by Him at the last day. He proceeds to reaffirm this as against the Jews' murmuring and says, "I am the living bread which came down out of Heaven: If any man eat of this bread, he shall live forever: yea and the bread which I will give is My flesh, for the life of the world ... Verily, verily, I say unto you, Except ye eat the flesh of the Son of Man and drink His blood, ye have not life in yourselves. He that eateth My flesh and drinketh My blood hath eternal life; and I will raise him up at the last day. For My flesh is meat indeed, and My blood is drink indeed. He that eateth My flesh and drinketh My blood abideth in Me, and I in him. As the living Father hath sent Me, and I live because of the Father; so he that eateth Me, he also shall live because of Me. This is the bread which came down out of heaven: not as the fathers did eat manna and died: he that eateth this bread shall live forever."

The disciples found this teaching to be "a hard saying," and they probably took it in a physical sense, as if He had taught a species of cannibalism. To correct this, He proceeds, "Doth this cause you to stumble? What then if you should behold the Son of Man ascending where He was before? It is the spirit that quickeneth; the flesh profiteth nothing: the words that I have spoken unto you are spirit, and are life." This explanation, since it appeared to leave unreduced the teaching that they must partake of His flesh and blood, failed to satisfy many of His disciples, who walked no more with Him.

The explanation appears to be that, since our Lord was to return to Heaven, a physical method of eating His flesh would be out of question. The eating was to be spiritual, and such as would be quickening and life-giving in effect. If Christ had been speaking metaphorically, however, He would surely have so phrased His explanation as to make this clear. He left unmodified a literal meaning which caused many to fall away from Him, and this meaning we may not explain away. He plainly meant that *somehow* we must truly eat His flesh and drink His blood in order to be quickened by the spirit of life that is therein conveyed. How we are to fulfil this requirement is revealed in His institution of the Eucharist, from which we learn that the feeding is sacramental. The faith that is required is therefore such as declares itself in receiving the Eucharistic sacrament.

§ 3. The earliest New Testament account of the institution [1] is given by St. Paul, who claims to have received it from the Lord. "The Lord Jesus in the night in which He was betrayed took bread; and when He had given thanks (εὐχαριστήσας), He brake it, and said, This is my body which is for you: this do for My memorial (εἰς τὴν ἐμὴν ἀνάμνησιν). In like manner also the cup after supper, saying, This cup is the new covenant in My blood: this do, as oft as ye drink it, for My memorial."

The variations in the accounts given in the synoptic Gospels are chiefly as follows. St. Mark and St. Matthew substitute for "when He had given thanks," the words "when He had blessed" (εὐλογήσας); and all three mention that He gave to them. St. Mark and St. Matthew respectively also add, "Take ye," and "Take, eat." These two Gospels, instead of "the new covenant in My blood," read "My blood of the covenant, which is poured out for many"; and St. Luke changes this last clause to, "even that which is poured out for you." St. Matthew adds still further, "unto remission of sins." St. Mark and St. Matthew omit altogether the phrases "for My memorial."

If we combine these accounts, it appears that before administering the elements Christ first blessed,

[1] On the institution, see S. *Hist.*, I. 4-11; H. L. Goudge, *First Epis. to the Corinth.*, pp. 102-108; W. B. Frankland, pp. 30-47, 116-119; W. Sanday, in Hastings, *Dic. of Bib.*, vol. II. pp. 636-638. The texts are 1 Cor. xi. 23-25; St. Mark xiv. 22-25; St. Matt. xxvi. 26-29; St. Luke xxii. 14-20. The words relating to the cup in St. Luke are possibly an interpolation.

or gave thanks over, each of them in language not reported; that He described the blessed bread as being His body given for them, and the blessed cup as being His blood of the new covenant; that He gave them to His disciples to eat and drink, directing them to do this for His memorial.

Our Lord plainly declares the blessed bread to be His body; and if He said, "My blood of the new covenant," He declared the blessed cup to be His blood. He implied this clearly enough, even if He said, "the new covenant in My blood." The protestant view that He spoke metaphorically only, after the analogy of His saying, "I am the door," does not at all answer to the interpretation to which the Holy Spirit has guided the Church from the beginning, and is too obviously the outcome of controversial reaction to be taken seriously. If by literal interpretation, however, we mean the grossly materialistic notion which the listeners to our Lord's discourse at Capernaum hastily deduced, this too is clearly foreign to the general burden of Christ's teaching. But we may not minimize the words of Christ so solemnly uttered. The fullest meaning that they can reasonably bear is to be sought rather than the smallest.

Our Lord was plainly speaking in the most formal way, and intended to provide His Church with "sound words," having the authority and inviolability of divine dogma. They are indeed symbolic, in that no human terms can adequately express what He was revealing; but for this very reason they have to be taken supra-literally, rather than infra-literally. That is, their meaning exceeds rather than falls short of a literal interpretation, but does not invalidate such interpretation. Translating the sacred words into terms of time, we learn from them that, by means of His blessing, the bread and wine do truly become His body and blood; but such a statement, final for us though it be, is an incipient proposition, for it symbolizes more than can be expressed in human language. In view of its divine source, however, we feel bound to accept it as being the highest available description of the mystery — the description that should permanently determine our faith in the sacrament. An abiding test of interpretations of our Lord's words is their effect when adopted upon our ability and disposition to retain, emphasize, and rejoice in, the double divine affirmation, "This is My body," "This is My blood."

This affirmation was made in a context of sacrificial connections and terms. Whether the last supper is to be identified with the feast of the Passover or not, their close association in time was not accidental. The sacrament which He then instituted perpetuates the memorial aspect of the Passover, although relating it to the redemptive death of Christ instead of to the deliverance from Egypt, the Old Testament type giving way to the New Testament mystery of which it was the prophetic figure. Used in such a context, the word ἀνάμνησις obviously has the sacrificial reference that belonged to it when used in connection with Old Testament sacrifices;[1] and the memorial instituted by Christ should therefore be understood as intended to be celebrated before God. The new rite also perpetuates the Paschal element of feeding on the sacrifice, and consecrates in its final meaning the communion element of sacrifice which was generally preserved in ancient religions. The institution meant that the new Israel, employing the customary elements of ancient meal and drink offerings, was to offer, and to feed upon, the bread of God, thereby at once offering acceptable sacrifice and partaking of the divine life.

The sacrificial reference of our Lord's calling the cup His "blood of the covenant" is especially clear and direct, for in the Old Testament this phrase had been applied to sacrificial blood poured forth and sprinkled on the people.[2] In this connection it is to be noticed that in describing His sacramental blood as poured out, He used a word ($\dot{\epsilon}\kappa\chi\upsilon\nu\acute{o}\mu\epsilon\nu o\nu$) more suggestive of the old covenant pouring of the blood of sacrificial victims at the base of the altar than of the effusion of blood in death.[3]

So far as the New Testament records tell us, neither

---

[1] Levit. xxiv. 7; Numb. x. 10. Different uses occur in Psa. xxxviii. 1; lxx. 1; Wisd. xvi. 6. It is the context, not the necessary meaning of the word, that determines. The only other N. Test. use is in Heb. x. 3. Cf. S. *Hist.*, I. 9-11.

[2] Exod. xxiv. 1-11. Cf. Jerem. xxxi. 31-34; Heb. ix. 15-21.

[3] The phrase " do this " ($\pi o\iota\epsilon\hat{\iota}\tau\epsilon$) has no sacrificial force in ordinary use. Its sacrificial reference here is due to the context, the sacrificial nature of which has to be established on other grounds.

Christ nor His Apostles specifically declared the Holy Eucharist to be sacrificial. There was no reason for doing so. The modern prejudice against such a doctrine did not exist. To the first Christian believers, both Jewish and Gentile, a religious system having no sacrificial ritual whatever was unknown. Accordingly, while the doctrine of Christ's death justified in their minds the abolition of bloody sacrifices, the unbloody ritual of worship which took their place came naturally to be regarded as sacrificial, especially after the abolition of Jewish sacrifices had been visibly accomplished through the destruction of Jerusalem — not that the Eucharist was regarded as having independent value apart from Christ's death, but as proclaiming it before God and as applying its benefits. They received no teaching that was inconsistent with such an inference,[1] and the doctrine concerning it both of Christ and of His Apostles was given in terms suggestive of sacrifice — of its being the promised pure offering of the messianic dispensation.

§ 4. The pentecostal Church is shown in the New Testament as at once assigning to the Eucharist the central place in its working system, as the one controlling factor of its regular corporate worship. We are told that those who had been baptized "continued stedfastly in the Apostles' teaching and fellowship,

---

[1] Heb. x. teaches only the abolition of bloody offerings and "sacrifices for sin," such as had been offered according to the old law

in the breaking of bread and the prayers,"[1] "the prayers" evidently referring to some generally accepted liturgical use. This use did not preclude some elasticity of precatory phrase,[2] but a certain fundamental and recognizable norm appears to be implied. The day of the week on which our Lord rose from the dead became the weekly Christian holy day, upon which the Eucharist was regularly celebrated. But there are possible indications of more frequent celebrations at home.[3]

The teaching of St. Paul is given in two chapters of his first Epistle to the Corinthians. In the tenth chapter[4] he is concerned to rebuke participation in pagan sacrificial feasts, with which he compares and contrasts the Christian Communion. He begins by describing the Eucharistic "cup of blessing" as "a communion of the blood of Christ," and the Eucharistic bread as "a communion of the body of Christ." He then describes the communion as a sacrament of Christian unity: "Seeing that we, who are many, are one bread, one body: for we all partake of the one bread." Just as the Israelites who partake of their sacrifices have communion with the altar, he proceeds to argue, so likewise, although gentilic idols are nothing, and the things sacrificed to them are nothing, these things are really sacrificed to

---

[1] Acts ii. 42. [2] 1 Cor. xiv. 15-17.
[3] Acts xx. 7; ii. 46; 1 Cor. xvi. 2; Revel. i. 10. Cf. St. Mark xvi. 9; St. John xx. 19. Cf. E. T. Green, ch. xiii.
[4] 1 Cor. x. 14-21. Cf. H. L. Goudge, *in loc.*

devils, and to eat of them is to have communion with devils. "Ye cannot drink the cup of the Lord, and the cup of devils: ye cannot partake of the table of the Lord, and of the table of devils." This all clearly implies some basis of comparison between pagan sacrifices and the Christian communion. Both are acts of communion, the one with devils and the other with the Lord. But such acts of communion he treats as communion with the altar, that is, participation in the sacrifice. The common basis is therefore sacrificial. The modern antithesis between communion and offering was unknown to the ancients. They viewed them as vitally interconnected, and constituting one sacrificial ritual.

In the eleventh chapter [1] St. Paul has occasion to rebuke the abuses that had arisen in connection with the Agape which preceded celebrations of the Eucharist, each one selfishly taking before other his own supper and thus nullifying the significance of the Eucharist as "the Lord's supper." To accentuate the gravity of their offence he reminds them of its immediate connection with, and consequent effect upon, their fitness for partaking of the Eucharist. He does this by describing the institution of that sacrament in language which we have already quoted and expounded, and by adding admonitory comments. "For as often as ye eat this bread and drink this cup," he says, "ye proclaim the Lord's death till He come. Wherefore whosoever shall eat the bread

[1] 1 Cor. xi. 17-30.

or drink the cup of the Lord unworthily, shall be guilty of the body and the blood of the Lord. But let a man prove himself, and so let him eat of the bread, and drink of the cup. For he that eateth and drinketh, eateth and drinketh judgment unto himself, if he discern not the body. For this cause many among you are weak and sickly, and not a few sleep."

The phrase "proclaim the Lord's death" does not of itself determine whether the proclaiming meant is before God, before men, or before both God and men; but the general teaching of the New Testament justifies belief that in fact we proclaim the Lord's death before both God and men. In going on to teach that one who partakes of the sacrament "unworthily" shall be "guilty of the body and blood of the Lord," and that failure to discern the Lord's body involves eating and drinking judgment to oneself, St. Paul implies that the body and blood are objectively present independently of the worthiness of reception of the sacrament. It is also implied in the rest of the admonition that unworthy reception causes the bread of life to act like a poison, in not a few cases with spiritually fatal results. In later terminology, the sacrament in any case is efficacious *ex opere operato*, the subjective state of the recipient determining whether the effect is beneficial or injurious.

It seems to throw side light upon St. Paul's conception of the Eucharist as sacrificial, that he elsewhere describes himself as having received grace to be "a priest ($\lambda\epsilon\iota\tau o\upsilon\rho\gamma\acute{o}\nu$) of Christ Jesus unto the

Gentiles, doing priestly work (ἱερουργοῦντα) in respect of the Gospel of God, that the oblation (προσφορά) of the Gentiles might be made acceptable, being sanctified by the Holy Ghost."[1]

The author of the Epistle to the Hebrews writes, "We have an altar, whereof they have no right to eat which serve the tabernacle."[2] The word altar (θυσιαστήριον) does not appear to refer to any material thing on earth, but to the Cross or to Christ Himself, in whom and through whom we offer our Eucharist. The reference to eating of this altar, however, is plainly Eucharistic, and the thought involved is that the Eucharist is a sacrificial feast — not a separate sacrifice, but our means of representing, feeding on, and making our own, the one true sacrifice of Christ. It is the priesthood of Christ, to the consideration of which the Epistle to the Hebrews is primarily devoted, in which Christians share, each in his appointed place in the mystical Body; and the sacrificial aspect of the Eucharist arises from its being the instituted means of formally exercising this priesthood.

II. *Patristic and Mediæval*

§ 5. The Eucharist retained the dominant and central place in the working system of the Church

[1] Rom. xv. 16. Cf. Sanday and Headlam, *in loc.;* W. Sanday, *Conception of Priesthood*, pp. 89–90; S. *Hist.*, I. 15.

[2] Heb. xiii. 10. Cf. B. F. Westcott, *in loc.;* R. C. Moberly, *Ministerial Priesthood*, pp. 269–270.

throughout the patristic period. Its doctrine also occupied a vital place in patristic thought, and was occasionally appealed to in controversies on other subjects, wherein intense polemical feeling was involved, in order to illustrate or confirm the arguments of various contestants. The fact is very significant, therefore, that no serious controversy as to Eucharistic doctrine itself arose in the Church prior to the ninth century. Accordingly no technical watchwords of Eucharistic orthodoxy were developed, but the subject was handled with the unanxious freedom that consciousness of a common mind and of unlikelihood of misconstruction alone can explain. Therefore we find a great variety of statements on the subject, and occasional phrases that seem vague and even unsound when tested by later and technical standards.

The rule by which such phrases should be interpreted is clear. Inasmuch as they are exceptional, are often fully offset by more exact statements of the same writers, and are rarely given in a formal or controversially assertive way, they should be treated as non-determinative, and as indicating free and uncritical writing rather than real deviation from the prevailing patristic doctrine. The exceptions are few and far between; and two general affirmations are dominant in patristic references to the Eucharist. These are (*a*) that the consecrated elements are truly — not in mere metaphor — the body and blood of Christ; and (*b*) that the Eucharist is a sacrifice —

PATRISTIC AND MEDIÆVAL

not independently of the Cross, but as the appointed memorial of it, and as the means by which Christians participate in offering it and in pleading its merits. To establish the correctness of this general summary would require much space; and we shall have to content ourselves with the briefest possible sketch of the several ways in which the ancients expressed their conceptions of the Eucharist.[1]

(a) The doctrine that the consecrated elements are the body and blood of Christ was affirmed along several lines. Categorical assertions of the fact are very frequent, and also allusions to the sacrament in which it is unmistakably implied.[2] With the progress of inferential theology the custom became common to translate these assertions into the terms of time. The bread and wine are frequently said by consecration to become the body and blood of Christ.[3] In this becoming the elements are sometimes said to be changed (μεταβέβληται), transmade (μεταποιεῖσθαι) and transelemented (μεταστοιχειώσας).[4] The last phrase suggests the later theory of transubstantiation, and St. Cyril of Jerusalem appears in one place to deny

[1] For witnesses, see S. *Hist.*, chh. ii–iii; E. B. Pusey, *Doctr. of the Real Presence . . . in the Fathers;* Archd. Wilberforce, chh. iii, viii–ix; and pp. 269–279; K. R. Hagenbach, *Hist. of Doctr.*, §§ 73, 138; J. Tixeront, *Hist. of Dogmas*, vol. I, *passim;* II. pp. 171–184; III. 226–242.

[2] St. Ignatius, *Smyrn.* 6; *Philad.*, 4; and Justin M., *Apol.* I. 66 afford significantly early witness. Cf. S. *Hist.*, I. 33–41.

[3] St. Irenæus, *Adv. Hær.*, V. ii. 2–3; and many subsequent writers.

[4] St. Cyril Jerus., *Catech.*, xxiii. 7; St. Gregory Nyss., *Catech. Orat.*, 37.

that the seeming bread and wine are any longer such after their consecration. Elsewhere, however, he speaks more guardedly to the effect that they are no longer *simple* bread, or *bare* elements, but the body and blood of Christ.¹ The patristic witness that they are still bread and wine after they have become also the body and blood of Christ is sufficient. Finally there is the witness that the sacrament is adorable, as being the body and blood of Christ, in which Christ is personally present.²

The passages that are cited against this manifold witness are chiefly those in which the consecrated elements are described by such terms as symbol (σύμβολον), "copy" (*exemplum*), "antitype" (*antitypum*), "figure" (*figura*), "represents," (*repræsentat*), "images" (εἰκόνας), "likeness" (ὁμοίωμα), "type" (τύπῳ), and "sign" (*signum*). But we have to remember that the ancients used these terms differently from moderns. As Dr. Harnack says, "What we nowadays understand by 'symbol' is a thing which is not what it represents; at that time 'symbol' denoted a thing which in some kind of way really is what it signifies." ³ The ancients did not speak of the consecrated elements as *mere* figures; and in

---

¹ Lec. xxii. 9. Cf. xxi. 3; and Justin M., *Apol.*, I. 66. On the doctrine of conversion, cf. S. *Hist.*, I. 102-105.

² St. Cyril Jerus., xxiii. 21-22; St. Augustine, *in Psa.* xcviii., *Enar.* 9. There are many others: S. *Hist.* I. 106-109.

³ *Hist. of Dogma*, II. 144; IV. 289. Cf. K. R. Hagenbach, *Hist. of Doctr.*, § 73. 3. S. *Hist.* I. 29-33, 61-67, gives these comments and the chief examples. Cf. J. G. H. Barry, pp. 129-132.

view of the generally acknowledged fitness of the outward elements to be used as sacramental "signs," we need not fear to say that after their consecration they retain their sign and figure aspects, even while becoming the things which they represent and signify. The well worn phrase of orthodoxy that Christian sacraments "effect what they figure" is pertinent.[1] That this view of the passages in question is correct is borne out by the fact that most of the writers referred to affirm in other connections the ruling doctrine, that the consecrated elements are the body and blood of Christ. As time went by, however, symbolic descriptions were felt to be inadequate, and were gradually abandoned. St. John of Damascus and others mistakenly supposed that the fathers had applied them to the unconsecrated elements only.[2]

The doctrine of the real presence of Christ in the sacrament, an objective presence challenging and justifying Eucharistic adoration, is undeniably patristic; but the ancients were more apt to use stronger language of identification, affirming that the consecrated species *are* the body and blood of Christ. They were not accustomed to regard what we call the two parts of the sacrament as two things, but viewed them as two aspects and descriptions, both true, of one and the same thing. They are still bread and wine, but they have also become the body and blood

---

[1] St. Thomas, III. lxii. 1 *ad primum*: *Efficiunt quod figurant*.
[2] St. John Damasc. *De Fid. Orth.*, IV. 13.

of Christ. St. Irenæus, indeed, distinguishes two things in the sacrament, an earthly and a heavenly;[1] but he appears to mean by the heavenly thing not the body and blood, but the Word or power which, when added to the elements, makes them to become the body and blood of Christ. The modern phrase that the body and blood of Christ are present in, *with*, and under the consecrated species cannot easily be harmonized with the patristic doctrine that the consecrated species *are* the body and blood of Christ, and not mere vehicles of them.[2] And their practice of reserving the sacrament for administration to the absent[3] shows that they believed this identification to continue so long as the species remained.

§ 6. (*b*) The ancients were not less emphatic than moderns are in repudiating carnal and bloody sacrifices; and also, after the example of both Old and New Testament writers, they applied sacrificial descriptions loosely and derivatively to various non-Eucharistic forms of devotion and action expressive of self-surrender to God. None the less they retained the more technical use of the term " sacrifice "; and, while asserting its spiritual nature, they plainly regarded the Eucharistic oblation as a true sacrifice in the formal sense of that term.

[1] *Adv. Hær.*, IV. xviii. 5.
[2] Cf. L. Waterman, pp. 32-34; and Note A (where he disputes the relevance of certain patristic passages used in support of the phrase by E. B. Pusey, in *op. cit.*, pp. 131-133).
[3] Already an established practice in the middle of the second century. Justin M., *Apol.*, I. 65.

The evidence of this is very abundant. The Eucharist is called "the sacrifice of Christians," and the Holy Table is called the altar (θυσιαστήριον), from the earliest sub-apostolic period, and by representative writers of every Christian type.[1] From the same early period these writers frequently speak of the Eucharist as the fulfilment of Malachi's prophecy, "In every place incense shall be offered unto My name, and a pure offering."[2] The sense in which the Eucharist is a sacrifice, according to patristic thought, is to be gathered partly from their connecting it with the death of Christ as the appointed memorial of it, the offering of what was then offered, which cannot be exhausted, and which avails for us by our offering it.[3] The patristic sense is also to be gathered from their associating the Eucharist with our Lord's heavenly priesthood. There is "an altar in the heavens," where Christ intercedes for us; and consecrates the earthly oblation, whereby we unite with Him in the heavenly oblation.[4] In line with the ancient general association of communion with sacrifice, the fathers treated the Eucharistic feeding on Christ's body and blood as a communion whereby we participate in the sacrifice.[5] St. Augustine defines sacrifice as a visible sacrament, that is a sacred sign, of an invisible sacrifice,[6] the essence of

[1] S. *Hist.*, I. 46–49, 109–123; K. R. Hagenbach, *op. cit.*, § 73.
[2] Mal. i. 11. S. *Hist.*, I. 49, 109–114 *passim*.
[3] *Idem*, I. 50, 114–116.
[4] *Idem*, I. 50–52, 116–121.   [5] *Idem*, I. 121–123.
[6] *De Civ. Dei*, x. 5.

which is the dedication of self to God — a corporate dedication, for the Church offers itself in this mystery, and its members are mystically participant in the oblation.[1]

§ 7. Throughout the middle ages and both East and West, the ancient doctrine that the consecrated elements have become the body and blood of Christ retained its hold upon the minds of Christian believers in general.[2] But two Western controversies occurred in the ninth and eleventh centuries respectively which had important results in subsequent scholastic developments.

(a) The first of these controversies was caused by statements made by Paschasius Radbert,[3] that after the consecration, "though the figure of bread and wine remain, yet these are altogether a figure, and . . . we must believe that there is nothing else than the flesh and blood of Christ . . . and . . . this certainly is no other flesh than that which was born of Mary and suffered on the Cross and rose from the tomb." In this language we have the germ of the later theory of transubstantiation. Its baldness seemed materialistic to his contemporaries, and

---

[1] S. *Hist.*, I. 123–124. The end of sacrifice, he says, is "that we may be united to God in holy fellowship": *op. cit.*, x. 6.

[2] On mediæval Eucharistic history, see S. *Hist.*, chh. iv–viii; K. R. Hagenbach, *op. cit.*, §§ 193–197; B. J. Otten, *Manual of the Hist. of Dogmas*, vol. II. chh. xviii–xix.

[3] In *On the Lord's Body and Blood* and *Epis. ad Frudegardum*. On this controversy, S. *Hist.*, I. 216–233; K. R. Hagenbach, *op. cit.*, § 193; Hastings, *Encyc. of Relig.*, vol. V. pp. 556–557.

caused alarm; although he expressly described the conversion of the elements as spiritual. Neither he nor his opponents were able to express their meaning clearly. The age was not one of accurate thought and terminology.

The chief replies came from Raban Maur and Ratramn. The former seemingly refused to identify the sacramental *res* with the body that was born of the Virgin and suffered and rose, and emphasized the spiritual nature of the presence. Yet with reference to the *res* he wrote, "That the body and blood of the Lord are real flesh and real blood, each Christian ought to believe." His divergence from Paschasius Radbert is perhaps not substantial. Ratramn in a more elaborate way also stresses the spiritual nature of the mystery. The body and blood received in the sacrament "are figures in respect of visible species; but in respect of invisible substance, that is, the power of the divine Word, they are really the body and blood of Christ." Using the authority of St. Ambrose, he distinguishes between the flesh in which Christ was crucified as "an external reality of nature" and the Eucharistic *res* as being "the real body and blood of Christ," but "*in sacramento*."

(b) The second controversy (1045–1088, A.D.)[1] was caused by Berengar of Tours. The general mode of expression of Radbert had by this time been widely adopted, but Berengar attacked it in a letter to Lan-

[1] On which, see S. *Hist.*, I. 244–259; K. R. Hagenbach, *op. cit.*, § 193; Hastings, *op. cit.*, vol. V. p. 557.

franc as contrary to the teaching of St. Ambrose, St. Jerome and St. Augustine. In the long controversy which ensued Berengar more than once recanted under pressure, and then resumed his teaching, the exact nature of which is somewhat obscure. His main theses appear to have been (1) that the bread and wine undergo no physical change by their consecration, remaining true bread and wine; and, (2) that the body of Christ is not "brought down from Heaven and carnally present on the altar." He declared that the bread and wine "are converted by means of the consecration into the real body and blood of Christ," but in view of his general attitude he was suspected of a purely figurative use of terms. The outcome was inevitable. The tendency against which Berengar protested gained general approval in the West, and was destined to be fixed by the use of the term *transubstantio* in defining the conversion brought about by the consecration of the bread and wine. This term was first employed in a treatise ascribed to St. Peter Damien of Ostia, but its formal adoption came later, and received official recognition at the fourth Lateran Council of 1215 A.D.[1]

Summarizing the general drift of ideas concerning

---

[1] On the development of the doctrine of transubstantiation, see S. *Hist.*, chh. vi–ix, *passim;* K. R. Hagenbach, *op. cit.*, § 194; Hastings, *op. cit.*, vol. V. pp. 557–560; B. J. Otten, *op. cit.*, vol. II. pp. 315–320; *Cath. Encyc.*, *s.v.* "Eucharist," I. (3); Chas. Gore, *Dissertations*, pp. 229–268. The Council referred to simply declared in its first chapter that the bread and wine are "transubstantiated" by the power of God. Hardouin, *Concilia*, vii. 15–18.

the effect of consecration, the tendency was to assert more and more emphatically that the bread and wine really become the body and blood of Christ, and to identify what they become with that which the Word assumed of the Blessed Virgin. But the protests against apparent materialisic implications in this development had effect; and the adoption of the term *transubstantio*, coupled with the distinction made by scholastic writers between *substantia* and *accidentia*, appears to have been due to desire to exclude the supposition that the Eucharistic conversion is a physical one. It was held, on the contrary, to be metaphysical; and this was apparently thought to guard sufficiently the spiritual nature of the mystery. As time went on, however, two difficulties emerged. In the first place, the term "substance" came in popular use to denote material substance, and this caused the doctrine of transubstantiation to mean for many the crude materialistic theory which is repudiated under that designation in the Anglican *Articles of Religion*. In the second place, the scholastic doctrine of the separability of substance and accidents came to be discredited in modern philosophy.[1]

Adhering to the metaphysical rather than to the physical use of the term, the Council of Trent declared that "by the consecration of the bread and wine, a conversion is made of the whole substance of the bread

[1] Various Roman Catholic writers acknowledge that this separability cannot be proved apart from supernatural revelation: e.g. P. Coffey, in *Ontology*, ch. viii.

into the substance of the body of Christ our Lord, and of the whole substance of the wine into the substance of His blood, only the species of the bread and wine remaining, which conversion is, by the holy Catholic Church, suitably and properly called transubstantiation."[1] The same Council affirmed the doctrine of concomitance, already developed by the scholastics and implied by earlier writers, that the *totus Christi*, body, blood, soul, and divinity, are present in both of the consecrated species and in every portion of them, there being no division of Christ, either because of the twofoldness of the species, or in their distribution.[2]

§ 8. The doctrine that the Eucharist is a true and proper sacrifice, representative and applicatory of the sacrifice of Christ, also retained its hold throughout the middle ages upon the convictions of Christian believers and writers in general both East and West.[3]

In the East the Eucharist was constantly described both as the memorial of Christ's death and as the earthly adjunct of the continuing heavenly oblation, wherein Christ intercedes for us and makes ef-

[1] Sess. XIII. ch. iv and Can. 2. The Council avoided the difficult term "accidents," substituting "species," meaning appearances.

[2] *Idem*, ch. iii and Can. 3. This doctrine was used in defending communion in one kind. See ch. iv. § 12 and pp. 179–180, below. For earlier statements of the doctrine, see S. *Hist.*, I. 140–141, 198, 269, 280–281, 284, 287, etc. Also St. Thomas, III. lxxvi. 1–4.

[3] On the mediæval doctrine of Euch. Sacrifice, see S. *Hist.*, chh. vi–viii, *passim;* K. R. Hagenbach, *op. cit.*, § 194; Hastings, *Encyc. of Relig.*, vol. V. pp. 560–562; B. J. Kidd, *The Later Mediæval Doctr. of the Euch. Sacrifice.*

fective our earthly memorial and self-oblation. The thought that Christ's heavenly oblation is the connecting link which unites our Eucharists with His death and unifies them in His sacrifice is occasionally expressed. The same general conception is found in early mediæval Westerns, Paschasius Radbert leading the way in doing ample justice to the heavenly oblation and being followed by several other writers.

But as time went by the heavenly priesthood of Christ fell into the background, and the practice became general in the West of reckoning only with the relation of the Eucharist to the sacrificial death of Christ. The externals of the sacrament were given symbolic interpretations as representative of the Cross, and a definition of sacrifice was furnished by St. Thomas Aquinas which with narrowing effect suggested two new notions. The first of these is that true sacrifice is propitiatory,[1] which obscures the larger conception of sacrifice as a form of self-oblation due to God from rational creatures *as such*, regardless of sin. The element of propitiation is wholly due to sin and to the necessity of somehow making the sacrificial homage of sinners acceptable to God. It is not an intrinsic element of sacrifice as such. The second notion is that sacrifice requires the destruction or physical modification of what is offered.[2] St. Augus-

[1] St. Thomas, III. xlviii. 3: *Sacrificium proprie dicitur aliquid factum in honorem proprie Deo debitum ad eum placandum.*

[2] *Idem*, II. II. lxxxv, 3 ad 3. "Sacrificia proprie dicuntur quando circa res Deo oblatas aliquid fit; sicut quod animalia occidebantur, quod panis frangitur et comeditur et benedicitur. Et hoc ipsum

tine had been content to regard sacrifice as a sacrament in which we offer ourselves to God, an effective form of self-oblation being the essential mark of true sacrifice.[1]

St. Thomas did not elaborate his conception, but his definition had evil effects upon later developments. The tendency to ignore our Lord's heavenly oblation was accentuated. The rhetorical statements of earlier writers that in the Eucharist Christ is mystically immolated, came to be used more seriously, although no one ventured to contend that Christ is actually slain again in the Eucharist. Rather the conversion of the substance of the bread and wine into the substance of Christ's body and blood was thought to be the modification required for the Eucharistic sacrifice, and the means by which it is connected with the sacrifice of the Cross.[2] This con-

---

nomen sonat, nam sacrificium dicitur, ex hoc homo facit aliquid sacrum." The stress is clearly on physical modification. Cf. B. J. Kidd, pp. 50–57.

[1] *De Civ. Dei*, x. 5–6.

[2] John de Lugo, S. J., in his *Treatise on the Venerable Sacrament of the Eucharist*, postulates that "in every sacrifice there must be some destruction of the thing that is offered" (XIX. i. 6–7). He proceeds "to explain how by the act of consecration itself the body of Christ is sacrificed; for, though it is not destroyed substantially, . . . yet it is destroyed in human fashion in so far as it receives a lower state of such a kind as to render it useless for the human purposes of a human body and suitable for other different purposes in the way of food." In brief, Christ is conceived to experience in the Eucharist a functionally destructive change of His body. Cited in S. *Hist.*, II. 373–377 (cf. for Franzelin's similar view, pp. 388–389). The present dominant view makes the mystical immolation

nection, however, had become less easy to exhibit because of forgetfulness of Christ's abiding heavenly oblation, which is the true connecting link between the Cross and the Eucharist. Accordingly, the sacrifice of the Mass assumed an independent and self-sufficient aspect in popular treatment which prepared the way for a most unhappy development. The multiplication of Masses came to be regarded as a multiplication of sacrifices having a certain species of absolute and independent value. The Cross, it was popularly thought, availed for original sin; but sacrifices of Masses were so many separate propitiatory remedies for actual sin. This opinion was never formally sanctioned, but it accounts for the thirty-first of our *Articles of Religion*, which is not directed against the catholic doctrine of Eucharistic sacrifice, but against this caricature of it.[1] But the older and larger conception did not wholly disappear, and various modern Roman writers have related the Eucharist to the heavenly oblation of Christ, and through it to His death.[2]

§ 9. The Greek and Latin Churches, in spite of in-

---

to consist of the separate consecration of the species (*Idem*, II. 389-393). According to Suarez and various recent writers, the essence of the sacrifice is the production of the body and blood of Christ by transubstantiation of the elements (*Idem*, II. 367-371, 393-397). Cf. B. J. Kidd, pp. 98-141.

[1] B. J. Kidd, pp. 6-41; A. P. Forbes, XXXI.

[2] Melchior Cano, Charles de Condren, John J. Olier, Louis Thomassin, V. Thalhofer and Abbé Lepin are quoted to this effect in S. *Hist.*, II. 356-357, 377-387, 397-405. And there are others.

cidental divergences, have retained to the present time a fundamental agreement that the bread and wine by consecration become the body and blood of Christ, and that the Eucharist is a true sacrifice. And in the first of these doctrines the Easterns have approximated the Latin terminology of transubstantiation. The *Orthodox Confession*, approved by the Eastern patriarchs in 1643 and by the Council of Jerusalem in 1672, used the term μετουσίωσιν to describe the change of the elements caused by their consecration. The Council of Jerusalem also adopted a decree of its own to the same effect. In accepting the decree of this Council the Russian Church in 1838 softened a phrase or two; but no real change of doctrine appears to have been intended.[1]

Certain minor divergences in Eucharistic practice and theory should be mentioned. The controversy concerning azymes or the use of unleavened bread,[2] which became usual in the West about the end of the ninth century, derived its heat from the general bitterness between East and West rather than from its intrinsic importance. In the East, except among the Armenians and Maronites, leavened bread has been used from ancient times. The Anglican use since

[1] These and other modern Eastern statements appear in S. *Hist.*, I. 177-192. The originals are in Kimmel, *Monum. Fid. Orient.*; and Hardouin, *Concilia*, xi.

[2] On which, see J. M. Neale, *Hist. of the Holy Eastern Church: Introd.*, pp. 1051-1076; D. Stone, *H. C.*, pp. 202-205. The Eastern use is described by F. E. Brightman, *Liturgies Eastern and Western*, I. pp. 571-572.

1552 treats ordinary bread as sufficient,[1] without excluding the pre-reformation use of unleavened bread. There can be no serious question as to the validity of either leavened or unleavened bread, if it is true wheaten bread.

Of more importance is the controversy over the "form" of consecration, as to whether it is completed by the recorded words of institution, as the Latins contend, or includes the subsequent invocation of the Holy Spirit (ἐπίκλησις), as the Easterns contend. The moment in the liturgy at which the consecration may be thought to be completed is involved. But the importance of determining this moment is undoubtedly exaggerated. Conventional usage in this matter, rather than scientific exactitude of time concomitants, determines the liturgical significance of ceremonial adjuncts. If some are found to employ acts of Eucharistic adoration while the consecration is still in process,[2] and others to defer such acts until it is finished, the intention and practical effect is the same in both cases. The consecration is to be viewed as a unit, its time-duration being due to the limitations of human speech rather than to the essence of the mystery. That a valid consecration requires some form of invocation or

[1] The modern yeast bread is different from the leavened bread of ancient use.

[2] Or even as anticipatory hailing of the Lord's expected presence, as in connection with the Minor Oblation. Cf. the explan. of Nicholas Cabasilas, in *Explanation of the Holy Liturgy*, c. 24 (S. *Hist.*, I. 167-168).

prayer along with the so-called words of institution, as doing duty for the unrecorded language with which Christ blessed the bread and the cup, appears to be certain; but this requirement is in some manner fulfilled in every catholic liturgy.[1]

A third controversy is connected with the administration among the Latins of the sacrament to the laity in one kind only, the cup being withheld.[2] This custom had begun in certain quarters early in the twelfth century, and gradually spread until it was enforced by the Council of Constance, 1415 A.D. In the ancient Church infants had been communicated in the species wine only, and from the third century at least the sacrament was reserved for the absent in the species bread only. These usages were justified on grounds of practical necessity, and on the theological ground that, since Christ is not divided in the sacrament, the substantial gift is not reduced for one who receives in one kind. The reasons originally advanced for the more radical practice under discussion were to prevent any accidental spilling of the consecrated wine and to prevent the unlearned from thinking that the whole Christ is not in each species. The doctrine of concomitance, thus accentuated, was set forth

[1] On this subject, see D. Stone, *H. C.*, pp. 221–230; *Eucharistic Sacrifice*, note 18; W. E. Scudamore, *Notitia Eucharistica*, pp. 572–594; E. S. Ffoulkes, *Prim. Consec. of the Euch. Oblation;* J. M. Neale, *op. cit.*, pp. 492–506; *Cath. Encyc.*, s.v. "Eucharist," II. 2.

[2] D. Stone, *H. C.*, pp. 213–221; A. P. Forbes, art. xxx; E. B Pusey, *Is Healthful Reunion Impossible*, pp. 328–331. Cf. St. Thomas, III. lxxx. 12.

by the Councils of Constance, of Basle, and of Trent.

That this doctrine is true, cannot be seriously questioned; but it would seem that no lighter reason than that of special necessity in given cases justifies disregard of the requirement of Christ "Drink ye all of it."[1] Moreover, the question arises as to whether a special grace is not conveyed by the administration of each species. That there is such grace has been acknowledged by some of those who defend the Latin practice. But to say that communion in one kind deprives the laity of grace necessary for salvation is evidently rash.[2]

III. *Modern*[3]

§ 10. The sketch above given has been confined to the more noteworthy lines of development. Before proceeding, therefore, the more comprehensive statement should be made that previous to the sixteenth century comparatively few writers are found to doubt (*a*) that the consecrated species are truly the body and blood of Christ; (*b*) that a real, although non-physical, change of the bread and wine is accomplished by the Holy Spirit through their consecration; (*c*) that the body and blood of Christ are really and objec-

---

[1] St. Matt. xxvi. 27.   [2] Cf. p. 94, above, and refs. there given.
[3] On modern developments in general, see S. *Hist.*, vol. II; Hastings, *Encyc. of Relig.*, s.v. "Eucharist," pp. 564–570; *Schaff-Herzog Encyc.*, s.v. "Lord's Supper," pp. 34 *et seq.*; K. R. Hagenbach, *Hist. of Doctr.*, § 259.

tively present in the sacrament, although in ineffable manner transcending physical and spatial analogies; (*d*) that the whole Christ is present and is communicated under each species; (*e*) that the body and blood of Christ are really, although spiritually, received by means of manducation of the sacramental species; (*f*) that the Eucharist is a proper, although representative, sacrifice, deriving its sacrificial status from its constituting the appointed memorial before God of the one true sacrifice of Christ; (*g*) that it is a propitiatory sacrifice — not absolutely *in se*, but derivatively, as being the formal rite whereby Christians acceptably plead the one self-sufficient sacrifice of Christ's death.

This general consensus did not prevent varying emphasis upon the several branches of Eucharistic doctrine. Speaking broadly, and ignoring numerous individual exceptions, the tendency of the patristic period was (*a*) to emphasize the identification of the consecrated elements with the body and blood of Christ, that is, to assert the literal force of our Lord's words; (*b*) to connect the Eucharistic sacrifice with our Lord's heavenly priesthood, as well as with His death, and to reckon with the non-propitiatory aspects of sacrifice. The mediæval tendency was (*a*) to stress the mystery of change in the elements; (*b*) to pay increasingly exclusive attention to the propitiatory aspect of the Eucharistic sacrifice, and in large measure to ignore its connection with the heavenly oblation of Christ.

An important change in the ordinary manner of reckoning with the sacramental side of the Eucharistic mystery was now to appear. The new method is to treat the doctrine of the real presence as the most prominent and determinative aspect. We ought carefully to note that our Lord did not reveal the Eucharistic mystery in terms of presence, but in those of identification. He did not say "My body is present in this," but "This is My body"; and that the consecrated bread and wine *are* the body and blood of Christ is the revealed premise of catholic theology *in re*. The two inferences, that some change of the bread and wine is involved, and that there is a real presence of Christ's body and blood in the consecrated species, are logically sound, of course.

But to shift the primary attention from the original mystery of identification to one or other of these inferential propositions, true though they be, can hardly fail to disturb perspectives, and to bring speculative problems to the front. Such considerations appear to explain, in part at least, the contrast between the patristic freedom from Eucharistic controversies and the confusing discord of later ages. A one-sided stress upon the inferential mystery of conversion ushered in the mediæval controversies; and the writer believes that an equally one-sided attention to the inferential mystery of presence partly explains the modern confusion of thought concerning the Eucharist. The ancients were at peace with each other because they attended in common to the Lord's words, the authority of which was not open to debate. Later Christians have lost that peace because they have taken their stand upon inferential propositions, which have not the same explicit basis in the *ipsissima verba* of the Word.

But there were additional causes of the many departures from the ancient doctrine concerning the Eucharist which appeared in the sixteenth century. The break with the Catholic Church which then occurred carried with it a rejection of catholic authority, a substitution of individualistic private judgment, and a violent recoil from every proposition supposed to be characteristic of papalism and mediævalism. That the Papal See was cherishing and defending abuses that tended to reduce the spiritual quality of Eucharistic teaching by connecting it with highly disputable theories and superstitions is a fact; and the consequent recoil was not less inevitable because of its deplorable consequences.

§ 11. Ignoring the manifold complexities of this recoil, as impossible to discuss within the space at command, the changes among continental Protestants and Reformers began with utter rejection of the doctrine of transubstantiation and of the proposition that the Eucharist is a proper sacrifice. Genetically speaking, the chief resulting theories concerning the sacrament were three.

(*a*) The Lutheran view [1] is often called consubstantiation, which implies an identification of the

[1] On which, see S. *Hist.*, II. 9–37; Hastings, *op. cit.*, pp. 564–566.

substance of the elements with that of Christ's body and blood. A more accurate description is that of co-presence. Luther did rhetorically insist that Christ's words are to be taken literally; but his actual theory was that the body and blood of Christ are *present* in, with and under the consecrated bread and wine. No real identification was held by him. He grounded his theory in his Christological error that the glorified body of Christ is ubiquitous, but contended for a special presence in the sacrament, differing from that elsewhere available. This special presence he declared to be not *circumscriptive* but *diffinitive*. The wicked, he contended, receive the body and blood in the sacrament, but not the benefit.

(*b*) The Zwinglian view [1] excluded any real presence of our Lord's body and blood, and reduced Christ's words to a mere figure of speech. That is, when Christ said, "This is My body," He meant "signifies" My body. The rite is celebrated in order to call to memory Christ's death, for human edification and to symbolize our faith in its benefits. But faith is the organ of benefit, and the sacrament confers no supernatural grace. It is an external expression of communion between the faithful — a mutual and social pledge of united allegiance. Thus a somewhat complete break with catholic doctrine took place.

(*c*) The Calvinistic view [2] also excluded any objective presence of Christ's body and blood in the con-

---

[1] On this, see S. *Hist.*, II. 37-43; Hastings, *op. cit.*, pp. 566-567.
[2] S. *Hist.*, II. 50-61; Hastings, *op. cit.*, pp. 567-569.

secrated bread and wine, but supposed their presence in power for the elect — a dynamic as distinguished from a substantial presence. The sacrament, in brief, is an appointed seal and pledge that the elect when they receive it also feed by faith and by the Spirit's operation on the body and blood of Christ. The sacrament is not the vehicle of the gift, although a sure sign of its bestowal upon the elect. Thus the traditional doctrines of real presence and, *a fortiori*, of identification and of sacramental conversion, are excluded; and, although the doctrine of communication of Christ's body and blood remains, it is given a novel interpretation and restricted in application to those communicants whom God has secretly predestined to glory.

This "receptionist" view, which limits the presence of Christ's body and blood to the heart of the receiver, was still further reduced in what is called "virtualism" — the theory that only the virtue or beneficial effects flowing from the body and blood are received.[1] There also appeared the contention that Christ's body and blood are present in the sacramental rite at large, rather than in the consecrated species, with the view that Christ is present in Person to bless faithful communicants, but not in His body and blood substantially considered. The sacramental phrase "body and blood" symbolizes, according to this theory, the life and virtue which flows from Him

[1] Put forth by Cranmer in 1550, and maintained by Waterland and others. S. *Hist.*, II. 127-129, 501-6, etc.

into us.¹ Then there is the strange opinion that Christ's body and blood are present in their slain or dead state.² The older impanation theory has also been received — the theory that the bread and wine become Christ's body and blood not by conversion, but by assumption into personal union with the Word, after the analogy of the assumption of flesh at the Incarnation. According to this theory, the sacramental body and blood constitute another body and blood, not identical with that in which Christ was crucified, raised and glorified. The implied premise is that Christ meant, "This *also* is My body."³

In this confusing babel of Eucharistic beliefs we see the consequences of forsaking the unifying guidance of the Catholic Church, and of giving rein to private judgment. Among Protestants the general tendency has been toward the Zwinglian standpoint; and the sacrament has been dethroned from its ancient central place in religious life.

§ 12. In dealing with Anglican developments [4] we

---

[1] Cf. the reverent statement of Dr. Handley Moule, given in Report of Fulham Conference on *The Doctrine of Holy Communion*, etc., 1900, pp. 72–73. Given in S. *Hist.*, II. 584–585.

[2] Bishop Andrewes, *Serm.* VII, on the Resurrection, and others. Cf. pp. 122–123, below; S. *Hist.*, I. 292, II. 223–225, 261–262.

[3] Defended as the postulate of patristic doctrine by L. Waterman, *Prim. Tradition of the Eucharistic Body and Blood*. Cf. ch. iv. § 4, below; K. R. Hagenbach, *op. cit.*, § 196 (2); *Schaff-Herzog Encyc.*, *s.v.* "Impanation."

[4] On Anglican developments at large, see S. *Hist.*, chh. x–xiii, xv–xvi; H. C., chh. ix–xi, *The Doctr. of the Real Presence . . . in the English Church* (erroneously ascribed to Pusey).

should remember (*a*) that the Anglican Churches claim to be provincial extensions of the Catholic Church, and base their reformation of mediæval doctrine upon appeal to the doctrine of the ancient Catholic Church; (*b*) that therefore, even in affirmations which appear designedly to fall short of full catholic doctrine, but which so far as they go are elements of such doctrine, the catholic standpoint should be assumed to be retained, especially in view of the seemingly catholic form and implications of the Anglican liturgy. *Lex orandi lex credendi*.[1]

With regard to Eucharistic doctrine the course of the Anglican reformation exhibits three operative factors: (*a*) the development among leaders of defective personal views corresponding to the limitations which appear in the positive affirmations of the *Thirty-Nine Articles;* (*b*) the eirenic purpose of framing statements which could be accepted by all types of English Christians except the distinctively Roman and the Zwinglian; (*c*) a conservative instinct, guided we believe by the overruling Holy Spirit, which saved the English Church from repudiating those elements of the catholic doctrine which were not fully and unmistakably reaffirmed.

Certainly the patent limitations of *The Articles of Religion*, and of the individual views of their framers, cannot in a Church claiming to retain the catholic faith commit Churchmen to a surrender of any verifiable element of the ancient catholic doctrine con-

[1] Cf. *Introduction*, pp. 182-189.

cerning the Holy Eucharist. The true mind of a Catholic Church is catholic; and, in the absence of undeniable official repudiations of catholic doctrine, the prevalence in a given period of defective personal views, and the consequent limitations of the eirenic documents put forth for stilling controversy, should not be taken to signalize an abandonment of it. The Church's mind is deeper and more static than passing demonstrations, and is protected by supernatural safeguards.

The Articles,[1] as finally adopted in 1571, contain the following negations.

(a) "The supper of the Lord is not only a sign . . . but rather it is a Sacrament," etc. — repudiating the Zwinglian conception.

(b) "Transubstantiation . . . cannot be proved by Holy Writ, but is repugnant . . . overthroweth the nature of a Sacrament," etc. The last clause shows that the notion of a physical destruction of the nature of the outward sign is what is repudiated.

(c) Reservation, carrying about, lifting up and worshipping of the sacrament are "not by Christ's ordinance." "The Sacraments were not ordained to be gazed upon," etc., "but that we should duly use them." It is not denied that such practices are allowable, when kept in due subordination to the instituted purpose of the sacrament.

(d) "The wicked, and such as be void of a lively faith, . . . in no wise are partakers of Christ."

[1] Arts. xxviii–xxxi. See treatises on the Articles by A. P. Forbes, E. T. Green, B. J. Kidd and E. C. S. Gibson.

(e) "The cup of the Lord is not to be denied to the lay people."

(f) "The offering of Christ" being sufficient "for all the sins of the whole world, both original and actual, . . . there is none other satisfaction for sin, but that alone. Wherefore the sacrifices of Masses, in which it was commonly said that the Priests did offer Christ for the quick and the dead, to have remission of pain or guilt, were blasphemous fables, and dangerous deceits." Both the reason given and the plural phrase "sacrifices of Masses" clearly leave us free to interpret this denial as directed against treating Masses as so many additional sacrifices, supplementing defects of the one sacrifice of Christ.

No one of these negations is inconsistent with full acceptance of ancient catholic doctrine. The affirmations are as follows.

(a) "To such as rightly, worthily, and with faith receive the same, the bread which we break is a partaking of the body of Christ, and likewise the cup of blessing is a partaking of the blood of Christ." This is so much of catholic doctrine as is retained in the "receptionist" view.

(b) "The body of Christ is given, taken, and eaten . . . only after an heavenly and spiritual manner: And the mean whereby the body of Christ is eaten . . . is faith." This is consistent with catholic doctrine, which does not teach a physical manducation of Christ's body and blood.

(c) The sacraments are "certain sure witnesses and

effectual signs of grace and God's good will towards us, by the which He doth work invisibly in us," etc. "Effectual signs," as shown by the history of the phrase, and "by the which," seem to mean that the sacrament as such is an instrument of God's supernatural working in us — a characteristically catholic doctrine.

If the articles were designed to afford a full and formal definition of ecclesiastical doctrine, the limitations of these statements would signify departure from antiquity. But they were not so designed, and such interpretation goes counter to the formal principle of the Anglican reformation, which is an appeal to catholic antiquity. Moreover, the context or working system of which the Articles are a sort of appendix has less of the protestant flavour, and perpetuates a liturgical use and an incidental discipline which directly suggests, although without formally defining, the inherited catholic standpoint and doctrine.[1]

The Eucharistic liturgy is sacrificial in form, this aspect being especially explicit in the liturgy of the Episcopal Church of Scotland and in that of the American Church. In the administration the sacramental species are designated severally as "the Body of our Lord Jesus Christ" and "the Blood of our Lord Jesus Christ." In the *Catechism* which candidates for Confirmation are required to learn,

---

[1] A. P. Forbes, Preface, is helpful in considering how the Articles are to be interpreted. Cf. Wm. Palmer, *On the Church*, Pt. II. ch. vi, and Pt. IV. ch. xiv.

the "inward part or thing signified" is declared to be "the Body and Blood of Christ, which are verily and indeed taken and received by the faithful in the Lord's Supper" — the words "verily and indeed" being changed to "spiritually" in the American version. These facts and phrases, while definitely catholic in their quality, do not, of course, shut out some elasticity of interpretation; but they give countenance to those who believe that the official mind of the Anglican Communion touching the Eucharist is catholic rather than either protestant or reformed.

§ 13. It is significant that those who most heartily conformed to the settlement of 1559-1571 developed into the historic "high" Church school; and the tendency of this school has been to recover and to give clear expression to those elements of catholic doctrine concerning the Eucharist which were obscured by the reactionary influences of the sixteenth century. But the catholic premise of real identification of the consecrated bread and wine with the body and blood of Christ, that is, with that in which He was born of the Blessed Virgin, suffered and was glorified, this premise has waited for its clear enunciation until our own time. Even the Tractarians of Oxford, while seeking to take our Lord's words literally, usually contented themselves with the affirmation of a real presence of the body and blood of Christ in, with and under the consecrated bread and wine. At the close of the sixteenth century Richard Hooker had set forth the receptionist affirmation as affording a platform of peace, deliberately refraining from saying whether his personal view went further than that towards the fuller ancient doctrine.[1] His theological prestige was great and lasting, and the limitations of his eirenicon afford a partial explanation, perhaps, of this slowness of catholic recovery.

The "low" Church or evangelical school, dominated by fear of the Roman Church and by much sympathy with Nonconformists, have refused to take a higher view of the sacrament than the undeniable contents of the Articles require, and have usually tended towards the virtualism of Archbishop Cranmer. Some have gone further in the Zwinglian direction, and some profess a doctrine of real presence, meaning a mystical presence of Christ's person in the rite at large as distinguished from the consecrated bread and wine. The tendency of Latitudinarians and "broad" Churchmen has been unmistakably to repudiate anything higher than the baldest Zwinglian conception.

The future is almost certainly in the hands of those who make the most of the Church's working system embodied in the Prayer Book, and we have given reasons for describing that system as catholic in its form and implications.

[1] *Eccles. Polity*, V. lxvii. 6–7.

CHAPTER IV

THE EUCHARISTIC GIFT

I. *The Mystery of Identification*

§ 1. In this chapter we discuss the meaning and implications of the description of the consecrated bread and wine given by our Lord — "My body" and "My blood." In the next chapter the sacrificial aspect of the mystery will be considered; and in another chapter the benefits of the sacrament, along with such incidental matters as ought to be included in any comprehensive survey of Eucharistic doctrine.

Our Lord's description of the consecrated species[1] affords the revealed premise by which all discussion of the Eucharist should be controlled. It furnishes our symbol of faith *ad rem*, the "form of sound words" to which we have repeatedly to recur in order to test the tenability of our theories. Its correct interpretation is of the utmost importance, even though we may not hope to exhaust its meaning, and to solve the problems which it suggests. The rule by which we are to be guided in this interpretation is the larger

---

[1] On its meaning, in addition to the refs. given on pp. 75-77, above, see J. Pohle, pp. 23-44; D. Stone, in Hastings, *Dict. of Christ*, s. v. "Lord's Supper," pp. 72-73.

THE MYSTERY OF IDENTIFICATION

rule of faith, which is to assume that the ascertainable mind of the Catholic Church on any saving doctrine is the authoritative and trustworthy basis of doctrinal interpretation of Holy Scripture.[1] We follow this rule as one that has been amply vindicated by the general results of its application through many centuries. It is, of course, based upon the Church's commission to teach, and upon the promise of the Spirit's sure guidance in this function.

In some sense our Lord plainly identifies the consecrated bread and cup with His body and blood; and the Church has always refused to consider this identification as merely metaphorical. Its reasons for this refusal are partly drawn from the teaching of Christ in His address at Capernaum, partly from the indications of apostolic understanding of them, and partly from the closer agreement of a more literal interpretation with the place and function of the Blessed Sacrament in the new covenant. Two initial problems, however, confront us.

(*a*) The first of them is created by the assumption frequently made that our Lord is not possessed of blood in His glorified state.[2] If this means merely that our Lord's blood is no longer in its earthly state, and no longer fulfils its earthly functions, it seems well grounded, but such a conclusion is non-relevant to the question as to whether He now possesses, and can impart to us as His own, a gift properly described

[1] Cf. *Authority*, etc., pp. 243-246, 255-257.
[2] E.g., L. Waterman, pp. 20-21.

as His blood. If, however, the assumption is that nothing really exists in any form or condition which can rightly be thus described, it is not susceptible of proof. It violates the implication of Old Testament ritual and prophecy that our High Priest enters the Holy Place "not without blood;"[1] and reduces even the metaphorical interpretation of the Eucharistic formula to unreality. Of what value is an ever recurring, even though purely figurative identification of sacramental wine with something which does not at all exist, coupled as it is with identification of the accompanying bread with an existing reality?[2]

(b) The other problem is suggested by the fact that when the Lord described the bread as His body, His flesh was not yet glorified but was visibly and physically there outside of the bread.[3] From this fact the inference is frequently made that He spoke metaphorically. And some of those who realize the weight of evidence for a higher interpretation, deny that the body which He made it to be is the body in which He sat before them and in which He is now glorified. These last infer that the consecrated bread is another

[1] Heb. ix. 7. Cf. Levit. xvi. 15. In Heb ix. 12, Christ is said to enter the Holy Place "through (διώ) His own blood." Cf. W. Milligan, *Resurrection of our Lord*, p. 242; M. F. Sadler, p. 66; St. Thomas, III. liv. 3.

[2] Cf. also the present cleansing function of His blood: Tit. iii. 5; 1 St. John i. 7; Revel. i. 5; vii. 14; Zech. xii. 1.

[3] *Crit. Review*, Sept., 1901, p. 403. Discussed by S. *Hist.*, I. 20 (who refers to H. N. Oxenham, *Cath. Doctr. of the Atonement*, Excurs. iv, on the condition of Christ's body while on earth); Chas. Gore, p. 312; H. L. Goudge, *op. cit.*, pp. 104-106.

body of His, a purely sacramental body. We may not venture to dogmatize as to how the Lord could make the bread to be the body in which He sat before them. But we are constrained to believe that He then accomplished and meant what He now accomplishes and means in every valid Eucharist, and that this is cannot be determined by the sensible conditions of that moment. It was no more impossible for Him to identify the bread with His body then visibly and locally present outside of it than it is for Him to identify it with that body now visibly and locally present outside of it to those who are with Him in Paradise. The two modes of presence, sacramental and physical, are equally to be reckoned with and equally beyond our adequate understanding in both cases. Therefore His being then visibly present to the disciples imports no intrinsic difficulty beyond that which confronts the understanding of catholic believers whenever the Eucharist is celebrated.

Some help may perhaps be derived from remembering that, although Christ had not yet been glorified, He appeared on one occasion to three of His Apostles wondrously transfigured. If He could for sufficient reasons anticipate certain conditions of His ascended state in this instance, we cannot rightly deny His power to anticipate other, although invisible, conditions of that state for the purpose of instituting the Holy Eucharist.

§ 2. In considering the double formula, "This is My body," "This is My blood," we should remember its symbolic status, as being the partial revelation in human terms of a mystery too profound to be expressed fully in such terms. Therefore we should be watchful against negations, lest in forgetfulness of our inadequate understanding we should exclude some vital aspect of Christ's meaning. Our task is to enter more and more fully into His meaning, rather than to erect negative barriers to further progress in apprehension. Historically the tendency to erect such barriers has almost always represented reaction from some crude caricature of the catholic doctrine. Having this caution in mind, we may rightly describe the consecrated bread and wine by an ascending series of affirmations, each of which is accepted by the Church as true in its positive aspects, and so far as it goes. Each is an incipient proposition, pointing further along a line of progress in apprehension the termination of which is not discernible to earthly believers.

(*a*) The consecrated bread and wine are figures, symbols, types, images, and so on, of what they are called — not less but more so after their consecration than before. They had pertinent figurative value beforehand, and therefore they are fittingly consecrated with a view to being religiously regarded and employed in such light for Christian purposes. Some of the ancients loved to dwell on this the initial proposition of Eucharistic faith; but they did not, as do certain moderns who appeal to their testimony, refuse to go further. They did not regard the consecrated species as *mere* figures of Christ's body and blood and nothing more.[1]

(*b*) They signify and represent, or do duty for, Christ's body and blood in the sacramental mystery, and thus have a sacred value and function for the faithful which cannot properly be ascribed to mere figures.

(*c*) They are so identified sacramentally with what they signify that they have the virtue and efficacy of Christ's body and blood; and those who rightly partake of the sacrament are enabled to receive this virtue by faith.

(*d*) By reason of their consecration, they are real vehicles of Christ's body and blood, and convey them in fact and substance to faithful communicants.

(*e*) They not only signify, represent and convey, but really are the very body and blood of Christ, although the manner in which they have become and are these things transcends human expression and conception. This in substance, is the ultimate affirmation of catholic doctrine in every age, so far as the mystery of identification is concerned. It implies a literal interpretation of Christ's words, but more. It treats them as being an incipient, although for our present needs a sufficient, declaration of what is insusceptible of more adequate human expression; and assumes that in the unrevealed and ineffable aspects of the mystery lies the solution of the problems which are involved. From this standpoint of belief in real as opposed to

[1] The Zwinglian view. Cf. pp. 86–87, above.

merely figurative and virtual identification, we adopt the oft quoted lines —

> "Christ was the Word that spake it;
> He took the bread and brake it;
> And what the Word did make it;
> That I believe and take it." [1]

§ 3. The doctrine of real identification above presented is a hard saying for many who feel constrained by the evidence of Scripture and catholic consent to accept it in terms. Accordingly, we find writers seriously debating as to what body and blood of Christ is meant, as if He might be thought to possess more than one. To catholic doctrine there is but one real body and blood of Christ; and the *res sacramenti* is no other than that which He took of the Blessed Virgin, in which He suffered, in which He now reigns in glory, and which is mystically extended for the incorporation of the baptized in the Christian Church. Of this body there has been a succession and plurality of states, and its content has varied according to the law of organic bodies in general; but the phrase "body," unless metaphorically used, cannot rightly designate any other than that which He wore on earth and has taken into Heaven. Its continuous identity with itself, amid all the changes of condition which it has undergone, is a postulate that cannot be dis-

---

[1] Ascribed to Queen Elizabeth, but is by John Donne, *Divine Poems*. So Vernon Staley says.

THE MYSTERY OF IDENTIFICATION

regarded without hopelessly confusing our conception of the Eucharistic mystery.

This thought will help us to find our way through the complexities created by the varying uses of certain adjectives and adverbs employed in describing the *res sacramenti* and the mode of its presence. Such adjectives as natural, physical, carnal, slain, dead, risen, glorified, super-physical, spiritual, mystical and sacramental ought to be used as adjectives, and as describing the body itself in one or other of its states. That is, they should describe in all cases one and the same body of Christ, even though severally intended to describe it at different stages, or in different conditions of its existence. The accent, however, may be one of identification merely, as it should be when writers insist that the natural or physical body of Christ is in the sacrament; or it may be one of description of its present proper state, as when we say that the risen, glorified and spiritual body of Christ is in the sacrament.

Unfortunately writers often fail to make their accent clear. Accordingly, those who with sound meaning insist that the natural Body of Christ is present in the sacrament, seem to others to be maintaining a physical and carnal mode of identification with the sacrament. In short, they carelessly use their adjectives adverbially, and sometimes the resulting confusion of thought has the effect of lowering their own conceptions in a materialistic direction.

Similar confusion of thought arises from inaccurate

use of adverbs. Thus some say that the body of Christ is naturally present, meaning either that it is really present or that it is the true body of Christ which is present, but seeming to mean that it is present in a physical manner — a crude and erroneous idea. From an opposite standpoint some say with verbal correctness that the body of Christ is present spiritually. They should mean either that the mode is not physical, that it is a supernatural mystery, that it is by the operation of the Holy Spirit, or all of these things together. In fact, however, they sometimes mean that the body of Christ is in the sacrament only in a figurative or virtual sense. The terms "spiritual" and "spiritually" are in this connection hopelessly ambiguous, unless used in a definitive context. The general result of this confused use of adjectives and adverbs is that we have need to be cautious in interpreting the statements of many writers, if we would avoid the injustice of ascribing to them sacramental ideas which they would reject.

For clearness in Eucharistic discussion it is best as a rule to confine our use of adjectives and adverbs to those which properly apply to, or are connected with, the body of Christ in its existing mode of being and presence. The body of Christ which the consecrated bread is rightly said to be is the body which is now supernaturally exalted in glory — the living and glorified body. This is no other body than that which was subject to earthly and natural conditions and was slain; but these conditions have been forever left behind, and to describe it by adjectives borrowed from them is apt to be misleading. For similar reasons, the manner in which the Eucharistic bread is identified with this glorified body of Christ should be indicated by such adverbs as supernaturally, mysteriously, sacramentally and (with definitive context) spiritually. Such terms as naturally and carnally suggest, and sometimes have really signified, materialistic error.

One description, in particular, is indefensible, that the Eucharistic body is the body of Christ *as slain*.[1] It is objectionable because the state of being slain has forever passed away. The body which we discern by faith in the sacrament is the living body of Christ. The mode of speech criticised is in some cases, perhaps, merely an exaggerated form of witness to the undoubted truth that both in Heaven above and in the sacrament the living Lamb of God exists in a manner that bears witness to His *having been slain*, and which makes His very appearance for us an effective pleading of His death. But to describe His body in the Eucharist as slain either involves an unreal use of terms or suggests a re-immolation of Christ — reversion to the conception of "sacrifices of Masses" which the thirty-first of our *Articles of Religion* condemns.

§ 4. There remains to consider the determinate assertion that the Eucharistic body and blood of Christ constitute another body and blood of Him,

[1] Cf. p. 107, n. 2, above, for refs.

other than that in which He was born, suffered and overcame death. In brief, it is said that the Eucharistic body, although closely identified with Christ's body in glory, is not numerically identical with it. The right name for this theory is "impanation,"[1] for it hypothecates in the Eucharist an assumption by the Word of bread, *panis*, into a hypostatic union analogous to that of the Incarnation. Its plausibility lies in its seeming to do justice to the so-called literal interpretation of our Lord's words, "This is my body," without involving the difficulty of explaining how a body locally present in Heaven only is produced, so to speak, on earthly altars.

This difficulty, however, is escaped only by bringing in the new and equally serious difficulty of explaining how the Word can bring into hypostatic union with Himself non-rational natures like bread and wine, and do this not once for all but repeatedly and on thousands of altars. No help can be had from the analogy of our own assimilation of such substances, for this assimilation destroys their specific nature, whereas the hypothesis in question postulates the continued existence of the bread and wine, as such, after their consecration.

We have indicated already that the argument for this theory which is based upon the visible presence of our Lord's flesh in the upper room when the sacrament was instituted is without real force.[2] The same

[1] Cf. p. 107, above, where refs. are given.
[2] Cf. pp. 116–117, above.

may be said of an argument based upon the alleged analogy of the mystical Body of Christ. The mystical Body is not properly described as another body of Christ, numerically other than His glorified body. Rather it is a mystical extension of His glorified body under the form of the Christian *ecclesia*.[1] So the Eucharistic body of Christ is a sacramental extension of His glorified body and truly one with it. We can and ought to distinguish the modes of existence of Christ's body in glory, in the Church and in the Eucharist, but the body which exists in each of these modes is one and indivisible.[2]

The theory under criticism is wholly lacking in demonstrable patristic support, and since its mediæval formulation it has been generally repudiated by catholic writers. For the purpose of argument at least, we feel free to acknowledge that a great array of patristic passages concerning the Eucharistic *res* can be found which might be made to fit in with the unexpressed assumption that the Eucharistic body is numerically other than our Lord's glorified body. But they also fit in, and that very readily, with the contrary hypothesis, with that which we are defending as the catholic doctrine *ad rem*. If the ancients neither explicitly repudiated the impanation theory nor took pains to avoid language which might be interpreted

---

[1] *The Church*, ch. iii. § 6.
[2] The Church is His body in that its members are vitally united with Christ's body in glory. The consecrated bread is His body as given objectively for our sustenance and for our oblation to God.

by moderns in seeming harmony with it, this was because it had not yet been formulated. Therefore it did not confront them as something to be reckoned with in their choice of terms. The non-emergence of undeniable assertions of the impanation theory during the patristic period is very significant in view of the fact that all the particulars of catholic belief concerning the Eucharist which have been developed in subsequent ages are anticipated in patristic literature in at least incipient forms.

II. *The Mystery of Conversion*

§ 5. The doctrine that the consecration of the bread and wine in the Eucharist brings about an invisible change in them, some kind of conversion of them into the body and blood of Christ, is a theological inference from the recorded facts and words of the institution of this sacrament. But the inference is so readily suggested that it began to be made at an early date, and in the middle ages came to have determinative effect upon ecclesiastical terminology. The argument is very clear and direct. Our Lord took into His hands mere bread and wine, and after blessing them He declared them to be His body and blood. If the Catholic Church is right in taking this declaration in what is called the literal sense, the bread and wine by His blessing *became* His body and blood; and what was then brought to pass constitutes a divine indication of what Christ achieves by His Holy Spirit in every valid Eucharist.

To say that in some proper sense — a sense not to be reduced to a mere metaphor — the bread and wine by consecration become the body and blood of Christ is one thing; to define the sense in which this is said, and the manner and incidental consequences of the becoming, is a different and far more difficult thing.

Many of the controversies concerning the Eucharist have grown out of attempts to define these things, and out of the coincident shifting of attention from the revealed premise of identification discussed in previous sections to the inference made therefrom which we are now considering. The most difficult aspect of the mystery has been brought to the forefront, and the uncertainties which attend its definition have tended to weaken men's faith in the original truth revealed by Christ when He solemnly declared the consecrated bread and cup to be His body and blood. An inference from revealed doctrine, even when, as in this case, it is undeniably clear, can be safely held only in relation to the premise from which it is deduced. When it is given the status of an independent proposition, and used as the basis of further speculation, it is liable to assume values and implications which obscure rather than correctly articulate the original premise.[1]

None the less, considered as an inference, and in the interpretative context of its premise, the proposition that by means of their consecration the Eucharistic bread and wine somehow become the body and

[1] Cf. *Introduction*, pp. 202-208.

blood of Christ cannot be denied without logical implications subversive of the original catholic doctrine from which it is deduced. Theoretically one might believe that this inference need not have been formulated, and that a simple resting in the Lord's words is preferable to the disturbing assertions of inferential theology. But, in practice, the inference in question could not have been prevented, if Christians were seriously to meditate upon the words of Christ. It was inevitable. We may regret that the inference had to be made, but once correctly made, theologians at least have to reckon with it; and they cannot deny its truth without inviting the subversive consequences above indicated.

What shall we say or not say, then, as to the manner and incidental consequences of the fact that the bread and wine become the body and blood of Christ? If we would be loyal to the certainties of faith, we must say negatively that the manner is non-sensible and non-physical, because the premised identification is such; and that no consequences follow which subvert the proper nature of the bread and wine, inasmuch as they continue to demonstrate their physical status to our senses.[1] Positively, we have to fall back upon the antecedent mystery, and say that, as the mode of identification is superphysical and supernatural, so the change and its results utterly transcend every process and consequence of the

[1] St. Paul says of the consecrated sacrament, "For as often as ye eat this bread and drink the cup," etc. 1 Cor. xi. 26–28.

THE MYSTERY OF CONVERSION 129

natural and physical realm. They are ineffable. To conclude, in whatever sense it is declared that the consecrated bread and wine are the body and blood of Christ, in that sense we infer that they *have become* these sacred things.

§ 6. This assertion, that the consecrated elements have become the body and blood of Christ, is so frequently made by the ancients that it may be reckoned as a patristic commonplace. Further assertions that the bread and wine are changed into the body and blood are also far from rare. More striking and distinctive statements are made by such writers as St. Cyril of Jerusalem, St. Gregory of Nyssa, St. Ambrose of Milan, and by quite a few later Eastern theologians, which cannot be taken literally without seeming to indicate a change in the nature of the bread and wine.[1] But in the earlier instances at least they perhaps represent nothing more than rhetorical emphasis upon the doctrine that the elements become the body and blood of Christ. Thus the statements occur that the bread and wine are transmade ($\mu\epsilon\tau\alpha\pi\sigma\iota\epsilon\hat{\iota}\sigma\theta\alpha\iota$), transelemented ($\mu\epsilon\tau\alpha\sigma\tau\sigma\iota\chi\epsilon\iota\acute{\omega}\sigma\alpha\varsigma$) and transfigured (*transfigurantur*), and that their nature is changed. St. Cyril goes so far as to say, "The seeming ($\phi\alpha\iota\nu\acute{o}\mu\epsilon\nu\sigma\varsigma$) bread is not bread, even though it is sensible to the taste, but the body of Christ."[2] There may be set against such language a number of clear

---

[1] Instances given in S. *Hist.*, I. 102-106 and ch. iv. Cf. E. B. Pusey, pp. 162-264.

[2] *Catech.*, xx. 9.

assertions that the bread and wine continue in their proper nature after they have become the body and blood of Christ;[1] and this appears to have been the ordinary patristic view.

But the middle ages saw a widespread shifting of emphasis from the mystery of identification to that of conversion, the new emphasis being intended to fortify the literal interpretation of our Lord's words, but creating a misleading terminology and new problems. In the West this development terminated in the scholastic doctrine of transubstantiation.[2] The Easterns also adopted an equivalent terminology, the term μετουσίωσις taking the place of *transubstantio*, and συμβεβηκότα that of *accidentiæ* and *species*.[3] The new doctrine hypothecated the distinction between *substantia* and *accidentiæ* or *species*—the former signifying the invisible substratum or noumenon of things, and the latter their phenomenal or sensible properties and effects. These two elements were regarded as separable by divine power, and the substance of the bread and wine was said wholly to be converted by consecration into the substance of Christ's body and blood, the accidents alone remaining. That is, the accidents after consecration were said to belong no longer to the substance of bread and wine.[4]

[1] See S. *Hist.*, I. 98–102; E. B. Pusey, pp. 75–90.
[2] This development is described in ch. iii. § 7, above.
[3] Cf. ch. iii. § 9, above.
[4] The Council of Trent used the term "species" instead of "accidents"; and the problem as to what supports the accidents of

Those who developed this theory were not seeking to assert a physical change, but a metaphysical and non-sensible one. They apparently thought that in so doing they were relieving the mystery of materialistic implications, while guarding the traditional and literal interpretation of our Lord's words. In short, they supposed that they were preserving a spiritual conception of the conversion.[1] Moreover, many of those who have maintained the doctrine of transubstantiation have attributed a reality to the remaining accidents or species that approximates, in some cases seems practically equivalent to, the continued existence of the physical matter commonly meant by the phrase bread and wine. Still further, various writers both East and West have denied that in affirming transubstantiation they intend any explanation of the mystery of conversion. They define their meaning as being simply an assertion that the bread and wine become the body and blood of Christ truly and really, not in a merely metaphorical sense.[2]

§ 7. How are we to regard this development? Our attitude is embarrassed by the fact that in popular use the term "substance" as used in the doctrine came to denote physical matter, and is still widely employed in that sense. Accordingly, the popular *doctrina Ro-*

---

bread and wine after the transubstantiation was not officially dealt with.

[1] Cf. D. Stone, *H. C.*, pp. 83–87.

[2] The Council of Jerusalem, *decret.* xvii, in asserting μετουσίωσιν, denied any further meaning than that the bread and wine really become the body and blood of Christ. See S. *Hist.*, I. 182.

manensium of the sixteenth century had become really materialistic, and meant that the bread and wine no longer really existed in the consecrated sacrament, the accidents being merely an accommodation of the body and blood, the only substantial reality present, to the limitations of our senses. Thus it was said that our senses deceive us in the Eucharist, if we suppose them to indicate any real presence of bread and wine. It was this carnal doctrine that was condemned in our twenty-eighth *Article of Religion*, and justly, as one that "overthroweth the nature of a sacrament" — presumably because it nullifies the outward sign.[1] Unfortunately the language of the Article does not distinguish between this crude view and other views denoted by the term "transubstantiation." An Anglican cannot therefore accept that term in any of its several uses without being obliged to make elaborate explanations in order to vindicate himself from accusations of materialism and disloyalty.[2]

Accordingly, under existing conditions a wise Anglican will avoid adopting the transubstantiation terminology in the normal definition of his position, whatever may be his opinion as to its orthodoxy as used and interpreted by Greek and Latin writers, and whatever acknowledgements he may feel under obli-

[1] Cf. A. P. Forbes, art. xxviii.
[2] Cf. J. G. H. Barry, pp. 132–134. Of efforts to harmonize Roman and Anglican doctrine as to transubstantiation, see E. B. Pusey, *Is Healthful Reunion Impossible?* pp. 75–90; and his correspondence with Newman, given in H. P. Liddon, Life of E. B. Pusey, vol. IV. pp. 166–172; G. F. Cobb and W. R. Carson, *opp. cit.*

gation to make in discussing the position of these writers. He will observe this course not deceitfully to conceal alien views, but honestly to avoid practically misrepresenting his actual position. And the transubstantiation terminology, soundly meant by many writers though it be, is open *in se* to adverse criticism. It is indeterminate and may be taken in at least three meanings: (*a*) the crude meaning in which our *Articles of Religion* condemn it; (*b*) the scholastic meaning, with its highly disputatious speculative assumption that the substance and accidents are different and separable things — a philosophical doctrine in any case, rather than a sure inference from Christ's words; (*c*) its more defensible meaning as intended merely to assert in an emphatic way, and without explanation, the doctrine that the bread and wine by consecration somehow truly become and are the very body and blood of Christ. So much we feel constrained to say by way of caution.

But a competent theologian will surely reckon with the fact, even though he regrets its being a fact, that a vast majority of catholic writers to-day, both East and West, employ the terminology in question, and do so in conformity with official decrees. The truth that a visible unity of doctrine within the Catholic Church is of the greatest importance, and should be cultivated by all legitimate means, may not be forgotten or neglected in practice. Therefore, we have need to go beneath the ambiguities and crudenesses which we suppose to inhere in this particular terminology, and to interpret its use by Eastern and Roman theologians, so far as the facts appear to permit, in accordance with sound doctrine. This will lead us to assume, in the absence of evidence to the contrary, that the doctrine of transubstantiation does not commit its defenders to the crude and speculative ideas associated with that term in ordinary Anglican interpretations of it, but means no more than an emphatic assertion that in the Eucharist the bread and wine become Christ's body and blood — in the same sense in which He declared them *to be* His body and blood, after He had blessed them in the night of His betrayal. On this basis we can take note of the acknowledgements that the accidents or species remaining in the Eucharist are not illusory, and can reasonably interpret them as virtually witnessing to the reality of the outward sign of the sacrament.[1]

§ 8. If the bread and wine truly become the body and blood of Christ, can they rightly be said to retain their former nature and still to be bread and wine? On the basis of a negative answer to this question, modern protestant writers vehemently repudiate the doctrine of conversion and, *a fortiori*, of identification as well. The imperfections of transubstantiation terminology, above indicated, serve to strengthen them in this negative answer and inference. On the other hand, the ancients clearly took for granted an affirmative answer; and, with a few uncertain excep-

---

[1] A very different line is taken by Chas. Gore, *Dissertations*, pp. 229 *et seq*.

THE MYSTERY OF CONVERSION

tions, they held, without being conscious of inconsistency, the doctrine that the consecrated elements are and have become the body and blood of Christ without ceasing to be real bread and wine.[1] There were giants in those days, and we are not justified in explaining their position as either careless or stupid. They were, however, more alive to the supernatural aspects of the mystery than are the majority of those who deny that such things can be.

To explain how they can be is a futile undertaking, for we are dealing with a mystery which transcends all natural analogies. There are, however, two supernatural analogies that may relieve our minds from feeling stultified in accepting this doctrine. We are taught that the divine Logos became flesh (Ὁ Λόγος σὰρξ ἐγένετο);[2] but that in becoming what He was not, He remained what He was, truly divine, is also taught in Scripture, and constitutes a stereotyped formula of catholic theology.[3] How this can be we do not pretend to say; but our inability to explain does not put us to confusion in accepting the fact that Jesus Christ is both God and Man, as truly one as the other, without division of His Person.

Again, the Church is visibly a society of men, and subject to the conditions and accidents of earthly societies; but it is declared to be the Body of Christ, and that in terms and connections which forbid our

---

[1] Cf. refs. in p. 130, n. 1, above. [2] St. John i. 14.
[3] Patristic examples are given in the writer's *Kenotic Theory*, pp. 5-6, n. 2.

taking the description as metaphorical.[1] It is at the same time both of these things; and, because it is, it exhibits in history a union of opposite qualities which baffles the understanding of carnal observers. How can this be? We do not know, but accept it as a mystery of the Holy Spirit's operations.

The Eucharistic sacrament is said to consist of two parts; but the phrase ought not to be taken as meaning that the inward *res* is separate or separable from the outward elements. A distinction of aspects and relations is involved, rather than a demarkation between mutually discrete substances.[2] The sacrament is one and indivisible, although substantially representative of two worlds. From the standpoint of this world, it is natural bread and wine to which an extraordinary thing has happened, insusceptible of verification by our senses. From the standpoint of the spiritual world, the self-same thing is the body and blood of Christ, marvelously accommodated to, and identified with, the forms and figures of bread and wine. The thing which we ought to avoid supposing is that, when our Lord declared the consecrated bread and wine *to be* His body and blood, He meant merely that His body and blood were present in them. In the *communicatio idiomatum* in which the consecrated sacrament is called either bread and

---

[1] Cf. *The Church*, ch. iii. § 5.

[2] The word "parts" is applied to "the outward visible sign, and the inward spiritual grace," a use which does not postulate two things, but one thing charged with grace.

wine or body and blood, we must not conceive of a substantial dualism. The sacrament has two relations and two proper descriptions, but the substantial reality is one in both. In saying this we break ground for discussing the mystery of the real presence.

III. *The Mystery of Presence*

§ 9. Like the doctrine of conversion, that of the real presence of our Lord's body and blood in the sacrament [1] belongs to inferential theology, and like it is too obviously deducible from the truth contained in our Lord's words to be denied without reducing these words to a metaphor. If the consecrated bread and wine are truly Christ's body and blood, it necessarily follows that His body and blood are really present in them; and this inference has been made and defended with general consent by catholic theologians in every age of Christian history. But, as in the case of the mystery of conversion, being an inference from our Lord's teaching rather than its explicit content, it is rightly understood, and given its just proportion, only when considered in derivative relation to the revealed premise from which it is deduced.

The modern tendency in many quarters has been

---

[1] On the real presence, see St. Thomas, III. lxxv–lxxvii; A. P. Forbes, *Thirty-Nine Arts.*, pp. 504–559; Archd. Wilberforce, chh. i–x; Wm. Forbes, *Considerationes Modestæ*, vol. II. pp. 378–507; D. Stone, *H. C.*, chh. iv, vi, viii–xi; W. R. Carson, pp. 15–31; P. N. Waggett, pp. 7–32.

to forget this, and to expound the real presence as if it were the fundamental premise of Eucharistic doctrine. The consequence has been a habit of defining this presence in terms that do not appear consistent with the original revelation. Our Lord did not say, "My body is present in, with and under this," but "This is My body." And His words, strictly taken, exclude rather than imply the supposition frequently apparent in modern assertions of the real presence, that the sacred things are to be distinguished numerically from the things with which they are said to be present. Christ affirmed identity, which surely excludes the theory of mere co-presence of the two realities involved. Some of these writers, with a happy inconsistency of language, have indeed continued to affirm that the consecrated bread and wine truly are the body and blood of Christ, even while also using the terms which we are criticising. But in employing this terminology they inevitably reduce the clear coherence of their general treatment of Eucharistic doctrine. In many cases this treatment seems practically to be controlled by the theory of co-presence, rather than by the literal interpretation of our Lord's words which with patent sincerity they profess to follow.[1]

Returning to positive definition, the fact remains that in the sense and manner in which the Lord declared the consecrated bread and wine to be His body

[1] The word "with" surely implies co-presence rather than identification.

and blood, in this sense and manner the Catholic Church has always taught that His body and blood are present in the consecrated bread and wine. The necessity of thus holding, if we take our Lord's words as more than a metaphor, is very clear. If one thing is rightly declared to be another thing, then that other thing is present in the thing first spoken of, for identification forbids separation.

And what is thus present? If the Lord's body and blood are present, then He is present in Person, for they are inseparable from Him. The presence under consideration, however, is obviously a special and sacramental presence, and is not to be confused with the omnipresence which is rightly ascribed to Him in His Godhead. It is a presence in His Manhood and as touching His body and blood.[1] It is not a branch of any ubiquity of His Manhood, for His human nature is not and cannot be ubiquitous while remaining truly human. The sacramental presence is not to be confused with His presence in His mystical Body, the Church, but is peculiar and adapted to the special purposes for which the Eucharist has been instituted.

§ 10. The various terms by which the presence is conventionally described in catholic theology require careful interpretation. They have been chosen for exactitude; but, thanks to modern controversy and other causes, they are often misunderstood. This misunderstanding has served to obscure the meaning

[1] Cf. Archd. Wilberforce, ch. iv.

of the catholic doctrine and to create artificial difficulties.

(*a*) The presence is called *objective* to signify that it is not merely subjective, or confined to the heart and understanding of the receiver of the sacrament, but is in the consecrated bread and wine previously to, and independently of, their sacramental reception.[1]

(*b*) It is called *real* as being the presence of a reality, called the *res sacramenti*. That is, it is a true presence of the very body and blood of Christ. It does not mean a realistic, or physical mode of presence.

(*c*) It is termed *substantial* in much the same sense. It does not mean either a physical or any other particular mode of presence; nor does it imply any philosophical theory concerning the nature of substance. It means simply that the thing signified in the sacrament, the *res sacramenti*, is not only signified, but is truly present in the consecrated bread and wine.

(*d*) It is sometimes, and with doubtful precision, called a *corporeal presence*. But in tenable doctrine the phrase cannot be used to define the mode of presence, as being physical, but should be intended to mean simply that what is present is truly the body (*corpus*) and blood of Christ.[2]

Speaking comprehensively, all the above terms con-

---

[1] It is not present *to us*, of course, unless we have faith to perceive it. Cf. P. N. Waggett, pp. 25-32; Chas. Gore, pp. 124-156. Both writers go further than the writer can in accepting an idealistic standpoint.

[2] Cf. Bishop Gardiner, *Explication and Assertion*, etc., p. 89, quoted in S. *Hist.*, II. 152.

stitute so many ways of saying that, because the consecrated bread and wine properly and truly are the body and blood of Christ, these sacred gifts are truly and properly said to be present in them. They do not describe the method of presence but the veritable fact of it. Moreover, each of these terms, except corporeal, can be, and is, used in adverbial form — objectively, really and substantially — without changing the meaning intended to be conveyed. For in each case the adverbial qualification of the verb "present" really denotes either the thing present or the fact of its being present. It does not in catholic use define the manner of the presence.

§ 11. The manner of the presence cannot be defined, although it can be described in the following relative and inadequate ways.

(*a*) Negatively speaking, it is not natural or physical, for in this mode the body of Christ is present in one place only, in Heaven. Accordingly, the presence is not properly speaking local, as if the body of Christ moved through space in order to be present in the sacrament. It is indeed said to be present on the altar, but this means simply that it is present in that which is on the altar, by virtue of the identification declared in our Lord's words. And all other phrases that connect the presence with either the locality or the movements of the sacrament must be taken in the same relative sense. The heavenly reality is present in a local sacrament, and in one that is carried about, but in the sense of the sacramental identification declared by Christ. The presence does not imply or involve any earthly localization, circumscription or spatial movement of the body and blood of Christ.[1]

(b) Negatively again, neither the presence nor the identification by which its reality is determined involves any interchange of the properties and functions which naturally belong, on the one hand, to the bread and wine, and, on the other hand, to the body and blood of Christ. Just as the Word became flesh without either humanizing His Godhead or nullifying the properties of flesh, so the bread and wine become Christ's body and blood without ceasing to have the properties of bread and wine and without changing the properties of the body and blood of the Lord. Accordingly, while making due allowance for the license of rhetoric, we may not in sober strictness speak of the body of Christ being broken, divided, immolated, crushed with the teeth, and so on, although we may say these things of the sacrament; and we may not ascribe heavenly attributes to the bread and wine, considered as such, although they may be ascribed to the sacrament, considered with reference to what it has become by Christ's action.[2]

(c) Positively, but relatively speaking, the presence is determined in mode by the sense and mode of the

---

[1] Cf. J. H. Newman, *Via Media*, ii. 220 (quoted in S. *Hist.*, II. 422); W. R. Carson, pp. 25–26.
[2] Cf. W. R. Carson, pp. 21–25, 27–31.

identification expressed in the words, "This is my body, This is my blood." We may call it sacramental, which means the same thing.

(*d*) Positively again, the presence is spiritual, a description which needs safeguarding, if it is not to be understood either as emptying the presence of objective reality or as excluding the body and blood of Christ from our notion of what is present. By spiritual presence should be meant a superphysical and non-sensible presence, perceived by faith, and supernaturally brought about by Christ through His Holy Spirit. In brief, it is mysterious, and transcends every earthly analogy by which we seek to describe it; although it is determinately objective, and sacramentally recognizable by faith.[1]

(*e*) Finally, the presence continues so long as the consecrated bread and wine remain in their proper nature, that is, until either by their appointed use in communion or by some other destructive cause they cease to be the species bread and wine. There is no express declaration to this effect in Scripture, but the fact that the presence in the sacrament endures at all — at least during the interval in the liturgy between consecration and communion, — coupled with the absence of any scriptural indication that the consecrated elements at any time cease to be what the Lord called them, has led the Church

---

[1] Cf. Roman Catholic witnesses to the spiritual nature of the mystery in S. *Hist.*, II. 420-425. See also St. Thomas, III. lxxvi. 4-7.

to the inference here given. Clear proof that this inference is catholic doctrine is found in the generally prescribed practice of reservation of the sacrament, and in the reverence with which the reserved sacrament has always been treated. The practice in question can be traced to a very early period, and from that period has been generally accepted in the Church as based upon, and justified by, the doctrine that the revealed effect of consecration continues so long as the consecrated species remain.[1]

§ 12. The statement that we may not ascribe the specific properties of bread and wine to the body and blood of Christ in the sacrament is nowhere disputed. To give a critical application, no reputable class of theologians would maintain that when the consecrated bread is divided and distributed the body of Christ is divided, so that the several communicants receive only broken parts of that holy gift.

The Catholic doctrine of concomitance,[2] as it is called in scholastic terminology, but which in substance is ancient, asserts in more comprehensive terms the truth which is involved in the application just given. This doctrine lays down the premise that the body and blood of Christ, although once separated in death, are no longer separable, and therefore are not separated from each other by the sacrament. Furthermore, Christ is wholly and indivisibly present

---

[1] On reservation, see ch. vi. § 12, below.

[2] On concomitance, see p. 94, above, and p. 180, below; D. Stone, *H. C.*, pp. 218–220; St. Thomas, III. lxxvi. 1–3.

in His body and blood, therefore the whole Christ, in all the fulness of both of His natures is present in each of the consecrated species and in every several particle of each. Such a definition may seem excessively logical and exact, in view of the mysteriousness of the subject; but wherein it is disputable is somewhat difficult to show.

The doctrine has been widely combated since the sixteenth century, even by many who believe in the real presence; but it has been rejected not on its own merits so much as because of its being emphasized chiefly in order to justify the practice of administering the sacrament to the laity in the species bread only. Something will have to be said concerning this practice in another chapter.[1] At present it seems sufficient to say that the truth of the doctrine is not overthrown by an objectionable use of it, and the use in question requires more reasons for its vindication than the doctrine of concomitance alone affords. In any case, whatever may be said of this doctrine in its elaborate form, its inital premise — that Christ is not divided in the sacrament — is certainly true.

This much of the limited space at our disposal has been used for setting forth the interrelated mysteries of identification, conversion and presence declared or implied in the phrases "This is My body" and "This is My blood," because only in the light of these truths can we rightly hope to discern sufficiently and

[1] In pp. 179-180, below.

without prejudice the richness, credibility and central value of the wonderful and comforting mysteries of the Eucharistic sacrifice and of sacramental communion — subjects to which the following two chapters are to be devoted.

CHAPTER V

THE EUCHARISTIC SACRIFICE

I. *Arguments*

§ 1. In this chapter we aim to vindicate and expound the catholic doctrine that the Holy Eucharist is a proper sacrifice.[1] It is indeed derivative, representative and applicatory; but by divine arrangement, under Christian conditions, and for Christian purposes, it fulfils an elementary requirement of religion — one which, under different conditions and with inferior results, was previously fulfilled by the sacrificial rites of the old covenant.

Our argument in behalf of this doctrine has for its first particular the proposition that some form of sacrifice is an integral and indispensable element of genuine religion, concretely considered;[2] so that the

---

[1] On the Euch. Sacrifice, see D. Stone, *H. C.*, chh. v, vii and *passim*; *Hist.*, *passim*; and *The Euch. Sacrifice*; Archd. Wilberforce, ch. xi; M. F. Sadler, *op. cit.*; W. J. Gold, *op. cit.*; J. R. Milne, *op. cit.*; A. P. Forbes on art. XXXI; *Theol. Defence*, pp 10–67; W. Sanday (Editor), *Different Conceptions of Priesthood and Sacrifice;* G. R. Prynne, *Truth and Reality of the Euch. Sacrifice;* B. J. Kidd, *op. cit.*; Chas. Gore, ch. iii; Wm. Forbes, *Consid. Modestæ*, vol. II. pp. 562–613; *Tracts for the Times*, No. 81. Of Roman Catholic works, see Jos. Pohle, *op. cit.*, pp. 272–397; and in *Cath. Encyc.*, *s.v.* "Mass, Sacrifice of the"; J. C. Hedley, *op. cit.*, chh. ix-xii; Chas. De Condren, *The Eternal Sacrifice.*

[2] Cf. J. S. Hart, *Spiritual Sacrifice*, Lecs. i–ii.

religious claim of Christianity, if valid, carries with it the presumption that it possesses some form of sacrifice. Religion means in the abstract a relation with God demanding, because of the social nature and solidarity of mankind, some form of generally recognizable public and corporate expression to God. In the concrete, therefore, or in working practice, a genuine religion should have some formal ritual in which its adherents can publicly and corporately express to God the relation in which they stand to Him. Moreover, the sacramental principle which has been expounded in the previous volume, grounded as it is in the necessities of human nature, requires that this expression shall be embodied in some corporately significant external action, thought to have divine sanction and calculated to show openly for its participants and before God the relations to Him in which they acknowledge themselves to stand. Without such ritual religion grows cold from lack of adequate expression.[1]

The history of ancient religions shows that men's natural tendency, even when no external prompting can be discovered, has been to fulfil this requirement by the twofold action of offering gifts to God, or to the gods, designed to secure His or their favour, and of feasting on what is offered, as a means of acceptable

---

[1] Cf. *Creation and Man*, pp. 216-217, 219-220. On sacrifice in general, see *Cath. Encyc.*, q.v.; J. A. Macculloch, *Compar. Theol.*, ch. viii; F. B. Jevons, *Introd. to the Study of Compar. Religion*, pp. 175-210; E. T. Green, ch. iii.

communion with Him, or with them. Sacrifice is the conventional name of such action, and when regarded from the Christian standpoint, it may be defined in a general way as a sacramental oblation and feast by which interior homage and self-surrender to God are suitably expressed, and filial fellowship with Him is cultivated. The cases in which ancient peoples are found to have no sacrifice are to be explained as due either to degradation so serious as to paralyze religious practice or to other adventitious causes, such as pantheistic beliefs that banish God from serious consideration,[1] and recoils from corrupted forms of sacrifice leading to mistaken views of its real nature and meaning.[2] We are justified, therefore, in regarding sacrifice as man's natural method of approach to God, the method which prevails when no evil, or at least accidental, cause interferes.

If sacrifice is natural to man, it seems to be this independently of sin and of the sense of need to placate God on account of sin. It appears to be so because sin is an *ex post facto* complication of human relations to God, and apart from such complication men owe to Him as His creatures the homage and self-oblation which sacrifice in its most elementary aspect is intended to signify and effect. But sin has occurred; and with the development of a sense of

---

[1] As in pure Buddhism.
[2] As in Mahommedanism and Protestantism. Cf. *Cath. Encyc.*, s.v. "Sacrifice," pp. 309, 317–318.

guilt among ancient races, the propitiatory element of sacrifice, shedding of blood, became general. So prominent did it become, and so strong became the general feeling of need to placate God on account of sin, that sacrifice often seemed to lose its primitive aspect and to become equivalent in meaning as well as in practice to sacrifice for sin. But the original idea of sacrifice — as the proper method in any case of creaturely homage and self-surrender to God — is of abiding validity, because men can never cease as creatures to owe the homage and self-surrender which in normal human practice has been thereby expressed.[1] Accordingly, whatever effect the sufficient sacrifice for sin of Jesus Christ may have had in modifying sacrifice, it cannot reasonably be understood to bring the need of any sacrificial rite to an end unless, as is not the case, a divine revelation to such effect has been given. And if the Christian religion has a sacrifice, it is surely to be found in the Eucharist, which alone of Christian rites resembles such a thing.

§ 2. The second particular in our argument is that the Christian system grows out of, and has unbroken continuity with, that of the old covenant, which was of divine institution and by divine prescription was sacrificial. The continuity of the Christian Church and dispensation with the Church and dispensation of Israel has been set forth in our last previous vol-

[1] On the obligation of sacrifice, see St. Thomas, II. II. lxxxv-lxxxvi.

ume.¹ The fact of such continuity is too well established to be disputed successfully. Baptized Christians constitute in Christ the seed of Abraham in which all the families of the earth by divine promise were to be blessed;² and they represent a catholic expansion and quickening of the spiritual remnant of Israel. Moreover, in order that the transition to a new covenant might not interrupt the continuity referred to, the Christian Church was nourished in the womb of Jewry for many years, until the destruction of Jerusalem put an end to the old ritual law. When this event had occurred, the Christian Church emerged in possession of a central corporate rite, the Holy Eucharist, which it regarded as taking the place of Jewish sacrifices, and as appointed of God thenceforth to be a modified and more effective sacrifice, which accomplished redemption had sanctified and established to continue until the end of the world.³

We have already seen that the sacrificial figures of Old Testament ritual, fulfilled by the death and heavenly priesthood of Christ, are taken up and exhibited in a new and more spiritual way in the Eucharist.⁴ The difference is that what the older sacrifices prefigured, and Christ's death and priesthood thereby consecrated make effectual, the Eucharist represents before God in behalf of Christians, and by

[1] *The Church*, ch. ii. § 1; ch. iii. § 4.
[2] Gen. xxii. 18; Acts iii. 25; Gal. iii. 8-9, 16, 29; Rom. ix. 8.
[3] For sub-apostolic witnesses, see S. *Hist.*, I. 42-52.
[4] In ch. iii. § 1, above. Cf. W. Milligan, *Ascension and Heavenly Priesthood of our Lord*, pp. 142-149.

the hidden operation of the Holy Spirit effectively applies to individuals.

There is no indication in Holy Scripture that the new covenant was to have no sacrificial rite;[1] and, in view of the fact that those to whom the Gospel was preached in apostolic days were accustomed to regard such ritual as an inevitable feature of any genuine religious system, the absence of any teaching calculated to correct this prevalent assumption affords the strongest presumption that the definitely sacrificial interpretation of the Eucharist which quickly prevailed among Christians after the older sacrifices ceased was justifiable — the more so that the Eucharist alone of Christian rites lends itself to such interpretation.

§ 3. That it does lend itself to sacrificial interpretation, appears in the terms utilized by our Lord at Capernaum and in His institution of the sacrament, and by St. Paul. As these have already been discussed in a previous chapter,[2] we need not here do more than briefly specify to what we refer. The circumstances and sacrificial associations involved have to be taken into account, of course, in reckoning with them. The circumstantial connection of both the address at Capernaum and the institution with the Passover seems to be more than accidental. The elements consecrated for the new rite were those of

---

[1] The sacrifices of the old law, especially the sacrifices for sin, were to be abolished. Heb. ix-x.
[2] In ch. iii. §§ 2-4, above.

the ancient meal and drink offerings, these having been kept continually before God on the table of show-bread in the Tabernacle and Temple. The feeding on the bread of God provided for in the Eucharist is in strict line with the sacrificial usage of the past both Jewish and Gentilic. The word ἀνάμνησιν, not conclusive in itself, is used in connections wherein it had sacrificial reference in the older ritual law. The cup was to be the blood of the covenant, a distinctly sacrificial association of ideas. This blood is described as poured out (ἐκχυνόμενον), suggesting the sacrificial pouring at the base of the altar rather than the physical result of violent death.

Other suggestions of sacrificial interpretation occur in the rest of the New Testament. The comparison made by St. Paul between the Eucharistic feast and the Jewish and Gentilic sacrifices gains point and force by such interpretation of the Christian rite.[1] When the sacrament is described in terms of communion with what is received, an integral element of ancient sacrifices is indicated. The modern antithesis between sacrifice and communion was then unknown. There is also the sacrificial description which St. Paul gives of his ministry. He claims to be a λειτουργόν, doing priestly work (ἱερουργοῦντα), that the oblation (προσφορά) of the Gentiles may be made acceptable.[2] This is in line with the statement in the Epistle to the Hebrews that a priest must have somewhat to offer.[3]

---

[1] 1 Cor. x. 18–22. [2] Rom. xv. 16.
[3] Heb. viii. 3. That the reference here is not to the past offering of the Cross, but to an abiding heavenly oblation, is borne out by

This writer is, of course, describing the priesthood of Christ; but the thought that Christ's Church shares in His priesthood is not without clear witness. St. Peter describes Christians as constituting a royal priesthood,[1] and St. Paul clearly does not treat His own priestly ministering as other than a ministry of Jesus Christ. There is no Christian action to which his mention of his ἱερουργοῦντα can strictly refer except that of the Eucharist. What can be said to offset this accumulation of suggestion, and the absence of teaching that in the new covenant religion was to lose its previously universal element of sacrifice?

(a) The New Testament instances in which sacrificial descriptions are applied to various non-sacramental forms of devotional expression and Christian conduct [2] are said to show that all sacrificial descriptions in the New Testament are figurative, representing simply an accommodation of language to existing forms of speech. But this proves too much, for a similar extension of sacrificial terms is found in the Old Testament,[3] without any reduction of the

---

the fact that the English R. V. of 1881 and the American Standard of later date, follow the Vulgate and King James in the rendering, "it *is* necessary that this High Priest also have somewhat to offer." The context is also decisive. Cf. *in loc.*, A. B. Davidson (in Exell's *Biblical Illustrator*); T. C. Edwards (in *Expositor's Bible*); Dean Alford; and Geo. Milligan, *Theol. of the Ep. to the Heb.*, pp. 139-146.

[1] 1 St. Pet. ii. 5, 9.
[2] E.g. Rom. xii. 1; Phil. ii. 17; iv. 18; Heb. xiii. 15-16.
[3] Psa. iv. 5; li. 17 (cf. verse 19); cvii. 22; Jonah ii. 9.

more strict use of such terms being involved. And there is no evidence whatever that the early Christians would regard a continuance of such derivative applications of sacrificial language as obtaining a new and negative implication.

(b) But, it is urged, the Epistle to the Hebrews definitely teaches that our Lord's death does away with sacrifice, as being a fulfilment of its requirement once for all.[1] This is surely a misinterpretation of what the sacred writer says. His subject is sacrifice *for sin*, not sacrifice comprehensively regarded. This sacrifice is indeed accomplished once for all. In fact, intrinsically speaking, the death of Christ is the only absolute sacrifice for sin in all history. The older sacrifices for sin were relative and prefigurative; but the fact that they were none the less divinely prescribed should put us on guard against hastily inferring, because the Eucharist is not an absolute sacrifice, or of sacrificial value independently of the Cross, that therefore it is not properly sacrificial. While the older sacrifices were prefigurative and gave way when their figures were fulfilled, the Eucharist is representative and, as earthly adjunct of the heavenly priesthood, applicatory of what has been fulfilled by Christ, and continues until the Lord comes again.[2] Like the older rites the Eucharist is a relative

[1] Heb. x. 5-18.
[2] 1 Cor. xi. 26. It is to be noted that the continuance of sacrifice in the messianic dispensation had been predicted. Jerem. xxxiii. 18-23; Isa. lvi. 7; lxvi. 20-21; Mal. i. 11; iii. 3-4. Cf. M. F. Sadler, ch. iv.

sacrifice only, but truly such in its relation to the Cross.

(c) Finally, the absence of any direct and explicit New Testament declaration that the Eucharist is a sacrifice is appealed to. The answer is twofold. In the first place, the New Testament was not written for moderns, but for people whose previous conceptions of religion obviated all need of asserting a continuance of sacrificial ritual. There was no controversy calling for such assertion. In the second place, such an assertion — and this argument is equally applicable to explain why Christian ministers were not definitely called priests in New Testament days — would have been taken probably as an obtrusive challenge to the Jewish hierarchy, as setting up a substitute for the older priesthood and sacrifices. True as such an impression would have been, the Holy Spirit guided the Apostles to refrain from unnecessary aggression, and, in Jerusalem at least, to observe the old law, as well as the new, until that city and its Temple ritual were destroyed.[1] This overlapping of dispensations served the wise purpose of visibly showing the continuity of God's dealings with His people. We know that, when that purpose had been fulfilled, the Christian Church quickly developed a most explicit sacrificial description of the Eucharist.

§ 4. This fact, along with the catholic consent which has continued through subsequent centuries that the Eucharist is the continuing earthly sacrifice

[1] T. T. Carter, *Doctr. of the Priesthood*, ch. xi.

of the Christian covenant, and fulfils the prophecy of Malachi concerning the pure offering which was to be made among the Gentiles in the messianic dispensation,[1] this fact and this consent complete the cumulative evidence of history and of Scripture that the Christian religion has an earthly rite properly entitled to the descriptive name sacrifice, and that the Eucharist is this sacrifice.

The consent referred to, at least so far as the centuries previous to the reformation are concerned, is so well established and so widely acknowledged that we need not consume space in establishing its practical universality and antiquity.[2] But one most important and official illustration of it calls for attentive consideration. We refer to the manner in which the Eucharist has been celebrated from the earliest times concerning which we have pertinent information. The catholic liturgies, variable as they have been in phraseology and minor details of arrangement, exhibit a remarkable similarity in their fundamental features and prescriptions.[3] The same characteristic actions are found in them all, and the language in each one is determinately sacrificial in reference, even when, as in the present English Church liturgy, other aspects are given new prominence.

[1] Mal. i. 11. Cf. S. *Hist.*, I. 49.

[2] Testimonies are collected in Archd. Wilberforce, pp. 262–278; M. F. Sadler, App. A; and S. *Hist.*, *passim*. For Anglican writers, see *Tracts for the Times*, No. 81.

[3] Archd. Wilberforce, ch. iii; *Ch. Quart. Rev.*, Oct. 1880, art. V; Geo. W. Hunter, *On the Divine Liturgy in the Book of Common Prayer*.

The liturgy of the American Episcopal Church, which in its determinative particulars is conformed to ancient analogies, affords a suitable illustration.[1] The leading elements are five: (*a*) a minor oblation of bread and wine; (*b*) a precatory or liturgical repetition of the known words of Christ by which they are designated to be His body and blood, the reference of this designation being made clear by accompanying manual acts; (*c*) a major oblation of these "holy gifts" thus designated, this oblation being described as "the memorial Thy Son hath commanded us to make"; (*d*) an invocation of the Holy Spirit upon these "gifts and creatures of bread and wine," which are such still, even if the Western opinion that they have already become the body and blood of Christ is true; (*e*) the feeding on what has been offered, under the designation, "The Body of our Lord Jesus Christ," "The Blood of our Lord Jesus Christ," that is, Christ being witness, on "the bread of God."

In other words, the Eucharist is a solemn action of offering sacred gifts to God as a memorial before Him of Christ's sacrifice, the oblation reaching its climax in an invocation of the Spirit which reminds us of the prefigurative fire with which Israel's offerings were consumed before God — this signifying God's acceptance of the sacrifice. It is also a feast on the sacrifice, such as is found in the sacrificial rites of all religions, both biblical and other.

But it is not simply a memorial representation and

[1] Geo. W. Hunter, *op. cit.*, ch. ix.

beneficial application of Christ's sacrifice for sin, although its acceptability is thus secured. In the prayer of oblation, it is described in terms which make it a fulfilment of the obligation of sacrificial homage and self-oblation which rests upon human beings independently of the complicating fact of sin. It is described as "our sacrifice of praise and thanksgiving." In it "we offer and present unto Thee, O Lord, ourselves, our souls and bodies, to be a reasonable, holy, and living sacrifice unto Thee." Acknowledging our being unworthy "to offer unto Thee any sacrifice; yet we beseech Thee to accept this our bounden duty and service."

Such is the Eucharistic worship of the Catholic Church, undeniably sacrificial in prescribed action and in phraseology. And what the Church universal has treated it as being, determines for us its proper meaning, a meaning which obtains confirmation by careful comparison with the general trend of biblical teaching.

II. *Its Constructive Place*

§ 5. Sacrificial descriptions have always been given in a general way to any acts or expressions of genuine devotion, whether public or private, which minister to the aim of sacrifice. This aim is to cultivate, and give expression to, the relations in which men should stand to their Creator. But this general use is derivative. In proper and strict meaning, sacrifice denotes a certain officially recognized and formal rite expressly designed for the fulfilment of this aim. It is a corporate rite or, when the offerer is a private individual, has an acknowledged relation to corporate ritual. As we have seen, it normally constitutes the central external function of all religions in which men seek to cultivate acceptable relations with a personal God, the exceptions being explainable on grounds that confirm the rule.[1] The Eucharistic rite is the Christian's continuing earthly sacrifice, being the final form of such sacrifice as modified and sanctioned by divine authority.

As such, it recapitulates and effectively represents and applies, on the basis of Christ's death, all the elements of sacrifice which more ancient sacrifices embodied in prefigurative ceremonial, but could not effectively apply previously to the consummation of the one and only absolute sacrifice of Jesus Christ. To His sacrifice they were made to point by the overruling providence of God. In so far as they expressed sincere self-surrender to God, and prefigured what was to come, they undoubtedly were accepted of God provisionally and until Christ's sacrifice for sin made possible the institution of a more effective representative and applicatory sacrifice — the Christian Eucharist.

The primary elements of sacrifice — those which are signified by the technical use of that name, and which are somehow recapitulated in the Eucharist —

[1] Cf. pp. 148-149, above.

are (*a*) an oblation of fruits of the earth which by artificial treatment have been made man's own, fruits symbolizing man's sustenance and life and widely consisting of bread and wine; (*b*) An accompanying offering of slain animals with the pouring of their blood as symbols of human guilt and as means of propitiating the offended Deity. This element appears not to have been strictly primitive, but to have been developed with the growth among men of a sense of sin; (*c*) A festal and vital communion with Deity through eating and drinking of the things offered to Him in sacrifice and supposedly sanctified by Him to that end.

By divine inspiration Israel was guided to co-ordinate these elements in a reformed ritual, wherein (*a*) An annual sacrifice for sin, directly prefigurative of the Cross, ceremonially sanctified once for all the sacrifices of the whole year; (*b*) A daily burnt offering made a continual memorial of the mystery thus symbolized, and gave validity to the primitive meal and drink offerings perpetually exhibited before God in the Tabernacle and Temple; (*c*) Sacrificial feasts identified the feasters with the things offered, and served as means of communion with God.[1]

The death of Christ has once for all fulfilled the propitiatory conditions of sacrifice thus prefigured; and it has consecrated an everlasting priesthood, and a sacrifice which can be continually exhibited with prevailing effect before God. It is thus ex-

[1] Cf. pp. 70–71, above, and refs. there given.

hibited in the Holy Place not made with hands by Christ's perpetual appearance for us. On earth also it is exhibited by the representative and applicatory sacrifice of the new law, whereby Christ's members are enabled to identify themselves with Him in offering His acceptable sacrifice.

§ 6. It is apparent, in view of the above considerations, that the Eucharist is a sacrifice only by virtue of its relations to Christ's sacrifice accomplished on the Cross, and to the heavenly oblation wherein the sacrifice lives on. These relations are both passive and active.

The passive relation of the Eucharist to the sacrifice on the Cross is one of substantial identification, inasmuch as in both the same Priest, Jesus Christ, is the Offerer and Victim.[1] Right here lies a chief explanation of the vital significance and value of the truth declared by our Lord, that the consecrated bread and wine are His body and blood. Because they truly are these sacred things, when they are offered to God in the Eucharist, the same substantial *res* is offered that was offered on the Cross, although in a different manner. And it is the same Priest who offers, for Jesus Christ is the invisible Offerer in every Eucharist, although He accommodates the

[1] A. P. Forbes, *Theol. Defence*, pp. 10–14. On the relation of the Eucharist to the sacrifice of the Cross, see A. P. Forbes, on art. xxxi, esp. pp. 614–624; M. F. Sadler, pp. 70–74 and chh. xi–xii; Archd. Wilberforce, ch. xi. *passim;* J. R. Milne, ch. i; J. C. Hedley, pp. 156–165; J. Pohle, pp. 332–340. Patristic passages, in S. *Hist.*, I. 50, 114–116.

mystery to our earthly conditions and acts through earthly ministers.

The active relation of the Eucharist to the Cross cannot be described as one either of literal identification or of repetition. The action of the Cross was fulfilled once for all. It can never be repeated, and no other action, as action, can be identified with it. In the Eucharist another and distinct action is performed, but one which is none the less related in a vital way to the action of the Cross. This relation is expressed in the conventional description of the Eucharist as a memorial before God of Christ's death, and as a representative and applicatory sacrifice.

It is a memorial of Christ's death because in it we exhibit before God the living body and blood of Christ in a manner that bears unmistakable witness to His having died for us, although now alive forever. That is, we offer His body and blood under mutually separate sacramental species.[1] Thus we do proclaim the Lord's death until He comes again, and represent it before the Father, in accordance with the terms of the covenant. Moreover, when we feed in this mystery on what we offer, we partake of Christ and, under the conditions of faith and repentance, thereby have the benefits of His sacrifice for sin applied to ourselves.

§ 7. The Eucharist is also related, both actively

[1] Passages from the following Latin writers who take this view are given in S. *Hist.*, II. 362 *et seq.:* Vasquez, Lessius, Perrone, Hedley, Thalhofer and Abbé Lepin. Cf. p. 96, n. 2, above.

and passively, to the heavenly oblation, wherein the Cross lives on.[1] And it is by means of the heavenly oblation that the Eucharist is effectively related to the Cross in the manner above indicated. Indeed, the living Christ and His heavenly priesthood constitute the connecting link between His death and whatsoever is now accomplished on earth for the salvation and bringing home to God of human souls.[2]

As has been shown in a previous volume, the perpetual intercession of Christ for us in Heaven is not to be understood as a mere praying for us.[3] It is the full exercise of a mediatorial priesthood, one which has been consecrated once for all by Christ's death, and in which the sacrifice of the Cross lives on. He there has somewhat to offer,[4] that is, the

---

[1] Attention to this aspect dates from the patristic period, but fell off in the West after the twelfth century, although various later Latin writers (cf. p. 97, n. 2, above) set it forth. Quite a few Anglican writers, especially in recent days, have emphasized it. A. G. Mortimer's *Euch. Sacrifice* describes the view here set forth as "modern," and ascribes its genesis to Socinus. This is hopelessly unhistorical, and because of its determinative place in the work referred to seriously reduces the value of that book.

On the relation of the Eucharist to the heavenly oblation, see D. Stone *Euch. Sacrifice*, note 11 (for a valuable list of refs. to patristic and later witnesses); and *H. C.*, chh. v, vii, *passim;* J. R. Milne, chh. ii, iv; W. J. Gold, Lec. iii; M. F. Sadler, chh. vii-x; P. N. Waggett, pp. 32-38; Geo. Milligan, *Theol. of the Ep. to the Heb.*, chh. vi-vii. Cf. *Passion and Exaltation*, ch. x, esp. §§ 9-12.

[2] P. N. Waggett, pp. 69-75.
[3] *Passion and Exaltation*, p. 317. Heb. vii. 25.
[4] Heb. viii. 3.

thing which He offered on the Cross, which is Himself in His Manhood. So far as we know this offering is not an external action. He is said to be appearing for us, and His appearance is described under the semblance of a lamb standing as having been slain.[1] In other words, there is that in His appearance which bears witness to His death for us, and which for this reason makes it to be a true and acceptable oblation and pleading of His passion, an effective intercession. Upon its continuance and prevailing power depends the value of the Eucharist, wherein we are enabled to identify ourselves with what He is doing above,[2] and thus also plead the merits of His passion.

Passively speaking, the relation of the Eucharistic sacrifice to the heavenly oblation, like that to the sacrifice of the Cross, is one of substantial identification. What Christ offers above is also offered in the Eucharist below, and the true Offerer in both cases is the heavenly Priest who suffered once upon the Cross. But the Eucharist enables us all through the action of His ministers to take part in offering.

Actively speaking, the Eucharist is related to the heavenly oblation as its earthly counterpart. This does not mean that the two transactions are externally the same, for while there is an abiding appearance above, the Eucharist below is an action

---

[1] Heb. ix. 24; Rev. v. 6.
[2] Heb. xii. 22–24. The Eucharist, it has frequently been noted, exalts us to Christ above, rather than brings Christ down from Heaven. Cf. P. N. Waggett, pp. 47–55.

in which things are done repetitiously, and in other regards in a manner that is accommodated to our earthly conditions. Thus we consecrate and offer repeatedly, not as multiplying Christ's sacrifice, but as being by reason of our conditions under the necessity of renewing our representation of it. Yet we do not consecrate the sacrifice again, for that was consecrated once for all on the Cross; but we consecrate creaturely elements in order to identify them, and ourselves through feeding on them, with what the Cross consecrated.

The Eucharist is the earthly counterpart of the heavenly oblation because, like that oblation, it is a memorial, a representation and a pleading of Christ's death before the Father, and not a repetition of it. As we have seen, that death cannot be repeated. But it does need to be represented, pleaded and applied.

§ 8. In all history there is but one true and acceptable sacrifice, although there have been several proper relative sacrifices whereby, with divine approval, it has been either prefigured or represented. In the death of Christ, and His heavenly oblation consecrated thereby, all relative earthly sacrifices are given unity, are interpreted, and obtain their appointed and derivative values. Even the ancient pagan sacrifices may be supposed to have been divinely prompted and overruled to express, however ignorantly, the necessity and desire of approaching God in the proper manner which Christ's sacrifice was to make possible. The sacrifices of the old covenant in any case were made by express divine appointment to prefigure truly the leading aspects of this same sacrifice of Christ.[1]

The Christian Eucharist, to which all previous relative sacrifices permanently give way, is determined in form by the accomplishment of Christ's sacrifice for sin; and, instead of prefiguring, this sacrifice represents and applies it in a manner solemnly instituted by Christ Himself. Furthermore, upon the basis of the mediation which Christ's death has made effective, it contains in acceptable forms all those elements which together make sacrifice to be the central and characteristic corporate function of religion, a "bounden duty and service" of creatures in relation to God.

But the oneness of the sacrifice is not upset by this comprehensive value of the Eucharist; for it is a derivative sacrifice, and is based upon Christ's death, which is thereby represented, pleaded and applied. The sacrifice, we repeat, is one. It was constituted and consecrated by Christ's death. It lives on in the heavenly Holy of Holies, where Christ has entered through the veil by His own blood. There, by His appearance for us, He represents it in our behalf; and upon its basis enables us, through the

---

[1] They constituted a kindergarten school, the pupils in which were too undeveloped to understand the meaning of its symbols, which none the less were fashioning the mind of spiritual Israel for the apprehension of later revelations.

veil of His flesh and by His blood, to gain access through Him to God. And so through this heavenly mediation the same sacrifice that was consecrated on the Cross is represented and pleaded by us also in the Eucharist. This rite, because of its divinely appointed relation to the Cross, has become the acceptable form of our homage, of our praise and thanksgiving, and of our self-oblation to God. In being this it represents all that our bounden duty and service requires us to perform in sacrifice on earth.

Finally, the oneness of the sacrifice is not at all removed by the multiplicity of Eucharists, whether temporal or geographical. Although the rite in question is properly sacrificial, that is in the relations above expounded, and although it is repeatedly performed at each Christian altar, and also at thousands of altars in different lands, in each and every instance the Eucharist is an earthly representation and application of one sacrifice, with which it is passively identical in substance, and with which even in action it is identified in purport. In all there is one Priest and Victim, one consecrating death and one oblation, wherever offered and by whomsoever pleaded. It is one in Christ Jesus, even as we who share in offering it are one in His mystical Body, and feed on Him in one sacrament of unity.

III. *Its Description*

§ 9. In indicating the constructive place and relations of the Eucharistic sacrifice we have inci-

ITS DESCRIPTION

dentally described in several aspects what the Eucharistic sacrifice is in itself. But it is desirable to recapitulate these aspects and to connect them with others in a more systematic and comprehensive description.

The Eucharist is described as a sacrifice because it is the divinely sanctioned method of offering up to God an external thing whereby is symbolically expressed, and also formally and sacramentally effected, an acceptable and thankful homage and self-surrender to Him, and because by feeding thereon we enter into sacramental and vital communion with Him.

In it the thing offered is a meal and drink offering of bread and wine, which by consecration become the body and blood of Christ, and which therefore constitutes an oblation of Jesus Christ, the Victim of the sacrifice of the Cross. By offering such an oblation we also effectively offer ourselves as sacramentally identified with Christ; and self-oblation is the creaturely obligation which the sacrifice is designed to enable us acceptably to fulfil.[1] In other words, we offer ourselves by offering Christ, with whom we are identified; and the acceptability of Christ makes acceptable what is offered to God in Him. But when we thus offer ourselves in Christ, we do so as mem-

---

[1] The inner purport of true sacrifice is the surrender of self, of the will, to God. W. J. Gold, pp. 3–9. For sinners such surrender involves shedding of blood, because the life is in the blood. Levit. xvii. 11. Cf. Heb. x. 5–10.

bers of His mystical Body. The action is a corporate one, involving the whole Body, and the Church offers itself up to God in every Eucharist.[1]

The sacrifice is offered exclusively to God, for to Him alone is such homage either due or allowable. And it is offered in a manner which is determined by the relations in which we stand to the three Persons of the Godhead. That is, it is offered to God the Father primarily, because in the divine economies He is designated as the Creator, and it is to God as Creator that sacrifice is due from creatures. Moreover, He is the fountain of Deity, and what is offered to Him is in effect offered to the undivided Trinity existing eternally in Him.

It is offered in and through God the Son, by whose death on the Cross the sacrifice gains acceptance, who is the one Mediator between God and man, and whose body and blood are made in this mystery to be the sacred thing in union with which we are enabled to offer ourselves effectively and acceptably.

Finally it is offered by virtue of the efficient operation of the Holy Spirit; and He is invoked that He may make the thing offered to be what it becomes in this mystery, and may also make our oblation both acceptable to God and life-giving to those who feed thereon.[2]

This recognition of trinitarian relations in sacrificial

---

[1] St. Augustine, *De Civ. Dei*, x. 6; Archd. Wilberforce, pp. 277–279; E. T. Green, ch. iv.

[2] *Trinity*, p. 309.

homage controls the arrangement and phraseology of the Eucharistic liturgy.[1] It also determines the ordinary methods of addressing God in other devotional approaches to Him; although it does not preclude incidental resort to language directly addressed either to the Son or to the Holy Spirit. Each divine Person contains the whole Trinity;[2] and these deviations from the liturgical order are permissible, and may be helpful, when they do not tend to subvert the normal order of divine worship. Examples of such deviations are fairly numerous in Christian hymnology.

§ 10. Various descriptive adjectives which have been applied by theological writers to the Eucharistic sacrifice require careful definition, if we are not to use them misleadingly.

(a) A *suppletory* sacrifice means one calculated to supply some want or defect in the sacrifice of the Cross. In this sense the Eucharist is not a suppletory sacrifice, although it fulfils purposes which the Cross does not fulfil. These purposes are two: (1) the representation and pleading of Christ's death before God by Christians, and the consequent application of its benefits to them; (2) the formal homage and self-oblation to God which in any case is obligatory for creatures, and which is made possible to fulfil

[1] That is, of Oriental liturgies and the Scottish and American. The invocation of the Spirit, if it can so be described, precedes the Lord's words in the Roman and English liturgies.

[2] *Trinity*, pp. 243-244; D. Stone, *H. C.*, pp. 273-274; H. P. Liddon, *Divinity of our Lord*, pp. 396-398.

effectively and acceptably in this rite by virtue of its relation to the Cross.

(b) The Eucharist is called a *derivative* and *relative* sacrifice because it is wholly dependent upon the absolute sacrifice of Christ, accomplished on the Cross and represented by Christ in Heaven, for the sacrificial status and value which are ascribed to it. The Eucharist cannot be celebrated in its appointed manner except in relation to the Cross and as deriving its validity and acceptability therefrom.

(c) But it is called a *proper* sacrifice because, derivative and relative in the above defined sense though it be, it has the form and, in relation to the Cross, the value of sacrifice in the stricter sense of that term. An *improper* sacrifice means an action, whether interior or exterior, which ministers to and expresses self-oblation to God, but which does not of itself fulfil the obligation of that formal and corporate oblation to which the name sacrifice is technically given. The word "improper" is not here used invidiously, but as indicating that the term "sacrifice" is used analogically and non-technically.

(d) The Eucharist is a *representative* and *memorial* sacrifice because by means of it we represent and proclaim Christ's death before God in the memorial appointed by Christ, as justifying and validating our appearance before Him and our self-oblation to Him. The representation is sacramental, and consists of a presentation of Christ's body and blood under divided species.[1] But Christ is not immolated again, nor

[1] Cf. p. 163, above.

does the division of species make any physical separation between the body and the blood with which they are identified.

(*e*) It is an *applicatory* sacrifice because by means of it we acceptably plead the merits of Christ's death and, through sacramental feeding on what is offered, we receive the cleansing, sanctifying and life-renewing grace which that death has won for us.

(*f*) The Eucharist is a *propitiatory* sacrifice not absolutely or independently, but relatively and derivatively, in that, as the divinely approved method of our representation of and feeding on the Cross, it sacramentally places before God that beloved Son of His who by dying for us has become for each succeeding generation the sufficient propitiation for sin.[1] The Eucharist makes God propitious to those who contritely participate in offering it, because their offering it is the means by which they identify themselves in Christ's appointed way with His offering of the one sufficient sacrifice for sin. To call the Eucharist a propitiatory sacrifice need not mean, and does not in catholic theology mean, that it is another and "suppletory" sacrifice for sin. It simply articulates the truth that this mystery is a representative and applicatory sacrifice by means of which we plead Christ's death and obtain divine favour thereby.[2]

---

[1] Rom. iii. 25; 1 St. John ii. 2; iv. 10.

[2] John Johnson, *Unbloody Sacrifice*, ch. ii. § 2. 2; A. P. Forbes, on art. XXXI, pp. 614-624; Wm. Forbes, *Consid. Modestæ*, vol. II. pp. 599-613; J. C. Hedley, pp. 157-160; J. Pohle, pp. 332-337. Patristic witnesses, in A. P. Forbes, *Theol. Defence*, pp. 57-63. Angli-

§ 11. As has elsewhere been indicated, sacrifice is a more primitive element of religion than propitiation, which, however vital, is of accidental necessity caused by human sin. We need not prejudge questions of critical exegesis in order to find in the narrative of Cain and Abel a convenient and pertinent parable. Sin had entered the world; and, in due recognition of the situation created thereby, Abel offered a bloody and propitiatory sacrifice of the firstlings of his flock. His sacrifice was accepted. Cain, however, offered the fruit of the ground, a sacrifice in which no propitiatory element was exhibited. It was not accepted, as it might have been had not sin lain at the door.

The fruits of the ground, in particular bread and wine, for ages previous to the institution of the Eucharist had been the generally recognized symbols by which men signified in sacrifice their creaturely relations to God, and by feeding thereon entered into vital communion with Him. And even when the propitiatory element became prominent, these ancient elements of sacrifice retained their place, although in what was felt to be a necessary validating connection with bloody offerings. The effect of Christ's death was to fulfil the condition of shedding of blood once for all, and with sufficient reparation for the sins of the whole world. Thenceforth, therefore, the offering of bloody victims was no longer a necessary accom-

---

cans who reject this description often have in mind an independent, suppletory and mactative sacrifice, which of course the Eucharist is not.

paniment of sacrifice, although men's future oblations had to be effectively related to Christ's sacrifice for sin, if they were to be acceptable.

Under such circumstances the thing which Cain, according to our parabolic interpretation, did too daringly, in offering the fruits of the ground only, has been appointed by Christ to be the proper and acceptable form of offering sacrifice. The ancient elements of bread and wine were consecrated by Him, as being the recognized symbols of what creatures must offer in sacrifice — symbols, that is, of themselves, their souls and bodies, which they were under religious obligation solemnly to devote to God. But by making them in His new rite to be His body and blood in separate figures, He also made their oblation to be for their offerers an effective representation and memorial of His death.

Thus in the Eucharist is restored the primitive and bloodless sacrifice of creatures, whereby they render dutiful homage to their Maker, and enjoy an earthly inception of the fellowship with God that constitutes the chief end of their creation. And they do this in a connection which assures them of acceptance with God by reason of Christ's death, without any further shedding of blood. The joyous mystery of sacrifice and fellowship, thus habilitated in spite of sin, is the wonder of the ages, the sign of God's unfailing love, and the central function and inspiring bond of unity in true religion, until the Lord of glory comes again.

§ 12. Because of its being all this, and because of Christ's institution of it, the Eucharist is the primary form of public worship in the Christian Church; and, except among modern Protestants, has been thus regarded and treated by all Christendom from the beginning. More than this, it has been celebrated in a manner to give expression to every form of Christian devotion. Its dominant note, apart from the oblation and communion wherein it primarily consists, is one of thanksgiving to God for all the natural and spiritual benefits which He bestows upon us; and because of this aspect it received in apostolic days the name Eucharist by which it is still called.[1] But other elements of devotion are also included in the liturgy, the didactic element in Epistle and Gospel; the confession of faith in the Creed; exalted strains of praise and adoration in the Tersanctus and Gloria in Excelsis; confession and absolution; and intercessions for all men, for the state, for the Church militant and at rest, and for the congregation present as well as for others. If there is any special purpose of prayer or thanksgiving which calls for attention on a given occasion, it is by common custom recognized in the particular intention with which the oblation is offered, or with which individuals take part therein. In brief, the Eucharist gathers into itself and recapitulates all Christian devotion, as being the sanctifying element of it all.

Furthermore, every other service of public devotion,

[1] 1 Cor. xiv. 16.

and every act of private devotion to God, is regarded by the catholic mind as sanctified and made acceptable by this central mystery. All the prayers and all the praises, thanksgivings and acts of penitence are branches of Eucharistic devotion, either preparatory for it or expanding it, and placed upon its oblation, so to speak, for acceptance by the loving God who has sanctioned it. The altar is thus what the Shekinah was to fleshly Israel, and the building of which it is the differentiating furniture is the new Israel's Tent of Meeting — the Holy Mount, where God in Christ meets His people, making Himself known to them in the breaking of bread, and in the bush that burns without being consumed.[1]

[1] On the central place of the Eucharist in Christian devotion and life, see W. C. E. Newbolt, ch. xii; D. Stone, *Euch. Sacrifice*, VI.

CHAPTER VI

BENEFITS OF THE EUCHARIST

I. *How Received*

§ 1. Unlike other sacraments the Eucharist conveys to its recipients a substantial gift or *res sacramenti*, the body and blood of Christ; and the benefits of the sacrament are conveyed in and by means of this gift rather than, as in other sacraments, by the rite at large.[1] To say this is not to deny that the rite is beneficial as such to those who devoutly take part in it. It is not only a sacrament but also an edifying act of worship, and as such it is a means of what is called "external" grace.[2] But its "sanctifying" grace, the grace of the sacrament strictly speaking, flows from the body and blood of Christ thereby received.

We ought not to be misled in this connection by the fact that certain of the ancients drew an overclose analogy between Baptism and the Eucharist, and, starting with the accepted doctrine that the bread and wine are converted into the body and blood of Christ, seemed to make the speculative inference that a parallel conversion of the water occurs in Baptism.

---

[1] Archd. Wilberforce, pp. 73-74, 279-280.

[2] St. Thomas, III. lxxix. 7. As the sacrifice is offered for all, its benefits presumably extend in part to noncommunicants.

Some moderns have appealed to this speculation as showing that the ancients believed the bread and wine to be changed only in the sense in which the water is changed in Baptism.¹ But the analogy in question should not be taken seriously. The Eucharistic doctrine involved, based as it is upon our Lord's plain teaching, has permanently retained its place in catholic consent. The baptismal theory in question, on the contrary, having no basis in revelation, and never having been generally accepted, gradually ceased to obtain serious consideration in any quarter.²

There is reason to believe that a special benefit is conveyed by each of the consecrated elements. How far we may press literally the distinction made in the words of the Anglican Prayer of Humble Access, "that our sinful bodies may be made clean by His body, and our souls washed through His most precious blood," is not certain. But that each kind has a beneficial value of its own is admitted even by Roman writers.³ In any case the Lord commanded both kinds to be received; and the presumption that, under normal conditions at least, He intended them to be received by all communicants seems overwhelming.

¹ So Daniel Waterland, cited by Chas. Gore, p. 294.
² Archd. Wilberforce, pp. 187-191; Chas. Gore, pp. 67-70, 294-295.
³ E. B. Pusey, *Is Healthful Reunion Impossible?* pp. 328-331; A. P. Forbes, *XXXIX Arts.*, pp. 599-600; D. Stone, *H. C.*, pp. 218-219; A. J. Mason, *Faith of the Gospel*, ch. ix. § 15.

The question is not determined by appealing to the doctrine of concomitance, that the *totus Christi*, both His body and His blood, are inseparably present in each species.[1] The question concerns the appointed manner of receiving the benefit, and that is reception of both kinds. To deviate from Christ's institution without real necessity does in any case reduce the basis of assurance that we receive all of the intended benefit.[2]

§ 2. The sacraments, as has been previously shown, have efficacy *ex opere operato*, by virtue of their divine appointment and the pledged action of the Holy Spirit, and men cannot nullify their efficacy by either lack of faith or other defective dispositions. The appointed instrument when validly administered operates according to its appointed law, whether the recipient is beneficially or injuriously affected thereby.[3] In the Eucharist, for example, a valid consecration makes the bread and wine to be the body and blood of Christ previously to its administration and independently of the mental and spiritual attitudes of minister and communicant. When the consecrated species are administered, therefore, the com-

---

[1] On which, see ch. iv. § 12, above.

[2] For history of communion under one kind, see *Cath. Encyc.* *q.v.*, II. Other defensive treatments, St. Thomas, III. lxxx. 12; J. Pohle, pp. 246-254. Sound treatments, A. P. Forbes, on Art. XXX; D. Stone, *H. C.*, pp. 212-221; Wm. Forbes, *op. cit.*, vol. II. pp. 508-531.

[3] On *ex opere operato*, *The Church*, pp. 163 (*d*), 322-323 and refs. there given.

municants, whether rightly disposed or not, take and receive what the bread and wine have become and continue to be so long as their specific nature remains, that is, until they are destroyed by consumption. Furthermore, we are compelled to believe that no one can thus take and receive the *res sacramenti* and be spiritually unaffected by such action. If he does not receive the appointed benefit, the reason is one that converts the sacrament into a source of condemnation and spiritual injury. He is guilty of the body and blood of the Lord.[1]

The question remains, Does one who receives the sacrament invariably partake of Christ's body and blood? It would seem not. We may surely distinguish between the physical manducation of the sacrament and the personal appropriation of the *res sacramenti*. The act of consuming the species destroys the sacrament, and thus brings to an end their identification with Christ's body and blood. But such destruction of the sacrament is not to be regarded *ipso facto* as identical with personal appropriation of the sacred *res sacramenti*. Such appropriation is indeed made possible by reception of the consecrated species; but in its own nature it is certainly a personal and spiritual act of laying hold on Christ, one which is dependent for possibility upon faith,[2] and upon the removal of all previous barriers of unrepented mortal sin.

[1] 1 Cor. xi. 27–31.
[2] A. P. Forbes, on Art. XXVIII, pp. 559–567; E. C. S. Gibson, on the same, pp. 661–662.

By such considerations we can help ourselves to perceive that when our Articles say that "the mean whereby the body of Christ is received . . . is faith," and that the wicked, and such as be void of a lively faith, . . . in no wise are they partakers of Christ," they assert nothing inconsistent with full assurance that all who receive into their mouths the consecrated bread and wine do thus receive what is rightly called the body and blood of Christ.

Needless to say the act of desecration committed by those who receive unworthily cannot injuriously affect the body of Christ which such recipients fail to discern. As the sunlight is neither reduced nor befouled by those who do wickedly in it, so the glorified Christ can suffer no injury from those who fail to discern His body and sinfully approach the sacrament.[1]

§ 3. The primary subjective conditions of beneficial reception of the sacrament are three: Baptism, faith and repentance.[2]

Baptism is essential for all subsequent sacraments because it is the means by which we are made members of Christ and enter into life — the life of grace. For this reason it is said to confer sacramental capacity. Sanctifying grace in every form, except that

---

[1] On reception by the wicked, see A. P. Forbes and E. C. S. Gibson, on Art. XXIX; M. F. Sadler, *Corinthians*, Excursus I. For various past opinions, S. *Hist.*, as referred to in Index, *s.v.* "Wicked."

[2] Cf. the last answer of the *Church Catechism* and the longer Exhortation in the *Holy Communion*. Cf. E. T. Green, ch. ix.

of new birth itself, is for the spiritually living; and one who has not been regenerate is incapable of receiving sacramental benefits because not possessed of the species of life to which such benefits exclusively appertain. It is for those who have become children of God by adoption and grace that these benefits are provided; and they are all dependent upon the membership in the mystical Body to which Baptism is the door of entrance.[1]

Faith also is necessary, so necessary that, as we have seen, it is described as the mean by which we partake of Christ's body and blood.[2] It is the mean in so far as it is the primary element in the spiritual attitude and action whereby we wholesomely appropriate the sacred gift. But this condition can be sufficiently fulfilled by those who are mentally incapable of explicit faith in its advanced degrees. What is required in all communicants who have reached the years of discretion is implicit faith, or docile acceptance of Christ and of sacramental doctrine so far as understood, coupled with readiness to be led on to such fuller explicit faith as the subject's mental capacity and opportunities make possible.

The third condition is that of repentance. This means in any case sincere sorrow for one's sins, because they are sins against God and man, along with

---

[1] Cf. pp. 23-24, above. Obviously a beast can neither appropriate the gift nor injure Christ by consuming the sacrament.

[2] Cf. pp. 181-182, above.

earnest purpose to use God's grace in resisting future temptations. Such a condition includes all that is necessary for the achievement of genuine contrition, for the obtaining of forgiveness and for due penance and making amends. To this end a resort to the sacrament of Penance may be practically necessary, and is necessary in any case where real contrition cannot otherwise be developed. The Anglican Churches do not require its use except when otherwise the subject "cannot quiet his own conscience." To "quiet" here means, of course, to clear one's conscience by true repentance.

In some parts of the Church the Communion is administered to infants, who are incapable of either faith or repentance. But neither can they erect barriers to the operation of grace — such as disbelief and actual sin. The same argument, therefore, can be advanced to justify administration of Communion to them that is employed to vindicate infant Baptism. And the further consideration is available that by Baptism the so-called guilt of original sin has been removed. Sacramental contact of innocent children of grace with Christ is, to say the least, in seeming accord with our Lord's taking little children into His arms and blessing them. We need not doubt that He blesses the innocent infants who sacramentally receive Him.[1]

§ 4. Two further conditions of profitable reception of the Eucharist are widely imposed by ecclesiastical

[1] D. Stone, *H. C.*, pp. 190-200.

prescription. The first of these is Confirmation. As has been shown in a previous chapter,[1] the Eastern Church administers Confirmation immediately after Baptism, thus emphasizing its close connection with, and complementary relation to, that sacrament. In the West the conditions are different and the postponement of Confirmation to the years of discretion has incidentally given rise to the abuse in the Roman Church of admitting children to Communion before Confirmation. That it is an abuse has been acknowledged by the Papal See. The Anglican rule is clear: "And there shall none be admitted to the Holy Communion, until such time as he be confirmed, or be ready and desirous to be confirmed." [2]

The reason both for the requirement and for the implied occasional exception is clear. Confirmation is ordinarily prerequisite because its grace is an appointed part of the normal spiritual equipment of Christians. As such it ought to be possessed, if possible, by any one who would exercise the most venturesome of spiritual privileges, the privilege of receiving the body and blood of the Lord. But the Church is convinced, none the less, that when Christians are ready and desirous to be confirmed and are reasonably hindered, without fault of their own, they ought not to be deprived of the bread of life and of sacramental participation in the Christian sacrifice. God's merciful protection is counted on for such

---

[1] See ch. ii. § 9, and pp. 46-48, above
[2] *Order of Confirmation*, last rubric.

cases. But this consideration cannot justify an admission of those who reject Confirmation altogether. If they do so through invincible ignorance, God is indeed merciful; but to relax the requirement involved is to sanction error, and the Church cannot do this without betrayal of trust.[1]

The other requirement is that of fasting communion,[2] which has been a matter of catholic precept from very early times; and it is usually understood to involve abstinence from all food and drink from the previous midnight, or at least during six hours previous to communion. The rule is not an arbitrary one, but has grown out of a very ancient and practically universal sentiment that fasting, considered as a means and symbol of subjecting the flesh to the spirit, is a notable duty of religion and a peculiarly appropriate preparation for extraordinary acts of devotion. Inasmuch as reception of Christ's body and blood is a very extraordinary devotional act, the general adoption of fasting as its antecedent was inevitable. So it is the devotional value of fasting that explains the precept, and not the semi-Manichæan idea that contact between the sacred species and ordinary food in the stomach has desecrating effect.

[1] A. C. A. Hall, *Confirmation*, ch. vi.
[2] On fasting communion, see D. Stone, *H. C.*, pp. 247-250, 304; F. W. Puller, *Concerning the Fast before Communion;* Frederick Hall, *Fasting Reception of the Blessed Sacrament;* J. W. Legg, *Papal Faculties Allowing Food before Communion* (Ch. Hist. Soc. Publications, No. lxxxvii). The chief contrary work is Tully Kingdon, *Fasting Communion*.

This precept has always been enforced, whether by canon law or by ecclesiastical sentiment, with peculiar rigour; and this seems to prove that the sentiment upon which it is based is too deeply grounded, too closely connected with religious instinct, to be lightly disregarded. And no one ought to violate the rule except under real necessity. Official dispensations from it have always been rare. Accordingly, it is quite unnecessary to cite Anglican canon law — a mediæval canon requiring fasting before communion is still technically in effect — in order to establish the existing force of this precept for those who acknowledge the binding authority of catholic consent in Christian practice.

Yet the limitation which inheres in all ceremonial precepts, where sacramental validity is not involved, ought to be acknowledged as inhering in this precept; for, in spite of the rigour with which it has been emphasized, it is of the ceremonial type. All such precepts are subject to the exception of necessity; and when choice has to be made between habitual reception of the sacrament without fasting and keeping the precept of fasting at the cost of entire, or at least ordinary, abstention from the sacrament, the higher obligation of receiving the sacrament ought to be observed. Our Lord's own example affords a justifying precedent. Even the divinely imposed precept which forbade plucking ears of corn on the Sabbath was allowed by Him to be disregarded on the plea of hunger, with the remark that the Sabbath was made for man and not man for the Sabbath.[1] Fasting is a generally recognized ceremonial precept of the Church; but it was made for Churchmen, and not Churchmen for it, and in real necessity mercy rather than sacrifice is required. The fact remains, of course, that, although the strenuous conditions of modern life make fasting more difficult than formerly, moderns are very self-indulgent; and peculiar care has to be taken lest self-indulgence rather than necessity should determine practice in this matter.

II. *Their Nature*

§ 5. We have seen that the benefits of this sacrament are conveyed to the soul by means of the *res sacramenti*, by individual reception of the body and blood of Christ through physical manducation of the sacrament and through faith, whereby the sacred gift is personally appropriated. It being presupposed that the habit of sacramental communion is duly maintained, and that failure to receive the sacrament on given occasions has a justifiable reason, there are benefits to be derived from devout participation in Eucharistic worship even by those who do not communicate in particular instances. Of these we shall speak when we discuss spiritual communion.[2] We

---

[1] St. Mark ii. 23–28 and parallels. The Papal See now dispenses those who by illness are hindered at least one month from fasting.

[2] In § 10, below.

are now concerned with the benefits of sacramental communion.[1]

The first which we consider, and the most comprehensive, is participation in the sacrifice, and in the sacrificial benefits, direct and indirect, of the death of Christ.[2] To feed on the sacrifice has in all ages been treated as the normal method by which individuals become effective participants therein. In fact there are reasons for believing that the communion aspect of ancient rituals, if it was not primary, was at least a very central and determinative element of sacrifice.[3] The modern antithesis between sacrifice and communion was unknown to the ancients, and would have been practically unintelligible to them. To eat at the sacrificial board was to participate in the sacrifice, and in no other way was full participation therein deemed possible. No doubt there were sacrifices on which no one fed, but such sacrifices were merely particular parts of a larger working system of sacrifice of which feasting on the things offered was an integral and determinative element.

Thus it was in the divinely appointed sacrificial system of the old covenant; and the sacrificial feasts of that system reached their climax in the Passover, with which the Eucharist in its institution was imme-

---

[1] On which, see Archd. Wilberforce, ch. xii; A. J. Mason, *Faith of the Gospel*, ch. ix. §§ 12, 14; St. Thomas, III. lxxix; J. G. H. Barry, X.

[2] Archd. Wilberforce, pp. 280–282; J. G. H. Barry, pp. 191–196.

[3] F. B. Jevons, *Introd. to the Study of Compar. Religion*, pp. 178–210.

diately associated. What Christ instituted was no purely external oblation, but a feast on His body and blood given and poured out for us in sacrifice,[1] a feast which was to constitute an abiding memorial of His death, and therefore the representative and applicatory sacrifice of Christians.

To feed on "the bread of God," "the bread which came down from heaven,"[2] in the Eucharist, accordingly, is the appointed method by which individual Christians unite in offering the sacrifice, and thereby appropriate to themselves the benefits of the one true sacrifice which the Eucharist represents, pleads and applies. And these benefits are not merely propitiatory — not merely the removal of barriers to an acceptable approach to God, — but include enjoyment, in such measure as is possible during our earthly pilgrimage, of the fellowship with God wherein our final beatitude consists.

§ 6. Out of the holy interchange of our acceptable oblation and homage, on the one hand, and of the corporate feast which God provides for contrite believers, on the other hand, flow all the sacramental benefits strictly so called, the benefits of sanctifying grace received by individual souls.

---

[1] The Israelites did not partake of the blood of their sacrifices, for the life which is in the blood (Levit. xvii. 14; Deut. xii. 23) had been forfeited by sin. But redemption has been accomplished, and we are allowed to receive the Redeemer's blood and may share in the life which was poured out and recovered once for all for our benefit.

[2] St. John vi. 31–33. Cf. Levit. xxi. 6, 8, 17, 21, 22; Exod. xvi. 4.

The first of these benefits is life (ζωή). This is not the animal life (ψυχή), but eternal life, the life which Christ came into the world in order to give and make more abundant, a purpose for which He gave His own physical life or ψυχή. The αἰώνιος ζωή consists, our Lord declares, in knowing the true God and Jesus Christ. This knowing clearly does not mean information about God, but personal experience of contact with God, a being alive to Him — a relation that constitutes the immortality which Christ brought to light.[1]

Baptism is the instrument by which this life is first imparted to men, and the Eucharist supplies the appointed supernatural nourishment of what is thus imparted.[2] It is the "food of immortality," for the resurrection life is the baptismal life, whereby we triumph over death and enter into the full enjoyment of the life with God in Christ for which we were created, our chief end. Our life is in Christ, and only he who hath the Son of God hath the life.[3] Moreover this having Him requires constant renewal, and the Eucharistic feast is the instrument of such renewal.

This is the burden of our Lord's discourse at Capernaum.[4] "I am the bread of life. . . . If any

---

[1] St. John x. 10–11; xvii. 3; Rom. vi. 10–11; 2 Tim. i. 10. On the Eucharistic benefit of life, see Archd. Wilberforce, pp. 282–286; E. T. Green, pp. 117–120; St. Thomas, III. lxxix. 1–2.

[2] *The Church Catechism* says that the benefits are "the strengthening and refreshing of our souls."

[3] 1 St. John v. 11–12.   [4] St. John vi, esp. 48–57.

man eat of this bread he shall live forever: yea, and the bread which I will give is My flesh, for the life of the world. . . . Except ye eat the flesh of the Son of Man and drink His blood, ye have not life in yourselves. He that eateth My flesh and drinketh My blood hath eternal life; and I will raise him up at the last day. . . . He that eateth My flesh and drinketh My blood abideth in Me, and I in him. As the living Father sent Me, and I live because of the Father; so he that eateth Me, he also shall live because of me."

The constructive relations between the Incarnation, the victory of the Incarnate over death and His glorification, the mystical Body and the sacraments of life are here apparent. The Son of God took our nature that He might make it for us the source of spiritual life in God. He perfected His Manhood by suffering, and immortalized it by resurrection from the dead. By His Holy Spirit He extended it mystically in the Church, which the Spirit united vitally with Him on the day of Pentecost. In Baptism we are incorporated into it, and made participators in its life; and in the Eucharistic feast we are fed on it, and have the baptismal germ nourished and strengthened for overcoming death and for attaining final immortality in God.[1]

§ 7. By this renewal of life we are sanctified and

---

[1] In the administration of each kind the priest says, "preserve thy body and soul unto everlasting life." Cf. J. G. H. Barry, pp. 203–205.

cleansed from sin.¹ Our justification is a justification of life. This is so because, although we are justified, accounted righteous, through our faith being imputed to us for righteousness, this faith is the initial manifestation of the grace of life whereby, if we persevere in it, we grow in actual righteousness.² This grace, the new life, sets us apart to God, and such setting apart is renewed and made more secure by the increase of life to which the Eucharistic sacrament ministers. Sanctification in its first stage and meaning is this setting apart to God,³ and because the Eucharistic food renews and deepens such consecration its grace is called sanctifying.

But it is sanctifying also in the sense of promoting the assimilation of its recipients to Him to whom they have been set apart.⁴ And assimilation of our characters to the divine character revealed in Him whose body and blood are received in this sacrament is a necessary antecedent condition of our complete enjoyment of the relations with God into which we are brought through Christ.⁵

This assimilation is conditioned by our voluntary response to grace, that is, by faith, repentance and persevering self-discipline. But it is made possible

---

[1] See E. T. Green, p. 116 and ch. xii; J. C. Hedley, pp. 112-120, 123-128; St. Thomas, III. lxxix. 3-6; *Cath. Encyc.*, s.v. "Eucharist," II. (3). (*b*)-(*c*).

[2] Cf. *The Church*, ch. viii. §§ 6-8, on justification.

[3] *Idem*, pp. 186-189.

[4] *Idem*, ch. viii. § 5.

[5] *Idem*, pp. 267-269.

by the flow of a stream of divine life into our nature — a life which not only rejuvenates but purifies all that it touches. The sacrament, therefore, is cleansing in its effect; and when its working is not hindered by impenitent hardness of heart, our sins are flushed away. Our bodies are cleansed by Christ's body, and our souls are washed by His most precious blood.[1] Moreover, the intimate personal contact with Christ which is enjoyed in the sacrament cannot fail to envelop those who realize His presence in a personal atmosphere of the most inspiring and transforming power. No influence can be more effectual for our assimilation in character to God than that of immediate and conscious contact with Him in the Person of Jesus Christ; and such contact is accomplished in its highest and most perfect earthly form in the Blessed Sacrament.

§ 8. The true mystic, one who seeks an immediate experience of God in Christ along the "way of union," finds the centre and primary instrument of his blessed experience in the Eucharist. This is necessarily so if the catholic doctrine concerning this sacrament is really true. If it is the appointed means by which Christ comes objectively, so to speak, to meet us, He being the one Mediator between God and man, then it is in this meeting that we have the covenant basis of faith that the highest experiences of God which we

---

[1] Cf. the Prayer of Humble Access, and the N. T. statements as to our sins being washed away by Christ's blood. Tit. iii. 5; 1 St. John i. 7; Revel. i. 5; vii. 14; Zech. xii. 1.

are severally permitted to gain on earth will be made available. A vast amount of Christian experience confirms this.

The laws which determine our several susceptibilities to the experiences called mystical are not open to scientific scrutiny and generalization, nor do we fully know the conditions under which God wills to grant such privileges. That they are privileges, and not to be obtained by all who seek, however earnestly, to enjoy them, is as certain as any empirical generalization can be.[1] But we may also be certain that they are granted for reasons, and under conditions, which are in harmony with the revealed laws of grace. We are justified in fearing, therefore, that any form of mystical experience which is dissociated from the appointed "way," or sacramental life in grace, is illusory and pathological rather than a genuine experience of the true God. In saying this we are not denying the possibility of exceptional mercies and privileges to those who are unblamably ignorant of the true way to God. What we mean is that no one is justified in expecting genuine experience of mystical contact with God who fails to approach Him in the appointed Christian way.

Returning to our main thread, history shows that countless devout souls have found the Eucharist to be the true Tent of Meeting, where God meets His people and affords to them the several forms and degrees of experience of Him which they can, and are

[1] A. Devine, *Manual of Mystical Theol.*, pp. 110-115.

permitted to, enjoy in this world.¹ Moreover, such experiences do not have to answer to the description signified by the term "mystical" in order to be very real, inspiring and helpful to those who enjoy them. They at least can recognize Him by faith in the breaking of bread; and, receiving Him into their hearts, they can go forth as having Him with them to encourage and help them in their earthly journey to God.

III. *Incidental Privileges*

§ 9. The primary benefits of the Blessed Sacrament we have seen to be four: (*a*) Participation in the sacrifice of Christ; (*b*) Renewal of baptismal life; (*c*) Sanctification and cleansing; (*d*) Communion with God.

Communion with God is the condition and sole effective means of the communion with each other which the members of Christ's mystical Body are privileged to enjoy. The communion of saints is the vital interaction and reciprocal inspiration and joy which is made possible by our baptismal incorporation into Christ, in whom we are united with God and therefore with each other. And of the earthly enjoyment of this communion the Blessed Sacrament is the primary instrument and sign. As St. Paul expresses it, "We, who are many, are one bread, one body: for we all partake of the one bread." ²

---

[1] Exod. xxix. 42 (R. V.). Cf. xxv. 22. On Eucharistic communion with God, see E. T. Green, ch. x; W. C. E. Newbolt, ch. i.

[2] 1 Cor. x. 17. On Eucharistic communion between the baptized, see E. T. Green, chh. vii–viii; J. G. H. Barry, VI.

The privilege of mutual communion here enjoyed is deeper and more vital than any purely external meeting together and than any manner of friendly relations or coöperation apart from common reception of the sacrament. It is the appropriation of a sustaining gift which is numerically and indivisibly the same for all who receive it, and which therefore unites them in one organic principle of life, action and growth. The union thus renewed and energized is interior as no other union between earthly persons can be, and is the chief and continuing source of the grace of mutual love.

For this reason the Eucharist is called the sacrament of unity. It is so treated in ecclesiastical discipline, which grants or withholds the privilege of receiving it according to the faithfulness of those who seek it to the common belief and life of the saints. The normal sign that a given individual is in full fellowship with the members of Christ's mystical Body is his acknowledged right and habitual practice of receiving the Lord's body and blood at the common altar. Moreover, when it is sought to attest in a formal way the unity between local or provincial portions of the Church, this is accomplished by their representatives receiving the Blessed Sacrament together.

When such acts of intercommunion are refused between Christian bodies, it is because visible unity has been broken, and schism between them has taken place. And the Church's visible unity continues to be broken so long as intercommunion is unrestored. The problem of restoring unity is therefore the problem of renewing intercommunion by removing the causes, whatever they may be, of its interruption. Unhappily the causes of the existing disunity are wider and more complex than a mere loss of mutual charity; and a revival of love and of desire for intercommunion, tremendously important as it is, cannot alone make its restoration possible. With all the desire for peace imaginable, Christians cannot communicate freely at the same altar without disregard of vital principles and violation of consciences until the existing divergences in fundamental faith and order are removed — a consummation to be reached by prolonged and persuasive education rather than by ingenious schemes and forcing methods. The unity of which intercommunion is the necessary form and sign is one of faith and hope as well as of love.[1]

§ 10. There can be no proper substitute for habitual reception of the sacrament in obtaining the benefits which are thereby received, and frequent sacramental communion is the chief means of Christian progress. The New Testament plainly implies that the sacrament ought normally to be received on at least every Lord's Day by all confirmed Christians who are not debarred from the privilege by some special cause, disciplinary or other.[2] Still more frequent communion is clearly desirable for those whose provi-

---
[1] Cf. *The Church*, pp. 66–77, 173–186.
[2] Cf. Acts xx. 7.

dential opportunities make it practicable. Even daily communion is desirable for many.

Perhaps the gravest abuse in the Church is the neglect and frequent positive discouragement of frequent communion that has for many centuries become widespread. So far as this has been due to a sense of need of adequate preparation for reception of the Lord's body and blood, it has seemed to many to be justifiable. But the real fact is that a false conception of the whole matter has been widely engendered. The Lord plainly wills that all who are penitent and believe shall receive Him freely. It is not our worthiness, but our need, and His desire that we should come to Him for help and communion with Him, that determines duty.[1] Penitence is an abiding condition of every form of divine blessing, and its absence is to be remedied at once in any case, whether sacramental communion is in immediate prospect or not. In other words the needed preparation for Holy Communion is the normal and daily condition of any acceptance with God; and Christ wills that all who are penitent and believing shall ordinarily receive His body and blood when they have opportunity to do so, and are not prevented by exceptional and sufficient momentary reasons.[2]

[1] The parable of the wedding feast (St. Matt. xxii. 1-10) is significant.
[2] The King provides the wedding garment, and all who are invited can secure it — can repent and approach with due devotion. On frequent communion, see D. Stone, *H. C.*, pp. 241-244; J. G. H. Barry, V and pp. 45-48; J. C. Hedley, ch. viii; *Cath. Encyc.*, *q.v.*; St. Thomas, III. lxxx. 10.

It is on the basis of habitual and reasonably frequent communion that the privilege called spiritual communion [1] is profitable, that is, when sacramental communion is for special reasons undesirable. Its form is noncommunicating attendance at the celebration of the Eucharist, and its profitable elements are subjective renewal of realization of the relation to Christ which previous communions have nourished, participation in the Church's worship, and such other devotional exercises as are appropriate to the Eucharistic atmosphere. The chief reasons which justify noncommunicating attendance are disciplinary requirements imposed by spiritual pastors, previous communion on the same day, and special circumstances that are either incongruous with sacramental reception or inconsistent with reasonable preparation. In this connection it is to be noted that frequent preparation, if sincerely undertaken, is more likely to be sufficient, than that which is rarely attempted. No doubt frequent repetition may become perfunctory, but there is much graver danger that infrequent preparation may be ineffectual through lack of practice.

§ 11. The Eucharist affords to Christians their highest and, both subjectively and objectively considered, their most effective means of worship, that is of suitably honouring and adoring the invisible God.

---

[1] On which, see Archd. Wilberforce, pp. 311-342; St. Thomas, III. lxxix. 7; lxxx. 1; J. G. H. Barry, pp. 177-185.

The public worship of Christians was focused in the Eucharist in apostolic days, and this rite has never ceased in the Catholic Church to be regarded as the validating centre of approach to God.

The obvious reason is that, according to New Testament and catholic doctrine, the adorable Lord, through whom alone we can approach the Father, makes Himself objectively present to us in the Eucharistic sacrament, and does so under no other earthly conditions. This fact is not at all reduced in its significance for our worship by the spiritual nature of the Eucharistic presence, elsewhere emphasized in this volume. Spiritual does not mean either unreal or non-objective; and the fact that there is no physical movement of our Lord's body and blood from heaven to earth, and no circumscription thereof in the consecrated species, does not nullify the revealed identification of the sacramental elements with His body and blood. He is present sacramentally and non-physically, in a manner beyond our ability to define or explain. But the objective and local conditions of the sacrament are the conditions under which in this wonderful mystery He permits us to apprehend Him by faith in the manner that normally challenges human adoration of the Invisible.

The sacramental principle lies at the root of effective expression of our creaturely relations to God. And that some form of external objectification is necessary in effective human adoration is plain when we reckon with the history of religion. This shows that the element of adoration gradually, often quickly, ceases to be present in creaturely devotion when this manner of worship is abandoned. Polytheistic worship is no doubt erroneous and idolatrous, but reflects a need in worship which is truly provided for in both the old and new covenants. Pure Buddhists do not adore any personal God. Mahomedans pray but do not properly speaking adore. Protestants have allowed worship to become a name for subjectively edifying exercises and preaching. They cherish no effective forms of worship in the historic sense. The exceptions therefore prove the rule that objective forms of adoration are necessary for an effective continuance of this element in religion.

In the old covenant the true Image of God had not yet been revealed, and the Israelites were forbidden to make images of God of their own devising. None the less the need of objectification was even then allowed for in the divinely prescribed worship of the Tabernacle and Temple. Such worship was directed towards a local Holy of Holies, in which an objective Mercy Seat, overshadowed by Cherubim, afforded suggestive symbols whereby human imagination was sacramentally assisted in apprehending the divine object of worship.

In Jesus Christ the true Image of the invisible God [1] became incarnate and objectively apprehensible to men. And, while it is true that His reason for coming on earth was not primarily or ostensibly that

[1] Col. i. 15. Cf. 2 Cor. iv. 4; Heb. i. 3.

He might be worshipped, the double fact is certain that His objective presence in flesh inevitably evoked acts of adoration determined in method by this manifestation, and that He never discouraged such acts on the part of those who dutifully performed them. The principle that wherever Christ makes an objective manifestation of His presence He is adorable *as thus revealing Himself* is undeniably implied in these circumstances. It is indeed indisputable.

Once revealed, the true Image of God becomes thenceforth the only proper objective medium of human worship, and the need of objectification in such worship is permanently met. But the manner in which it is met in the Christian covenant, after Christ's physical withdrawal from this world, is sacramental — a manner accommodated to human nature. By identifying consecrated elements of bread and wine with His own body and blood, doing this incidentally to His purpose of instituting a memorial of Himself, our Lord did establish a continuing mystery of objective presence of Himself among His people. And where He is objectively present He is not only adorable, but ought to be adored by all who apprehend Him as thus present in the Blessed Sacrament.[1]

This does not mean at all that the Eucharistic elements are in themselves adorable; nor that the body and blood of Christ are adorable apart from

---

[1] Cf. the act of St. Thomas, St. John xx. 28. Also see St. Matt. ii. 11; Revel. v. 9-14.

Him. The identification of the sacrament with Christ is the postulate of Eucharistic adoration, and only by recognizing this postulate can anyone correctly and justly consider the subject. It is Christ that is adored in the sacrament, and the external part thereof is the appointed sign of His presence and the guide of our worship.

It is perfectly true that the sacrament was not instituted expressly for such adoration, but it also entirely non-relevant. The adorable Lord, in the fulfilment of a certain purpose, makes Himself objectively present. To argue that He is not to be adored because His purpose in doing so is something else is to assume that this other purpose somehow reduces the honour which we should show Him when He comes to us. Such an inference is a *non-sequitur*. Christ is personally adorable because He is one in essence with the Father, and our adoration of Him does not at all displace worship of the Father. Rather it is the only reverent method of approach to Christ, as being the one through whom alone we gain access to the Father, and who is the true Image of the invisible God. "*Through* Jesus Christ" does not mean to the ignoring of His Person; and catholic Christians have always worshipped Christ in the sacrament before sacramentally receiving Him.[1]

[1] St. Augustine, *In Psa.* xcviii. *Enar.* 9. Cf. pp. 170-171, above, and refs. there given. On Euch. adoration, see S. *Hist.*, I. 106-109 (patristic); II. 553-559 (recent Anglican); John Keble, *Eucharistical Adoration;* Archd. Wilberforce, pp. 211-218; J. R. Milne, ch. vii; Wm. Forbes, *Consid. Modestæ*, vol. II. pp. 544-557.

It is not to be denied that untaught worshippers may so worship Christ as to separate Him in their minds from the Father ditheistically. No true practice is free from possibilities of abuse; and any worship which in effect makes Christ a substitute for the Father, in whom all creaturely worship should ultimately terminate — by implication at least — is not Christian. We should remember that Christ teaches that in Him we reach the Father, and through Him only.[1] Also that every form of Eucharistic adoration has for its background the liturgy, wherein the primary honour of the Father is duly conserved. Those who adore Christ in the sacrament (whether in the liturgy or in the reserved sacrament) are usually those who most regularly take part in the liturgy — in the worship of God the Father.

§ 12. Christ is present in the sacrament so long as the species remain, and this determines the attitude of catholic believers towards the reserved sacrament. The practice of reserving [2] for administration to the sick and unavoidably absent dates at least from the sub-apostolic period, and has for many centuries been of catholic precept. It is required by the mediæval English canon law,[3] which remains in force in the Anglican Communion, except so far as modified

[1] St. John xiv. 6-11. Cf. v. 23; x. 30.
[2] On reservation, see D. Stone, *H. C.*, pp. 250-255; *The Reserved Sacrament;* W. H. Freestone, *The Sacrament Reserved* (Historical); S. C. Hughson, *Reservation and Adoration; Cath. Encyc,*, *q.v.*
[3] By the *Constitutions* of Abp. Peckham. Cf. D. Stone, *Reserved Sacrament*, pp. 23-26.

either by political changes such as the American revolution brought about or by ecclesiastical legislation.¹ The only legislation which can reasonably be regarded as modifying the lawfulness of reservation for us is the rubric, "And if any of the consecrated Bread and Wine remain after the Communion, it shall not be carried out of the Church; but the Minister and other Communicants shall, immediately after the Blessing, reverently eat and drink the same."

If we disregard the ascertained purpose of this rubric, which was to correct the existing abuse of appropriating what remained of the consecrated elements for secular consumption,² it seems to prohibit reservation. But in view of its purpose, and of the evidence that more than one of those responsible for the rubric's adoption did not consider reservation for the sick to be abolished by it,³ we are justified in scrutinizing its phrases very closely. The apparent prohibition of such reservation was in any case inadvertent, and has been taken not absolutely to preclude a different interpretation. The phrase "the Communion," in view of the catholic precept

---

[1] Statutes of Henry VIII, 25. c. 19, declared the previous Canons etc., not contrary to the laws, etc., of the realm to be still in force. On the force of previous English Canon Law in America, see White, *Church Law*, chh. i–iii.

[2] D. Stone, *op. cit.*, pp. 32–33.

[3] H. Thorndike, *The Reformation of the Ch. of England better than that of the Council of Trent*, ch. xxxix (Angl. Cath. Liby., v. 578), pub. some years later, advocates the celebrating of the Eucharist "so frequently that it may be reserved to the next Communion." Cf. D. Stone, *op. cit.*, pp. 42–45; S. C. Hughson, ch. ix.

of reservation, has been treated as including provision for communicating the sick. That "it shall not be carried out of the Church," will then apply only to such consecrated elements as remain after any necessary reservation for the sick has been made. Were it not for the catholic precept referred to, such an interpretation would rightly be regarded as unjustifiable. But the catholic precept is justly to be taken as paramount over provincial legislation to the contrary; and the competence of a provincial part of the Catholic Church to prohibit reservation for the sick, especially in view of the catholic consent that such reservation is a spiritual necessity, is open to the very gravest dispute. Its regulation, as distinguished from prohibition, is of course under provincial jurisdiction and the episcopal *jus liturgicum*.

The fact of reservation being presupposed, it is in the light of the adorability of Christ in the sacrament, as above set forth, that the legitimacy of certain devotional developments in connection with the reserved sacrament has to be considered.[1] The fact that these developments are non-primitive, and the further fact that they are largely confined to the West, are non-relevant unless it can be shown that they involve new doctrinal implications. This cannot

[1] D. Stone, *op. cit.*, chh. iv-v and App. II; S. C. Hughson, chh. xiv-xvii. The most important contrary argument is that of Chas. Gore, *The Theological Bearings of Certain Extra-Liturgical Uses of the Blessed Sacrament.* Cf. discussions in *Chronicle of the Convocation of Canterbury*, Feb. 8-9, 1917, pp. 81-126.

be shown, for no other doctrine is implied than that anciently accepted by the whole Church — that Christ is objectively present in the sacrament, and is there to be adored.[1]

There is no standing ground whatever for the contention that such adoration must be confined to the public liturgy, and no evidence in its support has ever been presented. It being once acknowledged that Christ is always adorable wherever He is objectively present, the development of such adoration is doctrinally defensible, so long as it remains true to the initial premise that the object of adoration is Jesus Christ, as the true Image of the invisible God.[2] We cannot adore such an one excessively, and developments which are due to assured opportunities of enjoying His presence, and have His honour for their

[1] The doctrine of transubstantiation is merely an explanation of the mode of this presence. Its adoption did not create the doctrines of objective presence and adorability.

[2] Alfred Kelly, in *The Cultus of the Sacramental Presence in the Eucharist and in the Reserved Sacrament*, says that "the presence in the Reserved Sacrament is not, like the presence in the Eucharist, 'a presence of Christ in action.' It is a presence cut off from Christ's living and active relations with the Father and with us. The cultus, therefore, of the Reserved Sacrament cannot be grounded on the arguments which vindicate the cultus in the Eucharist" (as given in the *Church Times*). Such a plea postulates subversive doctrine and resembles that of certain Roman writers, above referred to, that Christ undergoes in the Eucharist a change of state into passivity. We cannot divorce Christ really present from His Person, which is intrinsically adorable. If we were to read that the disciples adored Christ when asleep in their boat — the wise men adored Him when a newborn babe, — would we regard their action as unjustifiable? Surely not.

controlling aim, cannot be regarded as superstitious.

The fact remains, of course, that the reserved sacrament is in the Church's keeping, and is incidental to the liturgical worship of the Church. The public use of it is subject, therefore, to ecclesiastical regulation. No public service can lawfully be performed in the Church which has not either been canonically prescribed or, as an extra-canonical service, been sanctioned by the bishop who exercises the local episcopal *jus liturgicum*. The service of Benediction of the Blessed Sacrament *in se* is no doubt a very special development,[1] and its lawfulness in given episcopal jurisdictions is conditioned by episcopal permission, either explicit or implicit. This is beyond intelligent denial.

In any case, the personal privilege of coming to Church for the purpose of private devotion before the reserved sacrament is very precious and helpful to many, and ought not to be hindered or discouraged. It does not in the slightest degree reduce the frequency of sacramental communion,[2] but does have the effect of drawing men more closely to the risen Lord. The attraction, we should remember, is His

---

[1] On its origin, see D. Stone, *op. cit.*, pp. 73-76; H. Thurston, in *Cath. Encyc.*, *s.v.* "Benediction of the Blessed Sacrament." It does raise the question of the reality of any specific blessing as resulting from making the sign of the cross over the people with the reserved sacrament.

[2] The lack of frequent communion among Roman Catholics antedates Benediction, and has other causes.

personal presence; and the notions that the sacrament becomes in these devotions a substitute for Christ, and that Christ becomes a substitute for the Father, are out of accord with their real purpose and normal effects.

CHAPTER VII

PENANCE

I. *Its History*

§ 1. Penance is the sacrament instituted for the remedy of post-baptismal sin.[1] Such sin is to the baptismal life what physical disease is to the physical life; and Penance is the medicine of the soul. The fact that Baptism does not in this life remove the liability to sin is undeniable, and the consequences of sin when left unremedied are fatal to the life of grace. True repentance, no doubt, will always secure

[1] On its history, see O. D. Watkins, *A Hist. of Penance* (very complete in source-material); Nathaniel Marshall, *The Penitential Discipline of the Primitive Church* (Ang. Cath. Lib.); T. T. Carter, *The Doctrine of Confession in the Church of England*, chh. i–v, xii–xiii; A. Boudinhon, *Sur l'histoire de la pénitence et des indulgences;* E. B. Pusey, *Advice to Those who Exercise the Ministry of Reconciliation*, pp. i–clxxiv; B. J. Otten, *Manual of the Hist. of Dogmas*, vol. I. pp. 183–189; vol. II. ch. xx.

On Penance at large, see T. T. Carter, *op. cit.;* H. U. Whelpton, *Sacrament of Penance* (popular); C. Bickersteth, *The Ministry of Absolution;* Ewd. T. Churton, *The Use of Penitence;* E. B. Pusey, *The Church of England Leaves her Children Free*, etc.; J. J. Elmendorf, *Moral Theol.*, pp. 593–606; W. W. Webb, *Cure of Souls*, chh. i–ii; St. Thomas, III. lxxxiv–xc, Suppl. i–xxviii; *Cath. Encyc., q.v.;* Jos. Pohle, *The Sacraments*, vol. III; H. Wace (Edit.), *Confession and Absolution* (Fulham Conference, 1901–1902); Hastings, *Encyc. of Relig., s.v.* "Confession" (in non-Christian religions).

divine pardon for Christians; but in its graver forms sin hardens men's hearts and makes repentance difficult, in many cases very unlikely, apart from the special aid of grace which this sacrament is designed to afford. Its value, therefore, and in some cases its necessity for salvation, is certain. .

The need of confession before men has always been felt by those who have acquired a proper sense of sin, and in the old covenant this need was taken for granted and duly provided for. The sinner was required to make his confession to a Levitic priest, and to make a trespass offering before the Lord. The priest then made atonement for him, and his sin was forgiven.[1] Certain graver sins indeed were not thus provided for, the apparent reason being that the Israelites could not enter fully into the benefits of Christ's redemption previously to its historical accomplishment. But the principle of sacramental ministration for the remedy of sins committed by the members of the covenant was clearly exemplified; and New Testament teaching confirms the permanent validity of this principle. The old law, in this as well as in other particulars, foreshadows the new.

In the teaching both of the Baptist [2] and of Christ the need of confession, and of ministerial agency in the remission of sin, is also taken for granted and re-enforced, and the New Testament at large every-

---

[1] Levit. iv. 1–vi. 7; Numb. v. 5–8. Cf. Rich. Hooker, *Eccles. Polity*, VI. iv. 4; T. T. Carter, pp. 8–12.

[2] St. Matt. iii. 1–6, etc.

where follows suit.¹ Our Lord worked a special miracle to support the claim that in His human capacity He had authority on earth to forgive sins;² and subsequently He transmitted this authority to His ministers, saying, "Whose soever sins ye forgive, they are forgiven unto them; whose soever sins ye retain, they are retained."³ The authority thus given is distinct from the general disciplinary authority of binding and loosing committed to the Church in the words, "What things soever ye shall bind on earth shall be bound in Heaven: and what things soever ye shall loose on earth shall be loosed in Heaven."⁴ That there is a difference between sins remitted or retained and things bound or loosed, that is, prohibited or allowed, seems evident. The power of binding and loosing may indeed be thought to include the power of remitting and retaining, but not necessarily nor when considered apart from Christ's specific teaching concerning the authority to remit sins.⁵

In the light of such teaching, we seem to find our Lord employing the symbolism of feet-washing in

---

[1] St. James v. 15–16; 1 St. John i. 8–9, and the numerous exhortations to repentance.

[2] St. Matt. ix. 2–8, etc.

[3] St. John xx. 21–23.

[4] St. Matt. xviii. 18. Cf. xvi. 19.

[5] The power of remitting and retaining sins constitutes the spiritual means of enforcing discipline, analogous to the penal element in civil laws. The connection of the two is therefore vital. On the power of binding and loosing, see J. K. Mozley, in Hastings, *Encyc. of Relig.*, s.v. "Binding and Loosing"; Fulham Conference, First Sess., esp. pp. 3–5 (H. B. Swete); O. D. Watkins, vol. II. pp. 8–10.

the night of His betrayal,[1] not only as an example of mutual service, but as exhibiting the relation of post-baptismal remission to baptismal cleansing. The example of mutual service was not difficult for His disciples at once to understand; but He said to Peter, "What I do thou knowest not now; but thou shalt know hereafter." The words that follow connect the washing with spiritual cleansing: "If I wash thee not, thou hast no part in Me." Refusing, however, to wash more than his feet — the members most liable to the stains of daily journeying — He added, "He that is washed" that is, all over, "needeth not save to wash his feet, but is clean every whit." The spiritual nature of the cleansing referred to is made clear by the further words, "And ye are clean, but not all." "For He knew," the writer adds, "who should betray Him."

In view of Christ's teaching and commission, the Apostles boldly exercised the ministry of reconciliation, not only in baptizing for the remission of sins, but, as exemplified by the case of the incestuous Corinthian, in dealing with post-baptismal sin. And St. James specifies among the ministrations which the presbyters of the Church are to fulfil when visiting the sick, "And if he have committed sins, it shall be forgiven him."[2]

§ 2. The external manner of administration or outward sign of this sacrament has not been divinely

[1] St. John xiii. 4-17.
[2] 2 Cor. v. 18; Acts ii. 38; 1 Cor. v. 3-5 with 2 Cor. ii. 6-11; St. James v. 15. Cf. the binding in 1 Tim. i. 20.

fixed;[1] and it has undergone various important changes by ecclesiastical authority. But in every age there has been catholic consent that the Christian priesthood has received power and authority from Christ to remit post-baptismal sins; that specific and contrite confession of such sins is the obligatory prerequisite of the administration of absolution to individuals; that such absolution confers distinct benefits, additional to the mere pardon which is promised to all who truly repent of their sins; and that in the case of those who fall into the more grave forms of sin priestly absolution is needed for due reconciliation and for full recovery to the state of saving grace.

In the earliest known sub-apostolic practice the order of procedure was (a) private confession to a presbyter or bishop; (b) if the matter was deemed sufficiently grave, public penance or exomologesis, sometimes extended through many years or even to the eve of death; (c) public reconciliation and absolution by the bishop and restoration to full sacramental privileges. At first there was a rigorist tendency altogether to withhold earthly absolution from those guilty of either apostasy, adulterous intercourse or bloodshed, but from the middle of the third century absolution was accorded to all penitents *in extremis*.[2] Moreover, priests were permitted to

[1] See *The Church*, pp. 333-336, on the external requirements.
[2] Dionysius of Corinth, about 171 A.D., was for mercy; and the decision of Pope Callistus to admit the impure to penance, gradually prevailed elsewhere. O. D. Watkins, pp. 128-129, 142, 468-469.

reconcile deathbed penitents, even when the performance of penance was impossible.

In the East, public exomologesis gradually disappeared during the fourth century. In 330 A.D. penitentiaries began to be established, that is, priests of special competence were appointed to hear confessions, to impose private penance, and when this had been fulfilled to absolve and reconcile. This institution was abolished in 391 A.D. and thenceforth the Eastern usage approximated that which now prevails.[1]

Public exomologesis was retained for several centuries later in the West, and the public reconciliation by the bishop took place during Holy Week. Certain permanent disabilities remained, even after such reconciliation. The prevailing rigour led to refusal in the West to admit sinners to penance more than once during a life-time; and there developed a widespread habit of postponing confession, even of the gravest crimes, until the eve of death. Notorious sinners, of course, continued to be subjected to public penance while in good health; but voluntary seeking of admission to penance previously to the hour of death became increasingly rare.[2]

In the Celtic and English Churches the system of public exomologesis never existed. Instead of it we find the modern use of private confession, penance and

---

[1] On early usages and tendencies, see H. B. Swete, in *Journ. of Theol. Studies*, Apr. 1903, 1st art.; O. D. Watkins, vol. I, esp. ch. x; T. T. Carter, ch. ii; N. Marshall.

[2] O. D. Watkins, pp. 481–483, 751–755.

absolution by a priest. The Celtic and English missionaries, for example, Columbanus and Boniface, transplanted their use to the continent. It became popular and gradually brought about a general abandonment, even in Rome, of the older system. The change was crystallized in Western Canon Law by the fourth Lateran Council, 1215 A.D., which also prescribed for all the practice of annual confession.[1] In both East and West the promise of performing the penance imposed by the priest came to be treated ordinarily as justifying an immediate absolution by the priest, and this is the present custom.

A distinctively mediæval development was the growing treatment of penances as in some sense satisfying the justice of God. The term "satisfaction" had previously signified a completion of repentance by acts of amendment and self-mortification. It came to be regarded as paying part of the temporal penalties which are imposed even upon reconciled sinners by divine justice.[2] As time went by, the whole subject of Penance came to be mixed up in popular imagination with the mediæval system of indulgences, wherein the penal aspect of divine justice obtained an excessively mechanical and quantitative description.[3]

§ 3. These last mentioned developments, and the making confession compulsory, provoked reaction, and helped to bring about the protestant revolution.

[1] O. D. Watkins, pp. 755–769.   [2] T. T. Carter, pp. 50–60.
[3] *Idem*, pp. 60–69. On indulgences, see *The Church*, pp. 275–278, and refs. given on p. 278.

The Calvinistic and Zwinglian reformers abandoned the sacrament of Penance altogether. They indeed approved of confession by those who cannot otherwise convince themselves of divine mercy, but the presbyter's part was limited to reassuring penitents by reminding them of Gospel promises. The power of absolution and sacramental grace through Penance were definitely repudiated.[1]

The Lutheran *Augsburg Confession*[2] says, "We teach that private absolution is to be retained in the Church, and we greatly extol its value and the power of the keys . . . we therefore carefully retain confession in our Church; but yet we teach that the numbering of sins is not necessary by the law of God, and that consciences ought not to be burdened by such numbering." Satisfactions, however, are repudiated as having "obscured the gracious gift of Christ, because the unlearned were wont to think that the remission of guilt was obtained through their own works, and, if anything were omitted, they were troubled." Unhappily the doctrine of justification by faith only reduces Lutheran absolution to a mere declaration of the Gospel of forgiveness for reassuring the individual penitent, and to a means of reconciling sinners to the Christian Congregation.[3]

[1] T. T. Carter, ch. iv.   [2] Pt. I. art. xii. Cf. II. iv.
[3] In May 1856 a Conference at Dresden affirmed "the necessity of reëstablishing the use of regular confession and absolution." T. T. Carter, pp. 88–90. This reflects the influence of an unhappily temporary high Church movement, coinciding with the Tractarian movement in England. See A. S. Farrar, *Hist. of Free Thought*, pp. 282–285.

The sacramental virtue of ministerial absolution, and its effect in reconciling penitents to God, are not acknowledged.

The Anglican Church retained confession; and, as will be shown in the next section, reaffirmed the ancient catholic doctrine concerning the power of priestly absolution, while abolishing compulsory confession. The penal conception of satisfaction was generally repudiated by the Anglican reformers. Reactionary influences operated among many to throw the sacramental conception of Penance into the shade; and the practice of auricular confession almost died out during the eighteenth century and until the catholic revival of the nineteenth century.[1] The recovery of sound doctrine and practice which then ensued was bitterly but vainly opposed by evangelical Churchmen. To-day a large section of Anglicans accept the catholic doctrine of Penance, and its habitual use is fairly widespread.[2]

§ 4. In surveying official Anglican doctrine concerning this sacrament,[3] it is desirable at the outset to remind our readers that, as has been shown in

[1] But, for examples of its continued use and recommendation, see J. W. Legg, *English Church Life from the Restoration*, etc., pp. 263-277.

[2] On the history of Anglican opinion, see T. T. Carter, chh. v, xii-xiii; E. B. Pusey, *Advice*, as cited, pp. lvii-cliii (catena); A. Priest, *Hints to Penitents*, pp. 7-61; Malcolm MacColl, *Reformation Settlement*, ch. viii. *Per contra*, see T. W. Drury, *Confession and Absolution, The Teaching of the Church of England*, etc.

[3] On which, see T. T. Carter, chh. vi-xi. Cf. Fulham Conference, Third Sess.

previous volumes, the tortuous language of the twenty-fifth of our *Articles of Religion* is not rightly to be interpreted as denying the supernatural efficacy of "those five commonly called sacraments," but only the divine institution in the Gospel of their "visible sign or ceremony." The plain implication, however, is that Penance is not to be ranked with Baptism and the Supper of the Lord, which alone, according to the *Catechism*, are instituted as "generally necessary to salvation."[1] In theological language, Penance was instituted by Christ not directly *in specie*, but *in genere*, or impliedly in His general teaching and in commissioning the Apostles to remit sins.[2]

The traditional catholic interpretation of this commission is officially accepted in the Anglican form of ordination of priests, wherein the bishop says to the ordinand, "Whose sins thou dost forgive, they are forgiven, and whose sins thou dost retain, they are retained." A softer echo of this same teaching is found in the first form of absolution prescribed in the Daily Morning and Evening Prayer, in which God is said to have "given power, and commandment, to His ministers, to declare and pronounce to His people, being penitent, the absolution and remission of their sins." The use of this and other forms of absolution is significantly and explicitly restricted by rubric to "the priest" — to one who, in the

[1] Cf. T. T. Carter, ch. ix; A. P. Forbes, art. xxv, pp. 448–453.
[2] Cf. *The Church*, pp. 290–292.

language of the American Church's Office of Institution is "possessed of full power to perform every act of sacerdotal function."

Of the meaning and effect of the general forms of absolution something will be said later, but that the undeniably sacramental rite of private confession and absolution is provided for is perfectly clear. In the English Order for the Visitation of the Sick the direction occurs, "Here shall the sick person be moved to make a special confession of sins, if he feel his conscience troubled with any weighty matter. After which confession, the Priest shall absolve him (if he humbly and heartily desire it) after this sort. Our Lord Jesus Christ, who hath left power to His Church to absolve all sinners who truly repent and believe in Him, of His great mercy forgive thee thine offences: And by His authority committed to me, I absolve thee from all thy sins. In the Name of the Father, and of the Son, and of the Holy Ghost. Amen." In the first exhortation of the Holy Communion the priest is directed to say, "If there be any of you, who by this means" (previous personal exercises of repentance) "cannot quiet his own conscience herein, but requireth further comfort or counsel, let him come to me, or to some other discreet and learned Minister of God's Word and open his grief; that by the ministry of God's holy Word, he may receive the benefit of absolution, together with ghostly counsel and advice, to the quieting of his conscience, and avoiding of all scruple and doubtfulness." The implication would seem clear that in such case the only form provided for private absolution, as above quoted, should be employed.

The American Church was organized towards the close of the eighteenth century, when sacramental beliefs and practices were at their lowest ebb. Unfortunately, therefore, in the revised Prayer Book which was then adopted the provision for administering absolution to the sick, above given, was omitted,[1] as was also the explicit mention of absolution in the exhortation of the Holy Communion. But we may not read into these omissions any repudiation of the teaching contained in the English provisions. The American Prayer Book expressly declares that in the changes made it will "appear that this Church is far from intending to depart from the Church of England in any essential point of doctrine, discipline, or worship; or further than local circumstances require." Obviously an abandonment of the mother Church's doctrine concerning the sacrament of Penance cannot be understood as required by local circumstances, for such doctrine, if true anywhere, must be true everywhere. Moreover, in all other particulars above given, the witness of the English Prayer Book as to confession and absolution is retained, with the added statement in the Office of Institution that a Parish

[1] In *Second Report of the Joint Commission on the Book of Common Prayer*, 1919, pp. 152–153, a Rubric is proposed, "Then shall the sick person be moved to make a special confession of his sins . . . after which . . . the Minister shall assure him of God's mercy and forgiveness."

ITS THEOLOGY

priest is "possessed of full power to perform every act of sacerdotal function."

The conclusion of the matter is that, in accordance with its general appeal to antiquity, the Anglican Communion retains the sacrament of Penance and the traditional catholic doctrine concerning the same. Its rejection of compulsory confession, and of certain mediæval conceptions concerning satisfaction, does not invalidate this conclusion.

II. *Its Theology*

§ 5. It is catholic doctrine that Christ's death has procured forgiveness of sins for all of His members who truly repent and believe in Him; and no reputable school of theologians denies that when baptized Christians really repent, they certainly and immediately secure complete forgiveness. Repentance includes an undertaking of self-mortifying works worthy of repentance, for in no other way can the sinner identify himself with Christ in His death and justly become a participant in its benefits. But when he contritely accepts this condition, Christ's death becomes for him a full satisfaction of divine justice. Indeed, no manner of satisfaction undertaken by sinners can avail, except it be undertaken upon the basis of Christ's reparation for sin, and as identifying its agent with His passion and moral attitude towards sin. The value of penitential satisfactions lies in their relation to what Christ has done. In themselves they are wholly inadequate; but when they represent genuine repentance and faith in Christ's death, full pardon is assured to baptized Christians independently of the sacrament of Penance.

The value, and in many instances the necessity, of this sacrament are not at all disproved by this doctrine; although its truth does have to be fully reckoned with in order rightly to understand them. The protestant repudiation of Penance was occasioned by theoretical and practical accretions which seemed to nullify the sufficiency of the Cross and the invariable readiness of God by reason of it to pardon unconditionally all genuine penitents. Catholic verity requires us to hold together in mutually interpreting relation the truth and the counter truth.[1]

God's pardon is in any case conditioned by true repentance; but inasmuch as sin often hardens our hearts so as to make such repentance difficult, or even impossible, without special assistance, God mercifully provides in the sacrament of Penance a means by resort to which we can repent more perfectly than is otherwise possible. Moreover, Penance is not merely an instrument of pardon. Sin is a disease as well as an act, and this sacrament is remedial as well as remissive. It also has high value as an aid to spiritual progress. Furthermore, as the appointed means of reconciling sinners to the Church on earth, it fulfils a very important part in the maintenance of the Church's divinely appointed discipline. By

[1] On which, see T. T. Carter, pp. 234-238, 252-255.

covenant arrangement, and for the sake of the Christian brotherhood at large, the Church is made to be an interested party in the divine discipline and reconciliation of sinners.[1] But its doctrine and practice *ad rem* must be in harmony with the freeness of pardoning grace, to which after all the sacrament of Penance is an adjunct.

Our Lord's teaching in the parable of the Prodigal Son [2] is vital, and its comforting tenour may not be discounted. But its scope is limited; and it must be viewed in connection with the rest of Christ's teaching, if it is not to become the basis of an inadequate conception of the effects of sin and of the task of repentance. The prodigal really repented. That is a vital point. And when our Lord exhibits the free pardon which such repentance secures, He should be understood to take for granted all that is elsewhere revealed as to the divine arrangements and adjuncts of the dispensation of pardoning and saving grace. In particular, the fact may not be forgotten that salvation from sin is not remission of its penalties. Sin has to be eradicated, and every available and pertinent means of grace is needed for the stupendous work of removing it. We may therefore be sure that it is dangerous, as well as presumptuous, to regard any instrument which Christ has provided for the remedy of sin as superfluous and unimportant.

[1] E. T. Churton, pp. 77-80; T. T. Carter, pp. 238-240; A. R. Whitham, *Holy Orders*, pp. 189-192.
[2] St. Luke xv. 11-32.

§ 6. The benefits of the sacrament of Penance, above alluded to, need to be defined in a more formal way.

(*a*) The primary benefit is an authentic, formal and plenary remission of sins. It is the primary benefit because all other benefits depend upon initial restoration of the penitent to the baptismal standing before God which he has forfeited. "If he have committed sins it shall be forgiven him."[1] The remission is authentic because visibly given by one who has been commissioned by God to bestow it. It is formal and sacramental in merciful accommodation to human nature, which depends upon the help of visible media for full assurance of spiritual blessings. It is plenary because divine forgiveness, if real, is always complete. God never forgives the slightest particular offence, unless conditions are fulfilled by the penitent under which forgiveness of all his sins is pledged.[2] Such fulfilment, as will be shown in another section,[3] is necessary for the beneficial reception of this as of all other sacraments.

(*b*) The Church has learned by Spirit-guided experience that sacramental absolution is curative as well as remissive. In the first place, it is often the means by which contrition, the necessary condition

---

[1] St. James v. 15. See T. T. Carter, ch. xvii; E. B. Pusey, *Entire Absolution of the Penitent;* St. Thomas, III. lxxvi and III. Suppl. x. 1; A. R. Whitham, *op. cit.*, pp. 119–124.

[2] St. Thomas, III. lxxxvi. 3.

[3] In § 9.

of forgiveness, is deepened and made sufficient in those who, without such assistance, are unable to turn to God with the right kind of sorrow for sin, although sufficiently moved by their sense of guilt to make use of the sacrament.[1] In the second place, the sacrament fortifies the sin-diseased soul with special grace, by means of which the sinner is helped to overcome his personal weaknesses and to make progress in forsaking his besetting sins. The proof of this is the experience of multitudes, who have found themselves to be helped in this way whenever they contritely resort to this sacrament. No other evidence is needed, especially in view of the strong presumption that a divinely appointed ministry of reconciliation will inevitably carry with it such curative benefits as are necessary.[2]

(c) A third benefit is the sinner's full reconciliation to the Church, and a restoration of his fitness and moral right to enjoy the privileges of grace which the Church administers, but should also guard from desecration.[3] One who is guilty of very grave sin may indeed escape detection, and while avoiding the tribunal of Penance may be admitted externally to all ecclesiastical privileges. But such an one is as truly alien to the Church as if his guilt were known, and he were under open discipline. When we remem-

---

[1] Cf. pp. 235–237, below.
[2] T. T. Carter, pp. 292–294; St. Thomas, III. lxxxix.
[3] Cf. W. R. Carson, *Reunion Essays*, III (on "The Social Aspect of Confession"); R. C. Moberly, in Fulham Conference, pp. 11–12.

ber that the Church is the Body of Christ, and that its discipline is Christ's discipline, the need and benefit of becoming reconciled to it under such circumstances by the method which Christ has appointed should be apparent to us. Then too, quite apart from the question of personal benefit, no one who realizes the extent to which the welfare and effective work of the Church at large depends upon loyal support and use of its chief instrument of discipline can fail to grieve at the widespread neglect of this sacrament. How can the Church's ministers intelligently and effectively look after the spiritual needs of those who conceal their spiritual diseases, and refuse to make use of the curative means which they are divinely charged to administer? [1]

(*d*) Finally, as might be expected in view of the benefits above described, a devout and recurrent use of this sacrament has been found to be an exceedingly effective means of progress towards perfection. And it does not cease to be this in the more advanced stages of the spiritual life.[2] That such a statement is in accord with experience is shown by the notorious fact that saintly souls who have once learned the value of Penance, so far from outgrowing the sense of need for it, find themselves more and more bene-

---

[1] Cf. John Keble's plaint as to the blind helplessness of pastors under such conditions, quoted in J. T. Coleridge's *Memoir*, pp. 202–203.

[2] T. T. Carter, pp. 238–240. Ascetic writers treat it as one of the means of perfection. Cf. J. B. Scaramelli, *Directorium Asceticum*, vol. I. art. viii; Arthur Devine, *Manual of Ascet. Theol.*, pp. 381–398.

fited and helped onwards by a frequent and regular resort to it.

Those who for various reasons deny or disparage the benefits of the sacrament of Penance — we do not refer to such as are moved by grave sin and wilful refusal to repent — almost invariably have wholly omitted to put it to the test of experience or sincere use of it. Their training and consequent unavoidable presuppositions may be pleaded by way of excuse, no doubt; but to reject a sacrament which is guaranteed by Christ's commission without proper experience of it is to reject it unintelligently. Those who have such experience find their faith in its value abundantly confirmed thereby. Countless examples confirm this assertion.

§ 7. It is *de fide* that our Lord's words, "Whose soever sins ye forgive, they are forgiven unto them; whose soever sins ye retain, they are retained," [1] were meant to confer on the priesthood a permanent authority and power to administer the plenary forgiveness of God to penitent believers in the saving priesthood of the Redeemer. This power is obviously judicial, inasmuch as its exercise requires the minister of Christ to determine whether the penitent is sufficiently fulfilling the conditions of remission.[2] For this reason the practice of auricular confession is conventionally described as a resort to the tribunal

---

[1] St. John xx. 23.
[2] He has power to retain as well as to remit, which implies judicial discretion. Cf. T. T. Carter, pp. 297–299.

of Penance. Furthermore, by ecclesiastical precept, in connection with absolution, and as conditioning its bestowal, the priest determines what penance or act of satisfactory self-mortification shall be required of the penitent.

But, although the remission of eternal punishment is a necessary effect of remission of guilt, and is thus indirectly an effect of the sacrament of Penance, the temporal penalties of sin which God imposes still remain to be endured.[1] The penances accepted from the priest are part of the work of repentance rather than penal, and do not at all remove the temporal consequences of sin. The conclusive proof that these are not removed is the universal experience of penitents that they are not relieved by Penance from enduring the just consequences of their sins. What is accomplished is that these consequences are no longer purely penal to contrite sinners. They become effectively purificatory and remedial and therefore cease when the sinner has been made perfect by suffering. They cannot wholly cease before such consummation, for until then the soul is still in an imperfect moral state which eternal justice does not permit to be free from penal consequences.[2] The remission of eternal punishment is due to a removal of its cause, which is guilt. Therefore this remission

---

[1] St. Thomas, III. lxxxvi. 4.

[2] Cf. St. Matt. v. 26; 1 Cor. iii. 15. The error of Roman doctrine concerning Purgatory lies in its over definite and mechanical aspects. We return to the subject in the next volume.

ITS THEOLOGY 231

is conditioned by the avoidance of subsequent sin; for whenever an absolved penitent falls again into sin he is once more liable to eternal punishment until he again repents and obtains pardon.[1]

The fact that the benefit of priestly absolution is always conditioned by true repentance does not, as disbelievers in the sacrament suppose, nullify the priestly power of absolution. The condition referred to is absolute in any method of divine pardon. God will not, and cannot in view of His righteousness and supreme responsibility for the moral order, forgive those who do not repent. Failure to repent is identical with obstinate guilt, a remission of which would be subversive of divine government. The minister of Christ, therefore, cannot remit the sins of the impenitent, but he is given power to do ministerially what God has promised to do for penitent sinners because of Christ's death; and Penance is the appointed means of thus doing.

There is another limitation. The priest is fallible, and may err in judgment so as to pronounce absolution upon one who is not really penitent. In such case the sinner's guilt is increased by his desecration of the sacrament rather than remitted. This is not at all inconsistent with the truth and efficacy of the sacrament, which like any other sacrament is a moral instrument, dependent for its benefits upon contrite

[1] The sins previously remitted are not thereby re-imputed, although their careless repetition cannot but bring a special guilt of ingratitude. St. Thomas, III. lxxxviii.

faith in its recipient. Every absolution is given *sub conditione*, and its promised heavenly ratification is to be understood in that light.[1]

§ 8. In technical description, while sins to be forsaken and remedied constitute the remote matter of Penance; its proximate matter is repentance or change of mind. This change requires and consists of contrition, confession, and satisfaction.[2] Contrition means true sorrow for sin as such, because of its violation of our filial relations to God, and the will by God's grace to forsake it. Confession so far as pertaining to the sacrament is the specific acknowledgment to the priest of one's sins, especially of each mortal sin and of all besetting sins whether mortal or not, so far as they can be recalled.

Postponing certain questions concerning these two, we now consider the meaning of satisfaction.[3] The word has been used since St. Anselm's time to denote the adequate reparation for sin which Christ made on the Cross, which is the historical basis of the baptismal covenant, and of divine forgiveness of penitent Christians.[4] In this sense of the word, no

[1] Its effect is also limited to removal of *previous* guilt. Until death has occurred, liability to further guilt remains. Only the final judgment of God is absolute for the future.

[2] St. Thomas, III. lxxxiv. 2. On the nature and parts of repentance, see *idem*, III. xc; W. W. Webb, ch. ii; W. W. Williams, *Moral Theol. of Penance*, pp. 12-15 and ch. iii; F. G. Belton, *Manual of Confessors*, Pt. II.

[3] On which, see besides the above E. B. Pusey, *Is Healthful Reunion Impossible?* pp. 69-73; St. Thomas, III. Suppl. xii-xv; Jos. Pohle, pp. 217-231.

[4] Cf. *Passion and Exaltation*, pp. 25-26.

sinner is capable of making satisfaction for sin to God, although he is enabled by grace and through repentance to identify himself with Christ in His death, and by voluntarily mortifying his corrupt affections to appropriate its benefits.

Satisfaction in its older meaning denotes that part of repentance in which we demonstrate our contrition and purpose of forsaking sin by voluntary acts of reparation to those whom we have injured and of self-mortification before God, whether public or private.[1] Its value does not lie, as does Christ's passion, in fulfilling the requirements of penal justice, but in completing repentance, and therefore in fulfilling the conditions under which the pardon won by Christ is extended to individual sinners. That we should make reparation so far as is possible to those whom we have injured is not at all in controversy, although it is not maintained that when such reparation is either partially or wholly impossible divine pardon will for that reason be withheld.

But under normal circumstances, and except *in extremis*, it is both possible and necessary that we should identify ourselves with Christ's great act of reparation for sin by some form and degree of self-mortifying imitation of His passion before God.[2] In the sacrament under discussion the self-mortifying

[1] So used by Tertullian, *De Pœnit.*, v; and by St. Cyprian, *De Lapsis*, xvii.
[2] Cf. Christ's command to take His cross, St. Matt. x. 38, etc. Also Rom. viii. 17; Col. i. 24; 1 St. Pet. v. 10.

element of such satisfaction is filled out by obedient acceptance from God's priest of the penance which he imposes. The point to be emphasized is that repentance should be adequately fulfilled, and it is not normally complete without some appropriate expression in specific acts of voluntary self-mortification. The pardon of God is not withheld, indeed, until our acts of penance are performed. God accepts the will for the deed, and priestly absolution is ordinarily given at once when the penitent indicates his acceptance of the assigned penance. But, as in the case of our first justification, the remission of post-baptismal sins postulates the subsequent fulfilment of "works worthy of repentance";[1] and its benefits will be jeopardized by avoidable failure to fulfil them. At least such failure will constitute a new offence requiring further repentance. We must align ourselves with the passion of Christ by action as well as by faith, and here, as well as elsewhere, faith without its appropriate work is dead.[2]

To regard the value of penitential satisfaction as lying in its external greatness or quantity, however, is a very serious error. Its value lies wholly in its completing the due and effectual expression of personal contrition, and in its thus completing repentance. For this reason a wise priest will not usually impose a penance that, because of its formidable nature, might be regarded as having a quantitative value for the

[1] Cf. *The Church*, pp. 261–263.
[2] St. James ii. 14–26.

reparative satisfaction of penal justice. It can have no such value.¹

III. *Certain Details*

§ 9. Contrition is the first and most obvious requirement of repentance.² It consists of sorrow for sin, taken together with the purpose of confession, whether sacramental or other, and that species of satisfaction which has been described in the previous section. Strictly speaking, it is not an act of virtue; but is metaphorically so described, as containing the moral purpose of recovering virtue.³ Its sufficiency for repentance, therefore, does not lie in any ideal perfection. Inasmuch as it presupposes a sinful subject, it cannot become perfect without becoming something else — that is, the state of fully restored harmony with God's attitude towards sin which may follow, but cannot precede, remission of sins.⁴

The sufficiency of contrition is analogous to that of a submissive patient's readiness for the physician's curative treatment. That is, it is sufficient when it makes the sinner susceptible to the pardoning and purifying grace of God. Contrition has varying degrees of adequacy, and because its sufficiency is wholly

---

[1] Cf. W. W. Webb, pp. 60–72; E. B. Pusey, *Advice*, pp. 353–373.
[2] On contrition, see W. W. Webb, pp. 21–31; E. G. Belton, *op. cit.*, Pt. II. ch. i. Blunt, *Dic. of Theol.*, *q. v.*; St. Thomas, III. Suppl. i–v.
[3] Cf. St. Thomas, III. lxxxv; III. Suppl. i. 2; *Cath. Encyc.*, *s. v.* "Penance," I.
[4] Cf. *Passion and Exaltation*, pp. 37–38.

moral and spiritual, no quantitative or mechanical measure thereof is available. To be sufficient contrition must at least be genuine. That is, it must contain some degree of true sorrow for sin as sin and a real purpose, however weak, of completing the work of repentance and of striving by grace to forsake sin. Unless these elements are present in some degree, the soul remains insusceptible of pardoning grace.

But sin often makes its agent incapable of contrition in its higher degrees, and God is very merciful and resourceful. He is ready to meet such weakness with special provisions, the appointed method of which is the sacrament of Penance, wherein a very imperfect degree of contrition is sufficiently enhanced by the infusion of grace. The proof of this is the experience of multitudes, who by resort to this sacrament have in fact come to feel a degree of contrition previously unattainable.

The lower degree of contrition which is thus enhanced is called attrition. Its distinguishing mark is that the sinner is more strongly moved by revulsion from the penal consequences of sin than by detestation of sin *in se*. In other words, it is akin to mere remorse, which consists wholly of servile fear — fear of consequences. But unless it is in some degree distinct from mere remorse, it cannot at all avail for repentance. To be sufficient even for beneficial reception of the sacrament of Penance, it must to some degree, however low, contain the elements of genuine contrition — sorrow for sin *in se*, and the will to fulfil the work of repentance and to forsake sin. Such considerations are to be presupposed in acknowledging the sufficiency of attrition for resort to the sacrament of Penance.[1]

Psychological analysis brings to light certain normal stages in the development of contrition. They include the following: (a) *Servile fear* or mere remorse, due to recognition of the consequences of sin to oneself. It leads often to detestation of the act which has such consequences, and even to certain degrees of external reformation in conduct; but the offence against the loving God, wherein the wickedness of sin primarily consists, is not in mind. Genuine contrition is not yet felt; (b) Attention to the Godward aspect and intrinsic wickedness of one's sins, dependent for development upon self-examination and upon consideration of one's filial relations to God and of His redeeming love; (c) Sorrow for sin as sin, growing out of some degree of quickening love towards God; (d) Filial or holy fear, which in this connection is a painful anxiety and purpose to please God by adequate repentance and abandonment of sin.[2]

Contrition is not needed for original sin, because the will of the penitent has had no part therein. It does not avail for others, because no one is susceptible of divine pardon until he himself is contrite. It has no prospective value, for contrition presupposes sins

---

[1] Cf. Blunt, *Dic. of Theol.*, s.v. "Attrition"; *Cath. Encyc.*, s.vv. "Attrition" and "Contrition."

[2] Cf. St. Thomas, III. lxxxv. 5.

already committed. Sorrow for sin should be habitual and life-long; but continued emotional brooding is sinful, because it induces discouragement and hinders the fulfilment of subsequent duties. It often conceals a subtle form of pride.

§ 10. Sacramental confession is obviously necessary whenever the gravity of one's sins makes their remedy otherwise impossible, or when by other methods the sinner "cannot quiet his conscience."[1] And it is required by ecclesiastical precept in the Roman and Oriental Churches at least once a year.[2] But it is not required in any part of the Church as an invariable antecedent of receiving the Blessed Sacrament. The obligation of confessing one's sins, in any case to God and in ordinary practice to others, is not limited, however, to the sacrament of Penance. It is an elementary part of repentance, which is not complete without some form of it.[3] Moreover, a proper fulfilment of this obligation requires the habit of self-examination by the rule of God's commandments and in the light of whatever means we have of knowing God's will and rightly judging ourselves.

The primary qualities required in confession, particularly in sacramental confession, are genuine contrition, wherein love towards God is vital, and integrity or unreservedly making clear to the priest the

[1] T. T. Carter, ch. xv. Cf. St. Thomas, III. Suppl. vi.
[2] So the Fourth Lateran Council, *decret*. 21: in H. Denzinger, *Enchiridion*, 363. Cf. *Orthod. Confess.*, Pt. I. Quest. 90.
[3] St. Thomas, III. Suppl. vii. 2-3; Blunt, *Dic. of Theol.*, *s.v.* "Confession of Sins."

whole state of soul which needs to be remedied. Moreover, sacramental confession cannot be made *in absentia*, whether by letter or by proxy. It has to be made with one's own mouth within the priest's hearing; although in case of necessity it may be made by signs which the priest can perceive and rightly interpret.

For integrity, a confession should specify, so far as they can be recalled, (*a*) every mortal sin; (*b*) all sinful habits or besetting sins, whether they result in acts of mortal sin or not; and (*c*) by implication, all other sins which escape the penitent's recollection. But the proper range of a sacramental confession, unless it is either a first confession or intended for sufficient reasons to be recapitulatory and "general," is expressed in the words, "since my last confession, which was . . ." If the penitent sincerely endeavours to make a clean breast, and to describe as truly and contritely as he can the nature and frequency of his sins, this is all that is to be expected of him.[1]

In particular, no penitent, and no human being, is competent to distinguish with invariable accuracy between mortal and venial sins. In technical parlance, a sin is mortal when it is so grave whether in kind (materially), in conscious deliberation (formally), or in both, that a mortal wound to the regenerate life of the agent is incurred thereby. A venial sin is one which, because of its relatively small matter and

[1] W. W. Webb, pp. 35–43; W. W. Williams, *op. cit.*, pp. 32–52; F. G. Belton, *op. cit.*, pp. 42–56. Cf. St. Thomas, III. Suppl. ix.

slight deliberation, is not fatal to the regenerate life, although it does, of course, hinder the soul's spiritual progress. In relation to God a mortal sin represents malignant defiance of His will, whereas venial sins represent only the weaknesses which remain, even in those who truly love God, until the perfecting work of grace is completed, and which inevitably betray us into occasional minor transgressions while we continue subject to this life's temptations.[1]

In making confession, a penitent fortunately does not need accurately to draw the line between his mortal and venial sins, provided he makes a full confession, and is sufficiently contrite. But he will err most dangerously, if his belief that a certain sin committed by him is venial leads him to think that it does not require earnest repentance. Contrition is fatally defective when not intended to be comprehensive in its reference, for God pardons no sin for which contrition is not somehow shown; and unless He pardons all our sins, He pardons none. The reason is that impenitence even for one sin represents an attitude which nullifies the soul's susceptibility to pardoning grace.

§ 11. The seal of confession,[2] or the secrecy which a priest ought to observe with regard to what he learns

[1] On mortal and venial sin, see T. T. Carter, pp. 245-246, 249; W. W. Williams, *op. cit.*, pp. 178-183; J. G. H. Barry, *Holy Eucharist*, pp. 48-58. Cf. 1 St. John v. 16-17.

[2] On the seal, see T. T. Carter, ch. xvi; F. G. Belton, *op. cit.*, Pt. III; St. Thomas, III. Suppl. xi; *Cath. Encyc.*, *s.v.* "Seal of Confession."

through hearing confessions, is of the utmost importance for the confidence which penitents should be able to have in their confessors. Moreover, confessions come under the category of privileged communications, the concealment of which is recognized by general human consent to be obligatory, even in law courts. The priest hears confessions not as a private person but as God's representative; and the secrets which he hears belong to God, who does not will that confessions made to Him, whether directly or through His appointed ministers, shall be made public. Even when it may be necessary for the priest to consult with another priest in order to deal wisely with his penitent, he is under obligation to avoid betrayal of the penitent's identity.

The seal extends not only to all the sins confessed, both mortal and venial, but to their circumstances, to the names of accomplices incidentally revealed, to the advice given and to every manner of self-revelation which is involved and implied in the penitent's words and manner of confession. Moreover, the penitent's death does not remove the seal. Knowledge thus gained is official, and the priest may make no other specific use of it than is required for immediate and judicious official treatment of the particular confession involved. He may not even recur to the subject in conversing with the penitent, without his previous free consent. If possible, such information should be forgotten, although it may lawfully afford subject matter for secret intercessory prayer.

There are indeed apparent exceptions; but, so far as the main principle involved is concerned, they are only apparent. (*a*) If the priest has personal knowledge of what is confessed, outside of the confessional, such knowledge is not brought under the seal, except so far as binding the priest to special care not to employ it without necessity in such wise as to imperil the seal; (*b*) When the good of others can thus be promoted, and the penitent freely consents, the seal may be broken for such good, but no further; (*c*) When the confession clearly reveals intention to commit in the future a crime that endangers others, it is widely held that such information does not come under the seal. The English Canon Law excepts cases in which a confessed "crime be such as by the laws of the realm his own life may be called in question for concealing the same."[1] Although various reputable theologians have defended such an exception, the present writer considers it to be Erastian and doubtful.

The seal obviously precludes any change in the priest's visible attitude and conduct towards the penitent outside the tribunal of Penance, especially where such change may injure the penitent. This involves that his sealed knowledge may not be used in other relations. For example, if the penitent is the priest's inferior — servant, pupil, or other subject —

[1] Canon 113 of 1604. Cf. T. T. Carter, pp. 273–275. The ancient exomologesis was apt to involve publicity in the graver cases. That is no longer a practical issue.

the priest may not allow such knowledge to modify his attitude and action towards him as his superior.

§ 12. Many troublesome questions necessarily arise in the ministry of Penance. They belong, however, to Moral and Pastoral Theology rather than to Dogmatic, and we treat only of such as pertain to a right understanding of that sacrament and to a due appreciation of its value and limits.[1] A priest is under the most solemn obligation to equip himself with sufficient knowledge of moral, casuistical and pastoral science; for his personal experience will in many cases fail to afford adequate basis for sound judgment, and errors in dealing with penitents may have the very gravest results. He should know, or be able readily to obtain information, how the problems which are likely to arise have previously been handled by wise moral guides; and this requires book learning.[2] He will also need to exercise personal discretion; but common sense, necessary as it is, when alone depended upon, is wholly inadequate. None the less, an inexperienced and unlearned priest, bound as he is to remedy his deficiencies as rapidly as possible, may not evade his divinely imposed pastoral office. And he may take courage from the fact that, *in ordinary cases*, a love of souls, a prayerful sense of priestly responsi-

[1] It is hoped to publish, after this series is completed, a work on *Moral Theology*, having the joint authorship of Dr. F. H. Hallock and the present writer.

[2] Useful books for immediate guidance are those cited above, by W. W. Webb, E. B. Pusey (*Advice*, etc.), W. W. Williams and F. G. Belton.

bility and earnest care will enable him to minister helpfully to penitents.

In order lawfully to administer this sacrament, however, a priest must have ecclesiastical jurisdiction as well as the priesthood. Under the Roman Canon Law this requires that, except in danger of death, a penitent must make his confession to his own priest, or to one delegated by competent authority to receive it.[1] The Anglican Churches, on the other hand, permit the penitent to go to a priest of his own choosing.[2] In prospect of death, when a priest is not available, confession to a layman is both permissible and salutary; for although a layman cannot give sacramental absolution, confession to anyone tends to deepen contrition, and under such conditions justifies hope of abundant divine mercy.[3]

Many reject sacramental confession on the ground that it necessarily tends to sap the penitent's personal strength and to weaken his sense of responsibility to be guided by his own conscience. The best instruments can be abused, and cases no doubt occur in which the penitent is made unduly dependent upon his priest; but these cases are comparatively rare. General experience shows that a sincere use of the

---

[1] *Concil. Trid.*, Sess. xiv, *De Pœn.*, cap. 7. Cf. St. Thomas, III. Suppl. viii. 4–6; D. Stone, *Outlines of Christ. Dogma*, pp. 328–329.

[2] The Exhortation at the end of The Communion, "Let him come to me, or to some other Minister," etc. Cf. E. B. Pusey, *The Church of England Leaves her Children Free*, etc.

[3] St. Thomas, III. Suppl. viii. 2–3; Malcolm MacColl, *Reformation Settlement*, pp. 211–214 (with refs. and examples).

sacrament of Penance as a rule not only deepens repentance, but enlightens and fortifies the individual conscience, and quickens instead of sapping the sense of personal responsibility for being guided thereby.[1]

It is, however, the duty of a priest to be most careful in this matter. A penitent's conscience may be in error and at the same time susceptible of enlightenment. In such case the proper instruction should be given. But in matters open to difference of judgment, the priest may not overrule consciences. Even in error, the conscience cannot be dethroned from its subjective authority without grave danger. Moreover, if its error is invincible, the priest has need to beware lest, by giving instruction which the penitent is incapable of assimilating, he convert ignorance into wilful resistance of truth and formal sin.[2]

[1] On "direction" or habitual guidance by a priest, acceptance of which is purely voluntary, see E. B. Pusey, *Advice*, etc., pp. clvi-clxviii; T. T. Carter, pp. 226-228; F. G. Belton, *op. cit.*, Pt. IV. ch. iii; J. G. H. Barry, *Holy Eucharist*, pp. 70-73.

[2] Cf. the works cited in p. 243, n. 2, above, on questioning and instructing.

CHAPTER VIII

HOLY ORDER

I. *Introductory*

§ 1. Holy Order is the sacrament by which a member of Christ's mystical Body is advanced to one or other of the orders of the sacred ministry which God has constituted for it, and receives the grace which is required for the due performance of its functions.[1]

In the last previous volume, the Christian ministry at large, its divine institution, the necessity and fact of its unbroken transmission through the Apostles by means of the episcopate, its threefold differentiation, and its prophetic, priestly and kingly functions, have been as fully considered as is practicable.[2] In the same volume, the external requirements of the sacrament of Holy Order have been summarized.[3] In this

---
[1] On Holy Order, see A. R. Whitham, *Holy Orders;* C. S. Grueber, *Holy Order;* T. T. Carter, *Doctrine of the Priesthood in the Church of England;* Wm. Denton, *Grace of the Ministry;* R. C. Moberly, *Ministerial Priesthood;* J. J. Elmendorf, *Elements of Moral Theol.*, pp. 610–619; St. Thomas, III. Suppl. xxxiv–xl; *Cath. Encyc.*, s.vv. "Hierarchy," I. A. and "Orders, Holy." Only the author's names are usually given in refs. in this chapter to these works.

[2] *The Church*, ch. iv, with refs. on p. 116.

[3] *Idem*, pp. 336–339.

chapter, we consider the twofold grace of the sacrament of Holy Order flowing from the gift of the Holy Spirit, the mission and jurisdiction which it conveys, and related matters. In order, however, that the connection of ideas may be duly preserved, we give the following recapitulatory propositions.

(a) In both the old and new dispensations, the Church and its ministerial organization have been divinely created, ordered and endowed with such authority and power as they have been entitled and enabled to exercise in divine things. And the same is to be said of the method by which the Church's ministry has been transmitted from one generation to another.

(b) Inasmuch as the old covenant was designed to be preparatory for the new, its arrangements in important regards were prefigurative of, and therefore somewhat analogous to, Christian institutions; although previously to redemption they could not, properly speaking, effect what they figured. Thus, while Circumcision admitted individuals to the old covenant, Baptism fulfils this mystery in the new; while the sacrificial ritual of the old law served for the formal maintenance of acceptable relations with God, the Eucharistic rite thus serves under the new law; and while a threefold tribal ministry of high priest, priests and Levites was constituted in the old dispensation, a threefold apostolic ministry of bishops, priests and deacons has been appointed for the Christian Church.

(c) The Incarnation and Christ's redemption of mankind, accomplished once for all, account for the differences between the old and new covenants and their arrangements. The Church is reconstituted to be Christ's Spirit-filled Body, as such becoming catholic instead of racial; and its ministry becomes an interior, organic and sacramental differentiation in that Body, deriving its validity from Christ by sacramental means rather than from tribal or family inheritance. No element of caste remains; but there is a participation, not less real because derivative and subordinate, in the prophetic, priestly and kingly ministry of the Redeemer and Saviour of mankind. Such a ministry needs no substantial alteration while the world lasts, being adaptable to the conditions and spiritual needs of every age and race.

(d) The sacrament of Holy Order is the instrument by which this ministry is perpetuated. By means of it chosen men are admitted to its several grades, and receive mission from Christ, along with the gift of the Holy Spirit and suitable endowments of grace.

§ 2. During the many centuries previous to the protestant revolution, no important body of professing Christians failed to accept and minister the sacrament of Holy Order in accordance with the doctrine and covenant requirements above indicated.[1] Such differences as emerged had reference

---

[1] On the history of this sacrament, see *The Church*, pp. 132-154 (where refs. are given); Hastings, *Encyc. of Relig.* and *Dic. of Apost. Ch.*, *s.vv.* "Ordination."

INTRODUCTORY

to certain incidental matters in the requirements of valid administration. The importance of loyal adherence to the apostolic ministry was emphasized before the end of the first century, in connection with certain disorders in the Church at Corinth, in a letter addressed to that Church by Clement of Rome; and this letter became classic as representing the consentient mind of the universal Church. The same position was emphasized some fifteen years later with the same general approval in several epistles of St. Ignatius of Antioch, who clearly set forth the threefold arrangement of the ministry as essential to a duly organized Church.[1]

During the second century the rise of Montanism and Gnosticism caused the Church to realize more fully and once for all the importance of regularity and validity in the ordination and uninterrupted continuity of its ministry for the preservation of apostolic doctrine among the faithful.[2]

The disorderly usurpation of presbyterial functions by confessors during the persecutions of the third century, weakly permitted for awhile in certain localities, soon passed away. In result it accentuated the general consent that episcopal ministration is necessary for the validity of Holy Order.[3] Whatever

---

[1] St. Clement, *Ep. ad Corinth.* xli–xliv (cf. *The Church*, pp. 144–145); St. Ignatius, *Ephes.*, 3–6; *Magn.*, 6–7; *Trall.*, 3; *Philad.*, 3–4; *Smyrn.*, 8.

[2] St. Irenæus, *Adv. Hær.*, V. xx. 1; III. iii. 1–3; Tertullian, *De Præscr.*, 32, 36.

[3] *The Church*, p. 143, W. H. Frere, in H. B. Swete (Editor), *Essays on the Early Hist. of the Church and the Ministry*, pp. 288–292.

may be the precise nature of a certain peculiar practice in electing and consecrating the Bishop of Alexandria during the first two centuries of that Church's organized existence, it was confessedly a unique custom. That it involved presbyterial consecration is not proved, and whatever was abnormal in it forever passed away in the third century.[1]

The Novatian and Donatist schisms did not involve any change in the previously acknowledged requirements of valid ordination, but raised important questions: (a) Is the validity of ordination, and of the ordinand's subsequent ministrations, affected by unworthiness of the minister who ordains? (b) Does heresy on the part of the minister of Holy Order invalidate that sacrament? (c) Is one who has received schismatic ordination validly ordained? Inasmuch as in this controversy Catholic and schismatic alike maintained the practice of episcopal ordination, the necessity of such ordination, previously acknowledged, was not at all brought into question.

St. Augustine carefully discussed these problems, and his conclusions were generally and permanently accepted. He concluded that since the real minister in a sacrament is Jesus Christ, His earthly agent's unworthiness cannot invalidate a sacrament which is otherwise rightly administered; that heresy and schism for the same reason leave the validity of sacramental ministrations unaffected; but that the personal benefits of such ministrations are hindered

[1] *The Church*, pp. 147-150 and refs. there given.

by the sinful conditions of their reception; and that due reconciliation to the Church is necessary before these benefits can be fully realized, and before the minister ordained in schism can lawfully exercise the ministry thus received.[1]

In subsequent theological development a part of St. Augustine's position was formulated in the doctrine of intention; which is that when a minister, otherwise competent, by seriously administering a sacramental rite of the Church in the appointed manner manifests his intention of doing what the Church does therein, the sacrament thus administered is valid. It is not necessary for validity that the minister's opinion as to what the Church intends to do in the sacrament shall be orthodox.[2]

Inasmuch as the outward matter and form, or essential actions and words, of Holy Order have not been divinely fixed, the Church has authority to modify them, so long as the original meaning and intention of the sacrament is preserved and the grade of Order to which the ordained is advanced is somehow indicated, whether in the form itself or in the rite at large.[3] In ancient ordinals the grade of Order was not designated in the form itself, although implied in the

---

[1] P. Pourrat, *Theol. of the Sacraments*, pp. 130–150, gives the whole controversy, with numerous refs. to St. Augustine's works against the Donatists.

[2] Cf. *The Church*, pp. 319–320; P. Pourrat, *op. cit.*, ch. vii.

[3] *The Church*, pp. 317–318; *Ans. of the Archbishops of England to . . . Leo XIII*, ix.

rite at large; but during the middle ages it came to be thus designated.[1]

In the West, the ordinal gradually became very elaborate, so much so that the question was sometimes debated without conclusive result as to the precise moment in the rite at which the necessary requirements of valid ordination had been fulfilled. Among the added ceremonies was the *porrectio instrumentorum*, or delivery into the candidate's hands of the chief instruments of his office. Pope Eugenius IV, in his *Decree for the Armenians*, declared this ceremony to be a necessary part of the matter, but this opinion is not now generally maintained by Roman writers.[2]

§ 3. The protestant revolution of the sixteenth century led to a complete break with the catholic hierarchy, to the setting up of new ministerial arrangements, and to an elimination of Holy Order from among the sacraments or divinely appointed instruments of supernatural grace. The change was truly revolutionary, and there is no continuity in Order between the ancient ministry of the Catholic Church and modern protestant ministries. These latter are plainly of modern origin, both in their externals and in the protestant theology concerning them.

The two leading ministerial systems thus brought

---

[1] *Idem*, xiii–xv; *The Church*, p. 337.
[2] E. Denny, *Anglican Orders and Jurisdiction*, p. 100; Thos. Richey, *Proper Gift of the Christ. Ministry*, ch. i; *Journ. of Theol. Stud.*, July, 1917, pp. 325–335.

to birth are the presbyterial and the congregational. The historic episcopate is eliminated from both. The originators of the presbyterial system maintained that presbyters are true successors of the Apostles and are possessed of the power of ordaining new presbyters. The historic episcopate they considered to be a human and post-apostolic development which, in its monarchical aspects, is prejudicial to the spiritual welfare of the Church.

The congregational system is an unauthorized development of the apostolic and ancient catholic recognition of the part which the Christian congregation at large ought to have in choosing those who are to be ordained and in accepting their ministrations. It also represents a reaction against the practical suppression of this privilege of the laity during the mediæval period. The congregational theory makes the local congregation immediately concerned to be the source of ministerial authority and the real ordainer, through agents of its own appointment. This is thought to be in accord with the mind of Christ and of His Apostles.[1]

There is indeed a third system, although not sufficiently widespread to rank with the presbyterial and congregational, which supposes a minister's ordination to consist in a direct call from the Holy Spirit, without human intervention, accompanied by charismatic gifts. In brief, the case of St. Paul is considered

[1] Cf. T. A. Lacey, *Unity and Schism*, Lec. v; D. Stone, *Christ. Church*, ch. xv.

normal and determinative of all ministerial ordination. The Church, according to this theory, has no authority to do more than to satisfy itself that the minister's claim thus to have been ordained is valid, and to use his ministry.

In catholic terminology a valid ministry means one that in its origination, whether in general or in individual cases, fulfils the pertinent conditions of the Christian covenant which God has historically appointed. What these conditions are is determined for catholic theologians by the general consent of the Catholic Church from ancient times, and by the harmony of ancient facts, so far as certainly ascertained, with this consent. On these grounds, and with this limitation of meaning, Catholics deny the validity of modern presbyterial, congregational and so-called charismatic ministries.

This conclusion need not, and generally speaking does not, imply that God refuses to employ these ministries and make them spiritually fruitful for those who sincerely use them, and who believe them to be appointed parts of the Christian covenant. But it does involve two practical deductions. The first is that real spiritual loss is involved in forsaking the appointed ministry and sacraments of God's Church, and this in spite of the excuses that certainly may be pleaded for modern departures. The second is that the organic ecclesiastical unity of Christians cannot be truly restored upon any other basis than that of a full restoration of the catholic ministry and sacraments to their former acceptance by all bodies of professing Christians.[1]

§ 4. In spite of powerful protestant sympathies and influences within, the English Church by official pronouncement and effective prescription definitely retained the sacramental conception of Holy Order and the threefold catholic hierarchy. And the Anglican Churches still adhere to the catholic settlement in this regard, whatever may be the occasional utterances and agitations to the contrary of certain active schools within them. This notable fact affords determinative evidence of the fundamental catholicity of the Anglican Communion.[2]

In the Preface to the Ordinal, the catholic intention of continuing and of reverently using and esteeming the ancient and apostolic orders of bishops, priests and deacons, and of recognizing no method of consecration or ordination except the episcopal, was, and continues to be, explicitly and unambiguously set forth. The Ordinal itself is in full accord with this declaration, and the uninterrupted faithfulness with which it has continued to be employed is undeniable.

The ancient laying on of hands by a bishop — by at least three bishops in consecrating bishops — is prescribed; and this has to be performed coincidently with a formula in which the catholic intention declared in the Preface is duly signified. In the Ed-

[1] Cf. *The Church*, pp. 25-26, 313-316; Chas. Gore, *Church and Ministry*, pp. 91-93, 304-307.
[2] *The Church*, pp. 241-242; A. W. Haddan, *Apostolical Succession*, ch. vi.

wardine Ordinal, which continued in use for a century, the intended grade of Order was not explicitly designated in this formula; but it was sufficiently indicated in the rite at large, and such an omission was in accord with ancient catholic precedents. In the revision of 1661, however, the designation referred to was inserted, and has since been retained. The motive for this insertion was not to remedy any intrinsic defect in the Edwardine formula, but to signalize in an explicit manner a rejection of presbyterian proposals to modify the Ordinal in a protestant direction.[1] The distribution of functions to the several Orders of the ministry as thus continued fully corresponds with catholic doctrine and practice. Moreover, the preservation of an unbroken succession of the Anglican episcopate from the Apostles through recognized catholic channels was provided for with painstaking care by the provisions carried out in the consecration of Archbishop Parker; and this line of succession has been reënforced by subsequent events.

It has been urged, however, that at a certain period various persons who had not been episcopally ordained were admitted to English benefices and permitted to act as ministers of the English Church. Such instances did occur, although they were very few indeed;[2] but they were cases of unlawful laxity of discipline which soon ceased and which cannot be made to offset the

[1] *Answer of the Archbishops . . . to Leo XIII*, xiii–xv; F. W. Puller, *The Bull Apost. Curæ and the Edwardine Ordinal*, pp. 5–22.

[2] Examined by A. J. Mason, *The Church of England and Episcopacy*, App. A. Cf. *The Church*, p. 241.

striking significance of the abiding general and prescribed rule that, whereas ministers who have been regularly ordained by Roman and Eastern Orthodox bishops are received into the Anglican ministry without re-ordination, protestant ministers of non-episcopal ordination have to be re-ordained before they can be recognized as ministers of Anglican Churches.

II. *Exposition*

§ 5. Reduced to essential terms, the end for which the rite of Holy Order [1] has been instituted and continued in the Church is a bestowal of the Holy Ghost for the office and work of a sacred minister of Christ in the Church of God, the grade of Order in each case being somehow indicated by the rite employed.

This end was defined by Christ Himself when He ordained the original Apostles, saying, "As My Father hath sent Me, even so send I you. . . . Receive ye the Holy Ghost: whosesoever sins ye forgive, they are forgiven unto them; whosesoever sins ye retain, they are retained." [2] The apostolic Church thus regarded ordination by apostolic laying on of hands; [3] and St. Paul twice declares that God hath set or given the ministers of Christ in His Church.[4] Although the setting apart of Barnabas and Saul at

---

[1] For bibliography, see p. 246, above.
[2] St. John xx. 21–23.
[3] 1 Tim. iv. 14 with 2 Tim. i. 6.
[4] 1 Cor. xii. 28; Ephes. iv. 11. Cf. 1 Cor. iv. 1–4; 2 Cor. v. 18–20; Acts xx. 24, 28.

Antioch for the work to which the Holy Ghost had called them was not their ordination to the ministry,[1] the direction then given by the Spirit demonstrates His part in assigning the ministry to its functions. Their sacerdotal nature is plainly indicated by St. Paul, when he describes himself as a λειτουργόν of Jesus Christ, ministering (ἱερουργοῦντα) the Gospel of God, that the offering (προσφορά) of the Gentiles might be acceptable."[2]

This conception of the origin, purpose and effect of Holy Order has never ceased to be retained in catholic doctrine and theology; and it is clearly borne witness to in the Anglican Ordinal. In the collects appointed to be used in ordaining deacons and priests, God's appointment by His Holy Spirit of the divers Orders of ministers in the Church is acknowledged; and the form of ordination to the priesthood reads, "Receive the Holy Ghost for the Office and Work of a Priest in the Church of God, now committed unto thee by the Imposition of our hands. Whose sins thou dost forgive, they are forgiven; and whose sins thou dost retain, they are retained," etc.

By no more determinate method could the Anglican Churches officially declare Holy Order to be a sacrament in the traditional sense of that term — a divinely appointed visible instrument of supernatural grace. To say in direct terms, "Holy Order is a sacrament," would undoubtedly disturb those who use the word

---

[1] Acts xiii. 2–3 with Gal. i. 1; ii. 9.
[2] Rom. xv. 16. Cf. *The Church*, pp. 131–132.

"sacrament" in the more restrictive sense of a means of grace generally necessary to salvation and having its outward sign fixed by our Lord in the Gospel. But such a pronouncement would add nothing to the Ordinal's unambiguous teaching *ad rem*. The fact that certain types of Anglicans freely hold defective views on this subject is due to the patient Anglican policy of toleration.[1] But in no particular does it reduce the officially expressed teaching of the Anglican Churches above indicated.

§ 6. It is an inevitable belief of those who acknowledge the bestowal of the Holy Spirit in ordination to the sacred ministry that such gift carries with it not only power and authority to be ministers of Christ and stewards of the mysteries of God, but also an endowment of grace for holy conduct in the ministry and for edifying exercise of its functions. Accordingly, catholic theology distinguishes between these two effects of Holy Order, describing the former as its *gratia gratis data* and the latter as its *gratia gratum faciens*.

The *gratia gratis data* of this sacrament is the grace which is thereby given for the ministry of grace, enabling Christ's ministers rightly to act in His name, and by His authority and power to administer valid sacraments of grace to the faithful.[2] That such grace is needed is very clear. No man may take upon

---

[1] Cf. *The Church*, pp. 233-235; *Introduction*, pp. 192-194, 198-199.
[2] On *gratia gratis data*, see Wm. Denton, chh. v-vi; C. S. Grueber, pp. 117-119; A. R. Whitham, pp. 81-83.

himself the office of priesthood except he "be called of God, even as was Aaron";[1] and no creature has in him the natural gifts which are required for the functions of this office. Moreover, the genuineness of ministerial authority and power is not sufficiently demonstrated by visible ministerial success as ordinarily understood, for the law that "by their fruits ye shall know them"[2] is more readily used to test personal sincerity, and the blessing which in any case God bestows upon it, than to authenticate the covenant validity of ministerial claims. Therefore an authentic and sacramental method of conveying to the ministers of Christ their ambassadorial authority and ministerial powers is needed and instituted for the protection of the Church from damage and the faithful from lack of covenant assurance of grace.

The grace of Holy Order which we are now considering, like that of Baptismal regeneration and that of the gift of the Holy Spirit in Confirmation, has a permanent and irreversible effect upon its recipient, stamping the soul with a spiritual quality and mark which forever differentiates him from those who have not received this sacrament. This distinctive quality is called character,[3] and because of its indelibility the sacrament should not in any particular grade of

---

[1] Heb. v. 4.   [2] St. Matt. vii. 15–20.
[3] On character and the indelibility of Order, see *The Church*, pp. 301–302 and refs. there given; C. S. Grueber, pp. 125–128; St. Thomas, III. Suppl. xxxv. 2; A. R. Whitham, pp. 84–86.

Order be repeated. Holy Orders are indelible; and deposition, while it makes the exercise of ministerial functions unlawful, does not in this regard nullify the effect of ordination or justify reordination in case of restoration to ministerial rank in the Church militant.

The character of Holy Order is considered to include that of Confirmation;[1] and that of a higher Order plainly includes that of a lower one. For this reason the lack either of previous Confirmation, or of lower grades of Holy Order, called *interstitia*, does not invalidate this sacrament, although such ordinations, *per saltum*, are irregular and unlawful; and the lower sacrament should not be subsequently administered to one who is thus ordained.[2] The case with Baptism is quite different, because no one previously unbaptized is capable of receiving any other sacrament, not having been made a member of Christ's Body.[3] It is necessary, accordingly, when a lack of Baptism is discovered in one who has been supposedly ordained, that he be baptized and then validly ordained.

§ 7. The *gratia gratum faciens* of Holy Order, as has been stated, has for its end that the minister of Christ may be able to maintain the personal holiness and conduct that befits his sacred office and to exercise his ministerial functions in an edifying man-

[1] St. Thomas, III. Suppl. xxxv. 4.
[2] C. S. Grueber, pp. 18–20; St. Thomas, III. Suppl. xxxv. 5.
[3] St. Thomas, III. Suppl. xxxv. 3. Cf. pp. 23–24, above.

ner.[1] Although official in connection, and in the distinctive conditions of the life which it is designed to sanctify, this grace is for immediately personal benefits, which are contingent in actualization upon contrite faith and sincere volitional response on the part of its recipient.

If the condition is unfulfilled, the minister himself will derive injury rather than benefit from his peculiarly close relation to the source of grace. But the principle of reviviscence[2] applies to the grace of Holy Order because of its irreversible effects, and when an unworthy minister repents and brings forth the fruits of repentance, he thereby comes to enjoy the benefits of the *gratia gratum faciens* of which we speak. In the meantime, just because he is Christ's minister, his sacramental ministrations are truly valid and beneficial to those who worthily receive them, in spite of his own unworthiness; and this is so because the source of sacramental grace is not the earthly minister, but Christ Himself.[3]

The need of special grace to enable a minister of Christ to exercise his office worthily and edifyingly is very great. Although ministerial unworthiness does not reduce the appointed effects of his sacramental ministrations *in se*, it does materially reduce, sometimes wholly destroys, his efficiency as pastor of souls

---

[1] On *gratia gratum faciens*, see Wm. Denton, chh. viii–xi; A. R. Whitham, pp. 83–84; St. Thomas, III. Suppl. xxxv. 1.

[2] P. Pourret, *op. cit.*, pp. 144–148, 201–203; *Cath. Encyc.*, s.v. "Sacraments," p. 304 (c); St. Augustine, *De Bapt. c. Donat.*, i. 2, 18.

[3] Cf. pp. 250–251, above.

and spiritual leader. That is, what is called external grace,[1] or the edifying influence of the personal quality of his life and manner of ministration, is either weakened or nullified. Furthermore, the peculiar conditions of ministerial life are inevitably attended by peculiar dangers; and without special help from God, Christ's ambassador may lose his own soul in the very work of saving others.[2]

§ 8. The ministry of the Church is called apostolic because its original members, through whom its authority and power have come from Christ by His Holy Spirit, were designated as Apostles. They were thus named because of their being sent by Christ; and the authority thus derived from Christ and transmitted to all subsequent recipients of Holy Order is called mission.[3] This mission in so far as possessed by the Church's ministry at large is plenary and catholic. It is plenary in that it includes all the spiritual authority and power required for officially administering the prophetic, priestly and kingly functions of Christ's Church on earth. It is catholic because Christ sent His ministers into all the world, to all mankind and to those of every generation of men until the end of the world. It is also inalienable and cannot at any time be rejected by an individual or class of men without rejection of Christ's appointments. "He that receiveth whomsoever I send, re-

---

[1] Cf. *Creation and Man*, p. 341.   [2] Cf. 1 Cor. ix. 27.
[3] On mission, see *The Church*, pp. 213-215; Blunt, *Dic. of Theol.*, *q.v.*

ceiveth Me; and he that receiveth Me, receiveth Him that sent Me."[1]

The authority to oversee and "to rule the Church of God, which He purchased with His own blood,"[2] thus received, is called jurisdiction;[3] and its immediate sources for each generation, and for such measures of it as are received by members of lower Orders of the ministry are the bishops. This is so because the apostolic succession is derived through bishops, and because they alone possess the fulness of apostolic mission and jurisdiction. For corporate purposes, in which the Church at large is involved, they possess it corporately and as colleagues in catholic authority; but within his appointed sphere and to those who are assigned to his chief pastorate, each bishop represents the entire episcopate;[4] and, subject to the canonical limitations accepted by the episcopate, whether of the whole Church or of his recognized autonomous province thereof, his jurisdiction is plenary. All inferior ministers within his jurisdiction derive their respective measures of mission and jurisdiction from him. These propositions are not reduced in principle, although they are determined in

---

[1] St. John xiii. 20.

[2] Acts xx. 28. Cf. St. Matt. xvi. 19; xviii. 18; St. Luke xxii. 29–30; 2 Cor. x. 8; 1 Tim. v. 17; Tit. ii. 15; Heb. xiii. 7, 17.

[3] On jurisdiction, see Wm. Denton, ch. vi; C. S. Grueber, pp. 151–164; Blunt, *Dic. of Theol.*, q.v.

[4] The classic patristic passage *ad rem* is St. Cyprian, *De Unitate Eccles.*, 5. "Episcopatus unus est, cujus a singulis in solidum pars tenetur." Cf. Chas. Gore, *Church and the Ministry*, pp. 152–156.

methods of practical application, by the Canon Law, whereby the government and discipline of the Church are rightly so regulated as to enlist the participation of inferior ministers, and of the laity as well, in the Church's legislation and practical administration.

§ 9. Ministerial jurisdiction is properly distinguished as habitual and actual. Every minister, in his Order and degree, derives habitual jurisdiction through the sacrament of Holy Order. That is, by virtue of His Order, he is sacramentally competent to exercise the authority and powers which appertain to his Order; and this competence is permanent, because of the indelible character which he has once for all received.

But actual jurisdiction, or lawful exercise of ministerial authority and power, is limited and determined by canonical assignment of the sphere within which he is appointed and permitted by ecclesiastical authority to minister. This regulation and restriction of actual jurisdiction grows out of the patent fact, confirmed by experience, that in no other manner can the unity and edifying value of ministerial work be preserved. The present disunion of Catholic Churches, however, unhappily makes a rigid insistence upon the rules of territorial jurisdiction practically absurd. And, until visible unity is restored, the theoretical aspects of jurisdiction must often practically give way to the necessity that no classes of catholic Christians shall be deprived of the sacramental ministrations which they believe to be valid. This necessity has especially to be reckoned with in America.

The jurisdiction which a minister derives from the Church is wholly spiritual. It is so because the Church has received from Christ no authority to enforce subjection to its rule except by persuasive appeal to consciences and by such measures of extending or withholding its privileges as lie within the competence of any society to regulate its internal concerns and to preserve its characteristic constitution and functions. None the less ministerial jurisdiction, when exercised in harmony with apostolic mission, and according to the Canon Law of the Catholic Church, has divine institution and sanction, and therefore cannot be rejected without material violation of the divine will.

The case is quite different with coercive jurisdiction, or authority to enlist civil machinery, and to enforce ecclesiastical judgments by external and physical measures and penalties. In their purely ecclesiastical status sacred ministers have no coercive jurisdiction whatever; and where they are possessed of it the source from which it is derived is wholly human and political. Its possession is an accident of those extraneous relations which are expressed in the phrase "establishment of the Church by the state." That state establishment, and the consequent possession of coercive jurisdiction by ecclesiastics, have wrought much harm, and have in many lands reduced the Church's spiritual prestige and success in winning souls, has been sufficiently indicated in the last previous volume.[1]

§ 10. The different measures and lines of spiritual jurisdiction and functioning which under any conditions can be exercised by the several Orders of the sacred ministry are fundamentally determined by the sacrament of Holy Order, and even the Catholic Church in its totality cannot substantially alter this sacrament and its several degrees. The differentiation of the catholic ministry into its three degrees comes from the Apostles, acting under the Holy Spirit's guidance and sanction. And, because the Catholic Church did not make itself, but is the Body of Christ, created and organically differentiated by its divine Creator, this Church cannot change its organic constitution and ministry, but can merely regulate and adapt actual ministerial jurisdiction, on the divinely appointed lines of habitual jurisdiction, to the conditions and needs of different peoples and of successive generations.[2] The range of such adaptation is potentially and significantly great, but it cannot alter the sacramentally derived functions of those who from ancient days have been designated bishops, priests and deacons.

As has been sufficiently shown elsewhere, the appointed functions of the ministry in general are prophetic, priestly and kingly.[3] That is, Christ's min-

---

[1] *The Church*, pp. 107–115, where other refs. are given.
[2] *Idem*, pp. 96–98.   [3] *Idem*, pp. 156–167.

isters are set to propagate the faith which He and His Apostles taught for the guidance of souls in the way of eternal life; to lead the faithful in corporate and sacrificial approach to God and administer the divinely appointed means of grace; and to exercise pastoral rule in holy precept and discipline. Each minister, however, exercises these offices according to his Order and degree.[1]

The bishop alone can exercise them in their apostolic fulness; and his distinctive functions include the perpetuation of the ministry itself by means of the sacrament of Holy Order; the general oversight of such part of the Church as is lawfully included in his actual jurisdiction; and full participation in the larger government and dogmatic office of the Church which pertains respectively to provincial and ecumenical gatherings of the episcopate. By virtue of his being the chief shepherd of souls within his actual jurisdiction, Confirmation is also normally reserved to him in the West, but can be, and in the East has been, delegated to priests. In practical polity his legislative authority is rightly subject, by consent of the episcopate at large, to constitutional adjustments calculated to enlist canonical coöperation by all the Church, clerical and lay. To these specifications should be added the

---

[1] On the functions of bishops, priests and deacons, severally considered, see J. Bingham, *Christian Antiquities*, Bk. II; Chas. Gore, *Church and the Ministry*, pp. 237–241; John Wordsworth, *Ministry of Grace*, ch. ii. The exhortations in the Anglican Ordinal afford classic summaries.

fact that, sacramentally speaking, every function of priest and deacon lies within his power and right to perform.

To the second Order, that of priests, pertains all the normal sacramental functions of the ministry, except those above described as either necessarily distinctive of the episcopal Order, or canonically reserved to it. In no case can a mere priest validly ordain other ministers; and he may not lawfully administer Confirmation, unless this function is delegated to him by competent provincial authority. But all other sacramental ministrations pertain to him, and within his canonically assigned actual jurisdiction he both can and ought to administer them. Subject to the Canon Law, his function includes a full pastorate of souls, as prophetic teacher, sacramental priest and spiritual overseer of his congregation. Moreover, under the Canon Law, he is entitled synodically to participate in the legislative government of the Church at large.

Deacons, as their name indicates, are ordained for assistant service only. Their sacramental power is limited to baptizing, although they can, when legally qualified, marry people, and can assist in administering the Eucharistic sacrament after a priest has consecrated it. They require a specific license from the bishop in order lawfully to preach;[1] and although

[1] That is, officially and in the Church's pulpits. All Christians have the right and, under proper circumstances, the duty to propagate Christian truth and practice.

they are authorized to perform such normal public services in the Church as involve no sacramental functioning, and to assist the priest in pastoral work, and in practice often act as missionaries, they are not entitled to receive an independent cure of souls, but must always retain the status of assistants to ministers of a higher sacramental Order. In a vast majority of cases, the ministry of deacons is in practice temporary only, and preparatory for ordination to the priesthood.

CHAPTER IX

HOLY MATRIMONY

I. *Introductory*

§ 1. Marriage is a lawful and enduring union and cohabitation between competent persons of opposite sexes for the purpose of procreation, upbringing of children, and domestic life. The sacrament of Holy Matrimony is such Marriage between baptized persons, sanctified to a supernatural end, and involving certain Christian requirements and obligations.[1]

By a lawful union is meant one that is allowable in the particular social state or states by the requirements of which the parties thereto are bound. In comprehensive terms, there are three such states, the natural, the civil and the religious or ecclesiastical. In so far as marriage is a natural union, and it always is this at least, it is subject to the physical and moral laws of nature, so far as understood. In organized society, or where civil law prevails, natural obliga-

---

[1] On Holy Matrimony, see O. D. Watkins, *Holy Matrimony;* J. J. Elmendorf, *Elements of Moral Theol.*, pp. 620–643; H. M. Luckock, *Hist. of Marriage Jewish and Christian;* T. A. Lacey, *Marriage in Church and State;* John Fulton, *The Laws of Marriage;* W. J. Knox-Little, *Holy Matrimony;* St. Thomas, III. Suppl. xli–lxviii; Hastings, *Dic. of Bible* and *Cath. Encyc.*, *s.vv.* "Marriage"; Geo. E. Howard, *Hist. of Matrimonial Institutions;* Hyacinthe Ringrose, *Marriage and Divorce Laws of the World.*

tions and conditions are supplemented by those imposed by such law. Finally in organized religious society, natural and civil obligations and conditions are supplemented and given higher reference by religious requirements, whether of revealed divine precept or of rightly imposed ecclesiastical Canon Law.[1]

In the forum of enlightened conscience, the immediate authority of which over personal conduct is paramount, any real or apparent conflict between these several lines of requirement has to be met in practice by preferring divine laws to the human, and religious and moral requirements when they are contradicted by civil laws and social customs. For example, a priest may not solemnize a marriage which the state requires him to perform, if it is forbidden either by the law of God, by that of His Church, or by natural morality. He is bound, in such case, to submit personally to the civil consequences of his refusal, when these are legally enforced; but this does not alter his duty in the particular considered.[2] Happily such conflicts are comparatively rare. Normally one can conform to the requirements and prohibitions of each of the three states mentioned, without thereby either doing what is otherwise unlawful or failing to do what is otherwise legitimately prescribed.

[1] On these three states, see Report of Joint Committee in *Gen. Conv. Journal of P. E. Church*, of 1886, pp. 784–785; T. A. Lacey, chh. i–iii; Wilhelm and Scannell, *Manual of Cath. Theol.*, vol. II. pp. 510–511.

[2] This is called passive obedience, exemplified in ancient Christian martyrdoms.

The principle here maintained — one upon which the truth and practical bearing of the catholic doctrine of Holy Matrimony depends — is this: When we learn that God has consecrated an existing institution to a special and supernatural end, and has either directly or indirectly imposed precepts in relation thereto, we are thereby committed to the obligation of accepting the theoretical and practical implications of such consecration, so far as discerned, along with the precepts thus imposed. The sacrament of Holy Matrimony represents such consecration, and is protected for its supernatural end by such precepts. And its distinctive end, implications and obligations have the highest of validities — that of divine authority — overruling lower laws that conflict.

§ 2. In sacred history Marriage has undergone three stages of development.[1] In the beginning God "made them male and female, and said, 'For this cause shall a man leave his father and mother, and shall cleave to his wife; and the twain shall become one flesh.' . . . What therefore," Christ says, "God hath joined together, let not man put asunder."[2] According to the primal law, therefore, one imposed upon mankind, Marriage was to be an abiding and indissoluble union; and the plain implication was that absolute divorce, followed by a substitutionary mar-

---

[1] See O. D. Watkins, ch. ii.
[2] St. Matt. xix. 4-6; St. Mark x. 6-9; Gen. ii. 18, 21-24. Cf. O. D. Watkins, ch. iii.

riage with another, was for every human estate contrary to the divine plan and will.[1]

The second or Mosaic stage is described by Christ in these words: "Moses for your hardness of heart suffered you to put away your wives."[2] The implication here is also clear. It is twofold: that human hardness of heart, rather than God's plan, was responsible for the change; and that the Mosaic license was a passing concession in view of men's fallen condition.

The third and permanent stage was initiated by Christ's own legislation — legislation which is morally binding upon all who have come to know His authority and will in the matter. His enactment is explicitly based upon the original law of God, and repeals the license of Moses. It is most clearly set forth in the second Gospel. "Whosoever shall put away his wife, and marry another, committeth adultery against her; and if she herself shall put away her husband, and marry another, she committeth adultery."[3]

---

[1] T. A. Lacey, pp. 16–19, 34.   [2] St. Matt. xix. 8.
[3] St. Mark x. 2–12. In the more difficult passage of St. Matt. xix. 3–10, the clause "Whosoever shall put away his wife except for fornication, and shall marry another, committeth adultery," has been taken to imply that the sin mentioned justifies absolute divorce and re-marriage. But the clause agrees neither with premise, "What God hath joined together, let not man put asunder," nor with the more coherent report in St. Mark. Of two scriptural passages on the same subject, one clear and consistent and the other difficult, the former is surely to be followed. The exception in St. Matt. has been regarded critically in three ways: (a) As referring to pre-marital unchastity, making the union null and void *ab initio*

A chief purpose of the primal law, thus reënacted, was clear to one Old Testament prophet at least — that the Lord "might seek a seed of God." [1] The true seed of God, of course, is Christ and those who have become children of God in His Body by adoption and grace. The primary divine purpose for which Matrimony is made holy, therefore, is that subjects of this adoption and grace may be brought forth and trained for their appointed sonship in Christ. Accordingly, a close relation is made to exist in the Christian covenant between the marriage union and the union betwixt Christ and His Church, wherein the children of God are gathered. St. Paul sets forth this interconnection.[2] The fact that the parties in Christian Marriage are members by Baptism of Christ's Body leads him to perceive a connection of their union with the great mystery of the union between Christ and His Church; and the right use of Holy Matrimony ministers to the enjoyment of this mystery and to the extension of such enjoyment to successive generations.

(Von Döllinger, *First Age of the Church*, App.); (*b*) As textually corrupt, not being fully quoted by any ante-Nicene writer and not used anciently as basis of license to re-marry after divorce for adultery (Watkins, pp. 152–167); (*c*) As probably due to misunderstanding by the Gospel writer of Christ's teaching (S. L. Tyson, *The Teaching of our Lord as to the Indissolubility of Marriage*). In any case, the apparent exception ought to be rejected in view of New Testament teaching at large. See also T. A. Lacey, pp. 23–25; H. J. Wilkins, ch. ii; A. Plummer, *On the Gospel . . . St. Matthew*, pp. 81–82, 259–260; D. Stone, *Divorce and Re-marriage*, note XI.

[1] Mal. ii. 14–16. [2] Ephes. v. 22–33.

It is only in this revealed connection that the Church's teaching concerning Holy Matrimony, and its vital place in the Christian system, can be rightly understood and adequately estimated. A common and spiritually disastrous error has been to disregard this connection and to treat Marriage, even when consummated between baptized Christians, as wholly determined in significance and effect by its natural and civil status and requirements. Even theological writers often fail to discern the full meaning of God's consecration of this estate to a supernatural end, and consequently overlook the vital dependence of the Church's success in its God-given mission upon due preservation of the distinctively religious nature and purpose of Christian Marriage.

§ 3. The secret of many disastrous vagaries and abuses in connection with mixed marriages, prohibited degrees and divorce lies in this isolation of the subject of holy Matrimony from its interpretative context. The history of the Church displays much inconsistency in canonical legislation and practice *ad rem*, although the New Testament doctrine on the subject has gained abundant acknowledgement in every part of the Church and in every age. We cannot tell the long and complicated story of Holy Matrimony in the Church. But it is easy to see that, human nature continuing to be what it is, and the social embarrassments of consistently enforced Christian discipline in this matter being so grave as they are, more irregularities and weaknesses are to be expected in handling matrimonial questions than in almost any other branch of ecclesiastical regulation.[1]

The overshadowing influence of a half-converted imperial court weakened the Marriage discipline of the Eastern Churches at an early date, and their general record in this matter is not edifying. Theoretically at least the Roman Church has consistently adhered to Christ's teaching. But in practice the technicalities of dispensations, nullities and the like have frequently been used to justify exceptions.[2] The Church of England is clearly sound in its doctrine and Canon Law, but notable deviations from consistency in practice, brought about by special bills in Parliament, have been acquiesced in; and to-day that Church, because of its connection with the state, has very grave difficulty in maintaining the integrity of its matrimonial discipline in the face of recent divorce legislation. The American Church, like the English, inherited the Western Canon Law,[3] which forbids the remarriage of a divorcee while the other party lives. But in 1868 the General Convention

[1] On the history of marriage and divorce in the Church, see H. J. Wilkins; H. M. Luckock, Pt. I; T. A. Lacey, ch. iv; O. D. Watkins, ch. vii.

[2] For the existing Roman Canon Law, see *Codex juris canonici*, Lib. III. Tit. vii; and H. A. Ayrinhac, *Marriage Legislation in the New Code of Canon Law*.

[3] Anglican Canon Law includes so much of the Western (Roman) Canon Law as had been received in England up to the commencement of the reformation, and was "not contrariant or repugnant to the laws, statutes and customs of this realm," etc. (Statute of Henry VIII. 25, c. 19). See *Ch. Q. Review*, Jan. 1898, art. X.

enacted a canon in which it was provided that such prohibition "shall not be held to apply to the innocent party in a divorce for the cause of adultery."[1] Several efforts have been made to remove this proviso, but no more has been accomplished than to qualify it with conditions designed to prevent haste and collusion.[2] We should remember that the American Church is overshadowed by denominational bodies that have very lax ideas of divorce. It is also greatly embarrassed by evil divorce legislation in most of the states, and by having to deal with many cases of divorcees remarried previously to their entrance into the Church and with numerous mixed marriages of its members. Inevitably the lax ideas of American society at large infect the minds of many Churchmen.

Throughout the Anglican Communion it has fortunately been possible for those who have sought to maintain the teaching of Christ and of St. Paul to fall back on the plain language of the Marriage service. And it is here that Anglican doctrine concerning Matrimony is officially indicated. In the opening address the congregation is taught to consider Holy Matrimony as "instituted of God in the time of man's innocency," and as "signifying unto us the mystical union that is betwixt Christ and His Church." In the pledges demanded of the parties to be married it is required of each that he or she will keep only to

[1] *Digest of the Canons of the Protestant Epis. Church of 1868*, Tit. II. Can. 13.
[2] Canons of 1919, 42, § III.

the other "so long as ye both shall live." The same life-long obligation is again accepted in the giving of troth, "for better for worse, for richer for poorer, in sickness and in health . . . till death us do part." The man has to declare that he weds the woman in the name of the Trinity, thus making God a party to the achievement of the union. The minister embodies these sacred obligations in a prayer to God for their faithful fulfilment, and proceeds to apply the law of Christ to the union which he is solemnizing by saying, "Those whom God hath joined together let no man put asunder." No trace can be found in the service and terms of union of the notion that Marriage is merely a contract, which can be lawfully abrogated by mutual consent or by legal process. On the contrary, there is explicit witness and agreement that the union is of divine making and significance, and is indissoluble by man.[1]

§ 4. Holy Matrimony has always been regarded by the Church as eliciting a special divine blessing and grace. Accordingly, when it was coördinated with other visible means of grace under the sacramental category, no innovating doctrine concerning it was introduced, but merely a development of scientific theological terminology. It is a sacrament according to this terminology because it is a visible means by which divine and sanctifying grace is elicited. It is not, of course, a sacrament in the narrower application of that designation to those particular means

[1] On divorce, see § 13, below.

of grace which are generally necessary for salvation, and the signs of which have been determined by our Lord in the Gospels. But it is a sacrament in the sense above indicated, in the sense in which it has thus been described for centuries in both the Eastern and the Western Churches.[1]

On the one hand, Holy Matrimony has a determinate outward sign, the completion of which is properly verifiable. This sign consists of lawful Marriage between baptized Christians, and the variety of laws which control the accepted methods of Marriage in different lands, and under different legal and social conditions, in no wise reduces the determinateness of this formal part of the outward sign. Everywhere the event of lawful Marriage is susceptible of recognition and verification, and in its lawful accomplishment lies the formal element of the outward sign. But its sacramental value and effect depends upon the Baptism of both parties, because no unbaptized person can be a subject of sacramental grace other than that of Baptism itself. Accordingly, when Marriage is achieved between persons one or both of whom are unbaptized, their union does not constitute the sacrament of Holy Matrimony until both have been baptized. In such cases, subsequent Baptism completes the outward sign —not less really because an interval of time separates the accomplishment of its two elements, those of Marriage and of baptismal status.[2]

---

[1] Cf. *The Church*, pp. 296–298.   [2] *Idem*, p. 339.

On the other hand, Holy Matrimony confers or elicits sanctifying grace. This is an inevitable inference from the fact that, as both Scripture and catholic doctrine assert, God Himself unites the parties in a significant relation, and with a supernatural end. The action of thus consecrating the Marriage union, apart from any added grace which He may be thought to impart to its human subjects, is itself sanctifying. But if He thus consecrates the union to a supernatural end, we are driven to believe that He also affords in it whatever aid of supernatural grace its participants may need in order to fulfil that end. Revealed doctrine does not, however, enable us to define this grace more narrowly.[1]

II. *Essentials and Obligations*

§ 5. We have summarized the essentials of the outward sign of Holy Matrimony as consisting of lawful Marriage and the Baptism of its parties. Whatever may be the temporal order of their fulfilment, both of these conditions are necessary to constitute a sacramental union; but when both have been fulfilled, the sacrament has been validly accomplished.

A lawful Marriage here means one which when once achieved is recognized by the laws under which it

---

[1] If Matrimony effected no more than a distinctive application of baptismal grace to a specific end, it would be sanctifying — sacramental. On the grace of Matrimony, see T. A. Lacey, pp. 50–54; O. D. Watkins, pp. 74–76, 137–150; W. J. Knox-Little, pp. 61–68; Jos. Pohle, *The Sacraments*, vol. IV. pp. 168–171.

falls as valid. A Marriage may have been contrary to laws designed to regulate its performance, but if these irregularities or illegalities do not under the law nullify the consummated Marriage, it is a lawful Marriage in the sense here meant. But the law which has to be considered includes divine as well as human law,[1] and ecclesiastical as well as civil law — all relevant laws to which the parties married are properly subject. In practice this means that, in order to be lawful in the sense required for a sacramental union, a Marriage must be such as will be recognized as valid by both the state and the Church — that is, the particular civil and ecclesiastical authorities to the jurisdiction of which the parties concerned are responsible according to the will and providence of God. It is true that actual submission to the spiritual jurisdiction of the Church is properly voluntary, and ought not to be coerced; and an exclusively secular Marriage is not adulterous by virtue of its being secular. The point is that its being *sacramental* depends upon its being at least valid according to ecclesiastical as well as civil law. In civilized nations the conditions of validity which satisfy civil law will usually satisfy ecclesiastical law, although there are unhappy exceptions, for example, in connection with forbidden degrees and divorces.[2]

[1] "For be ye well assured, that if any persons are joined together otherwise than as God's Word doth allow, their marriage is not lawful": Marriage Service.

[2] T. A. Lacey, chh. iii–v, *passim*.

The validity of Marriage in one nation is not dependent upon the laws of another nation, and that of Marriages in one autonomous part of the Catholic Church is not dependent upon the Canon Law of another part thereof. Anglican Marriages, for example, do not have to conform to distinctively Roman Catholic requirements in order to be ecclesiastically valid and sacramental. To think otherwise is to import an unreasonable confusion into the whole subject. If the catholic claim of the Anglican Communion is valid in general, it is valid in the particular of regulating and recognizing sacramental Marriage, subject to ecumenical doctrine and precept.

As might be expected, in view of all that has been said, the conditions necessary to be fulfilled in order that a Marriage may be lawful in the sense required for its sacramental status vary in different lands and in different parts of the Catholic Church. The ideally desirable unification of marital requirements everywhere is not within the range of practical possibilities. But those who marry do not in practice have to reckon with foreign laws, and the consummation of lawful Marriage is not ordinarily difficult, either *in se* or in subsequent determination of its validity. That is, the sacrament of Holy Matrimony has a readily verifiable outward sign.

All requirements of lawfulness and validity fall under the following heads: (*a*) The parties thereto must be legally competent, there being no nullifying impediments; (*b*) The method of achievement of the union must be valid. In particular, voluntary consent must be signified in a lawfully recognized manner; and, wherever the laws thus condition validity, the Marriage must be officially performed or solemnized, and in the manner required by them.

Holy Matrimony is more than a legal contract, but its contract aspect is essential, and the lawfully signified consent of the parties to be married is determinative both positively and negatively. The parties married are the earthly ministers, and the function of one who, in common parlance, "performs the ceremony" is that of giving legal sanction to the consenting action of these parties and, in the case of a priest, of solemnizing their union before God. We say that the parties married are the *earthly* ministers, but a sacramental union has for its chief minister God Himself, who alone can make them man and wife in the sacramental sense.

§ 6. A Marriage is a contract, but it is far more; for it initiates an estate the fundamental conditions and obligations of which antedate the contract and can be neither annulled nor modified by the will of the contracting parties. Moreover, the contract is not a private one, and the laws against clandestine marriages register the protest of society against its being thus treated. God is concerned, since even in the order of nature Marriage plays a vital part in the fulfilment of His plan. Society at large is concerned, because its moral welfare cannot be safeguarded unless it can protect Marriage from ill-advised exploiting and abuse. Society is built upon, and determined in moral complexion by, the family, which is its unit. In particular, the kindred and neighbours of the parties married are concerned, for the results of Marriage affect them in ways that are too serious to be unnecessarily disregarded.[1]

Accordingly society in civilized lands concedes to parents the authority to withhold consent to the Marriages of their offspring during minority, and the moral right of parents to be consulted at least continues even longer. They are the immediate agents of human society in safeguarding its interests in the Marriages of their children. Their authority expires in due course, and their subsequent moral right to be consulted does not nullify the right which children acquire at majority to marry according to their own choice; but, subject to these limitations, the authority and influence referred to cannot be put aside consistently with either the welfare of society or the will of God.[2]

If parents are thus set to prevent their children from marrying hastily and ill-advisedly, they are also responsible positively for preparing their children by wise education and adequate instruction for their prospective task of choosing their life-partners and of entering the Marriage estate intelligently and right-

[1] On all which, see W. J. Knox-Little, pp. 3-11 and chh. xv, xx-xxi.

[2] On parental authority *ad rem*, see G. E. Howard, vol. I. *passim;* J. J. Elmendorf, p. 629; Thos. Slater, *Moral Theol.*, vol. II. pp. 257-259.

eously. Ill advised prudery and timid reserve on the part of parents must result in grave evils. The children will gain sexual instruction at an early age in any event; and whether it shall be trustworthy and wholesome instruction or vicious and morally misleading depends almost invariably upon whether the parents exercise wise and courageous forethought or are supinely negligent. Finally, parents have it in their power to determine to an important extent the quality of the intimacies which their children acquire, and thus indirectly to promote a suitable and worthy choice by them of their life-partners. It is chiefly along such lines that their authority can be exercised effectively; for when that type of mutual affection which normally leads on to Marriage has once been developed, the power of parents to change the ultimate result is seriously diminished, and even during minority can be successfully exercised only at the cost of grave distress — perhaps sinfully rebellious discontent. Marriages of convenience, and such as are brought about by arbitrary parental management, regardless of the wills and affections of the parties directly concerned, are of course unjustifiable, and rarely result in due fulfilment of God's purpose in Holy Matrimony.

§ 7. The obligations incurred in the sacrament of Holy Matrimony[1] include those which pertain to

[1] On marital obligations at large, see W. J. Knox-Little, chh. xii–xiv; W. W. Webb, *Cure of Souls*, pp. 165–169. Cf. 1 Cor. vii. 3–5; Ephes. v. 22–23; vi. 1–4.

ESSENTIALS AND OBLIGATIONS 287

Marriage in the natural and civil order; but these are to a degree transfigured in reference and quality, and are significantly enlarged, by the sacrament. Although the classification is a cross-division — its branches partly overlapping — all these obligations may be brought conveniently under three heads: mutual, parental and religious, the last named colouring and enlarging the other two with determinative effect.

(a) In the natural order the first mutual obligation of the Marriage estate is the procreation of offspring, for this is the primary natural end of the conjugal union. The complex demands and pleasures of modern life have tempted many to evade this obligation; and various grave sins prevail, of which abortion or procuring premature gestation is the climax.[1] No doubt temperate marital intercourse is permissible for cherishing and expressing mutual affection, as well as for procreation. But every imaginable artifice for indulging in such intercourse without permitting nature to take its normal resulting course is sinful. Sufficient reasons may exist in particular cases for not producing offspring; but the only virtuous course in such event is self-restraint and such regulation of the frequency of indulgence — entire abstinence, if necessary — as will meet the difficulty without interference with nature's processes. Marriage does not legalize lust, but has a contrary end.

[1] Hastings, *Encyc. of Relig.*, s.v. "Fœticide"; *Cath. Encyc.*, s.v. "Abortion."

It leaves the laws of temperance, mutual allowance and self-control in unabated force. And no other use of sexual organs is lawful except that which is practiced in a chastely regulated Marriage union. All this is of the utmost gravity for the physical, moral and spiritual welfare of mankind.

(b) Mutual fidelity is also of the gravest necessity; and monogamy, or permanent and exclusive union of one man and one woman so long as both are alive, is a fundamental Marriage law of God.[1] Every species of carnal indulgence between the wife and any other man than her husband, or between the husband and any other woman than his wife, is mortally sinful — not less so for one partner than for the other.

(c) A third mutual obligation is the cultivation of mutual regard and affection. Mutual affection should indeed be the antecedent of Marriage, for without it the obligations of married life cannot properly be fulfilled. In particular, a loveless Marriage cannot exhibit the type which God wills it to exhibit of the union between Christ and His Church, and the Marriage union is an appointed school for the practice of Christian charity. This obligation involves for its due fulfilment that the man and his wife should spend their earthly days together. Mutual absences should, if possible, be exceptional, and should not be unduly prolonged.[2]

---

[1] Cf. T. A. Lacey, pp. 12–16; O. D. Watkins, ch. ix.
[2] Sailors at sea and travelling agents cannot, of course, spend their days at home.

(*d*) The common enjoyment of earthly goods and advantages is also obligatory. The legal title and control of property may indeed be rightly vested in one or other of the parties. But the enjoyment of all wealth possessed by either should be mutual and equal.[1] The happiness of each should be promoted by the other, and the twin virtues of unselfishness and helpfulness should be practiced by each towards the other — "for better for worse, for richer for poorer, in sickness and in health."

(*e*) In value before God, and in level of being and destiny, husband and wife are equals. Moreover, the ineffaceable difference of functions which nature and grace alike assign severally to them is not intrinsically speaking an inequality. The glory of a wife and mother is one thing and that of a husband and father another; but both are equally precious and honourable in the scale of essential values, and each is dependent upon glad adjustment to the other for its own perfection. The two are complementary, and their diversity is part of their several values, of the common welfare of the husband and wife, and of their naturally assigned functioning in the procreation and successful upbringing of children. When these fundamental truths are practically kept in view, the law of God and of man, which undeniably makes the husband to be the working head of the family, is not felt

---

[1] Such is the real intent of the man's marital pledge, "with all my worldly goods I thee endow." No legal transfer of title is involved.

by the wife as involving for her a servile status, nor by the husband as exalting him above his wife. Rather it is perceived to be a necessary safeguard against dualism in the family and the method of unity between equals which the complementary gifts of the sexes require. The obligation to preserve the husband's executive status in the Marriage union is clearly taught in Scripture; and no change of social conditions can make a disregard of this obligation otherwise than prejudicial to the natural and supernatural ends for которых Marriage is instituted.[1]

§ 8. The parental obligations of Holy Matrimony[2] may be summarized under four heads.

(a) First in temporal order is the eugenic obligation to produce healthy offspring. If there is previous reason to believe that under given circumstances this cannot be done, the method of self-restraint, with such degree of abstinence from marital intercourse as is necessary to avoid having offspring, should be pursued.[3] But, in view of the natural purpose of Marriage, if this difficulty is inveterate, and is known before Marriage, the proposed Marriage union should not be consummated. Modern Eugenics is associated, no doubt, with secular and essentially pagan ideals. But it represents also a fundamental moral and Christian right of children to be started in life with whole-

---

[1] 1 Cor. xi. 7–12; Ephes. v. 22–33.

[2] On which, see W. W. Webb, *op. cit.*, pp. 161–164; Thos. Slater, vol. I. pp. 275–283; *Cath. Encyc.*, *s.v.* "Parents."

[3] Cf. pp. 287–288, above.

some bodies and minds. Wittingly or carelessly to inflict hereditary diseases upon offspring, and to connect prejudicial conditions and abuses with the process of procreation and pre-natal growth, are not less gravely sinful because modern science has first brought into clear light certain of the natural laws of wholesome procreation.[1]

(b) Children are also entitled to as wholesome a physical upbringing as the parents can lawfully provide. This means nourishing food, proper clothing, healthy surroundings, and proper education and training in the laws of health. It means also the promotion of the children's real happiness in such degree as is consistent with providential circumstances and their proper moral and spiritual development. And the children should not be forced avoidably into the labour of earning their living before they have attained sufficient physical maturity.

(c) An additional reason for avoiding a hasty forcing of mature responsibilities upon offspring is their right to such educational equipment, mental, moral and spiritual, as their parents can reasonably afford. A fair chance to enjoy the higher advantages of this world's school of life is an elementary right of all — a right limited in the case of children only by the legitimate means and opportunities of affording these advantages which their parents possess.

(d) Finally, parents are under obligation to facilitate such permanent settlement in life as will be most

[1] On modern Eugenics, see *Cath. Encyc.*, vol. XVI. pp. 38-40

conducive to their children's general welfare and abiding happiness. Their own position and temporal advantages necessarily determine and limit the responsibilities of parents in this direction; and they have no legitimate authority or moral right to interfere with the natural bent and abiding choice of their children in determining their life-vocations.

§ 9. Our analytical survey of the obligations incurred in Holy Matrimony may seem more appropriate to Moral than to Dogmatic Theology; but the end in view is strictly dogmatic — to enforce the Christian doctrine that Holy Matrimony is necessarily a permanent union, indissoluble except by death. It is necessarily this, for upon no other basis can the obligations involved in Marriage, as we have been describing them, be justly and adequately fulfilled. And the religious obligations of Holy Matrimony to which we now come accentuate its indissoluble nature and sanctity to a striking degree.

(*a*) The supernatural end of Holy Matrimony is that its divine Founder may "seek a seed of God" — may obtain subjects of adoption and grace in His Church, which is the Body of Christ.[1] So it is that the ultimate purpose for which God makes of twain one flesh is hindered of fulfilment when parents neglect or repudiate the obligation involved in this divine purpose of their union, which is the religious education and training of their children. There is no more

[1] Mal. ii. 15.

dangerous heresy than that which leaves children to purely secular influences on the plea that their right to choose their religion for themselves when they come to mature years ought not to be prejudiced. If catholic Christianity is true the moral obligation to accept it is fundamental, and no really sincere parent believes that he should refuse to train his children morally for fear of prejudicing their freedom of moral choice in later years. God gives us children that we may bring them to His grace, and no plea for neglect of the educational measures needed to predispose the young towards their Christian calling can rightly be regarded as otherwise than a satanic illusion. To provide specific education in the doctrines and duties of Christianity as they are taught by the Church and confirmed by Scripture is as obligatory for parents as is any other parental duty.

(b) For the same reason parents are under obligation to have their children baptized into Christ's Church as soon as practicable, and in due course to bring them to Confirmation, in order that they may receive the equipment divinely provided for them of the sevenfold gifts of the Holy Spirit. When this obligation is rightly fulfilled, that is, under the conditions of wise and careful religious training, the personal liberty and integrity of the children involved is not at all undermined, but rather is enhanced and enlightened. The predispositions which proper education produce are the normal conditions of human progress and of personal liberty.

(c) These obligations cannot be properly fulfilled in a family wherein religious unity is lacking.[1] For this reason, if for no other, agreement in acceptance of true religion — the religion of Christ and His Holy Catholic Church — is plainly an obligation of Holy Matrimony. Christians are coming to realize the gigantic evils of Christian disunity at large; but nowhere do these evils more directly undermine the eternal welfare of souls than in a family of mutually discordant religious beliefs and practices. The clear note of saving truth is there made uncertain; and the compromises and comities which are frequently adopted for the sake of peace result necessarily in deadening religion, and usually are followed by the upbringing of a godless generation. There is a pressing call to-day for bolder and more persistent teaching in this matter than has hitherto been customary.

III. *Impediments and Divorce*

§ 10. A lawful Marriage in the sense here meant is one which, when it has been consummated, is recognized both in civil and in Canon Law to be valid and binding. Such a Marriage may have been in some respect unlawfully consummated, but if allowed to stand it constitutes valid Marriage; and if the parties are baptized, the union is sacramental, even though the unworthy manner of its consummation suspends until repentance the spiritual benefits of

---

[1] Cf. § 11 (e), below.

the sacrament. The impediments of Marriage[1] are of two kinds: those which make Marriage irregular without nullifying it, and those which nullify it altogether.

Nullifying impediments, *impedimenta dirimentia*, arise either from the incompetence of one or both of the parties concerned or from some invalidating circumstance of the Marriage contract. In some cases the impediment can be remedied, but unless and until it is remedied the Marriage is null and void *ab initio*. Yet the discovery of such an impediment by the parties concerned, while it makes their subsequent carnal intercourse formally adulterous, neither wholly releases them from temporal obligations nor permits them to marry otherwise until a declaration of nullity has been lawfully made. The moral welfare of society and of the Church of God requires that the freedom to marry after such a complication shall be lawfully and publicly made clear in both Church and state before its exercise.

Nullifying impediments which arise from human legislation are, of course, subject to change, whether of enlargement or of reduction, by the legislative authority which imposes them; and they differ in various civil and ecclesiastical jurisdictions. Those, however, which are due to divine law or to the na-

---

[1] On which, see O. D. Watkins, pp. 103-107, 136-137 *et passim*; J. J. Elmendorf, pp. 629-640; Blunt, *Dic. of Theol.*, *s.v.* "Marriage," VI; W. W. Webb, *op. cit.*, pp. 240-251; St. Thomas, III. Suppl. l-lxii; *Cath. Encyc.*, *s.v.* "Impediments."

ture of things cannot be changed; and they cannot be disregarded without sin. The following are examples of nullifying impediments.

(*a*) Error as to identity of one or other of the parties to the Marriage nullifies the union, because no true mutual consent is accomplished. But voluntary acquiescence after the identity of both parties has been mutually ascertained validates the union, and precludes any subsequent contrary plea on the ground of error.

(*b*) For the same reason compulsion, or such fear as is really equivalent thereto, nullifies the union, subject to the same proviso that subsequent free acquiescence remedies the impediment.

(*c*) Consanguinity and affinity, or relationship either by blood or by Marriage, within forbidden degrees nullifies the union, because parties thus related are incompetent to marry, and such unions are incestuous and adulterous.[1] Unhappily civil and ecclesiastical legislation does not wholly agree in listing the prohibited degrees. Christians are bound, however, to observe both forms of legislation, and this precludes them from taking advantage of permissions of the state to marry within degrees prohibited by the Church and *vice versa*. For example, many states permit a man to marry his deceased wife's sister, but

---

[1] On consanguinity and affinity, see O. D. Watkins, ch. x; Blunt, *Dic. of Theol.*, *s.vv.* "Degrees Forbidden" and "Affinity"; W. J. Knox-Little, ch. xi; A. C. A. Hall, *Marriage of Relatives* (Episcopal Charge, 1901).

the law both of God and of His Church makes such a Marriage unlawful for Christians.[1] On the other hand, the Anglican Communion permits own cousins to marry, but in certain states such unions are forbidden, and are there unlawful for all. The Roman Church has a more extensive list of prohibited degrees than either the Anglican Church or civil law in a majority of states.[2] Only Roman Catholics are bound by that list. The Anglican list is designed to include only the specifications and implications of the Levitic law. Because the law of God makes a man and his wife to be one flesh, and for morally safeguarding the intimate associations apt to occur between a married person and the kindred of his or her partner in Marriage, the Church conforms the list of prohibited degrees of relationship by Marriage, item by item, to that of relationship by blood.[3] The frequent prohibition by modern states of Marriage between own cousins is based upon eugenic grounds; and even where this prohibition does not exist, careful regard for eugenic requirements ought to be observed before entrance upon such unions.

[1] F. W. Puller, *Marriage with a Deceased Wife's Sister;* O. D. Watkins, pp. 648–656.

[2] *Cath. Encyc.*, s.vv. "Consanguinity," and "Affinity"; H. A. Ayrinhac, *op. cit.*, pp. 116–178.

[3] The Anglican list is given in the English Prayer Book and reaffirmed, until contrary legislation (never enacted), by the American House of Bishops in 1808. It includes all relationships of blood and of marriage in direct line ascending and descending, and in collateral lines as far as own cousins exclusive.

(d) Impotence, or physical inability of one or other party to perform his or her part in procreation, affords basis for a legitimate plea of nullity on the ground of incompetence to fulfil the Marriage contract. But such impotence must be initial and irremediable — not first incurred at a date subsequent to the physical consummation of the union. It must also be pleaded within a reasonable time.

(e) Immature age, prior to puberty, is a nullifying impediment for the same reason;[1] and parental consent does not usually validate a Marriage thus impeded. The recognition of this and of the last mentioned impediment clearly implies that physical intercourse is necessary for a full consummation of the Marriage union. The Roman Church, indeed, regards itself as justified, when sufficient reasons exist, to declare any Marriage null and void which has not thus been consummated.

(f) Existing Marriage, validly accomplished, necessarily nullifies a subsequent Marriage of either party while the other lives. By the teaching of Christ and by catholic doctrine this impediment is absolute, if the existing Marriage is sacramental, because death alone can dissolve it. In other cases, the impediment is moral, and is based upon what Christ describes as the primal law of God. Civil divorce, therefore, does not for Christians make a subsequent

[1] Justinian's *Code*, v. 60, 3, forbade Marriage under the age of fourteen for males and of twelve for females; and such is the Western Canon Law. See O. D. Watkins, pp. 128–130.

Marriage of either party morally lawful in any case.[1]

§ 11. Various impediments make a Marriage either irregular or inexpedient but do not, in most jurisdictions at least, nullify it when once fully consummated.

(a) Disparity of social status and culture, especially if racial inequality is involved, ordinarily makes Marriage inexpedient, because of the hindrance afforded to mutually congenial relations and to the relations of each party with his or her own social equals. There may, of course, be exceptions which justify themselves. Difference of caste in certain lands is a legal bar to Marriage, and some states forbid Marriage between one who is free and a slave.

(b) An elopement, even where both parties have attained legal majority, makes the ensuing Marriage irregular; but does not invalidate it, unless either the consent of the abducted party is nullified by force or by equivalent fear or, in case of minors, parental consent is withheld. In all Marriages of minors whose parents are dead, the consent of legal guardians is necessary for validity.

(c) Clandestinity, or failure to have an official agent, civil or ministerial, present to give public sanction to the Marriage, makes it irregular and highly inexpedient. In some jurisdictions such unions are also unlawful and invalid.[2]

---

[1] Cf. pp. 273-275, above, and § 13, below.
[2] Roman Canon Law treats as clandestine any Marriage not

(d) A duly given religious vow of chastity ought always to bar the way to Marriage, unless proper dispensation is obtained, but does not invalidate it either in the Anglican Communion or in a majority of civil states.

(e) As has been shown, disparity of worship, *disparitas cultus*, or difference of religious faith and practice, inevitably prevents an adequate fulfilment of the religious obligations of Matrimony, and is therefore a serious impediment, for these obligations spring from the revealed will of God.[1] If one of the parties is unbaptized, and until this defect is remedied, the union is non-sacramental.

(f) It is contrary to ecclesiastical precept, and inconsistent with loyalty to Christian discipline, to be married without grave necessity during the more solemn seasons of public devotion in the Christian year.[2] The intense preoccupation which inevitably attends Marriage is highly prejudicial to the due observance of these seasons.

§ 12. The obligations and impediments of Matrimony, as we have endeavoured to describe them,

contracted before the proper priest and two witnesses. H. A. Ayrinhac, *op. cit.*, p. 232.

[1] Cf. § 9 (c), above. Strictly speaking, disparity of cult means that one of the parties is an infidel or unbaptized. But in principle it includes "mixed marriages" between those of different Christian Communions.

[2] Bishop Cosin specifies (a) from Advent Sunday until eight days after Epiphany; (b) from Septuagesima until eight days after Easter; (c) from Rogation Sunday until Trinity Sunday.

will seem formidable to those only who do not sufficiently consider the degree to which many vital interests, social, moral and spiritual, depend upon careful protection of the Marriage union from abuse.

This union affects many relations and interests, and fundamental elements of right demand that society, both civil and religious, shall have duly recognized part in providing that it be not entered into hastily, passionately and capriciously, or without regard for the sacred obligations involved — to God as well as to man, to unborn children as well as to each other, and to the several social circles affected, whether immediate or remote. Marriage is not, and cannot be, a private affair betwixt the two who are most directly concerned. The whole social order is to some degree involved in every Marriage, and more than one generation of human beings as well.

§ 13. It is in the light of such considerations that we ought to consider the troublesome subject of divorce.[1] There are two kinds of civil divorce: (*a*) *a mensa et toro*, or separation from bed and board without right to remarry; and (*b*) *a vinculo*, or absolute divorce with right to re-marry.

The catholic doctrine here maintained is that, while divorce *a mensa et toro* may in certain cases be necessary for the legal protection of one or other

---

[1] On divorce, see §§ 2–3, above, and refs. there given. See also D. Stone, *Divorce and Re-marriage;* Chas. Gore, *The Question of Divorce;* F. E. Gigot, *Christ's Teaching Concerning Divorce; Cath. Encyc.*, Hastings' *Dic. of Christ*, and Blunt's *Dic. of Theol.*, *q.vv.*

party and of the children, if there be any, absolute divorce, when followed by re-marriage during the life-time of both of the original parties, is consistent neither with the primal law of God, with the indissolubility of Holy Matrimony which Christ taught, with the obligations to offspring that are involved, nor with the moral welfare of society at large. History shows that a notable increase of divorce in a nation has normally been attended by, and has hastened, that nation's decadence and ruin. The abiding sanctity of the family and of domestic life is the *sine qua non* of moral civilization; and this sanctity absolutely depends upon the assurance that the Marriage union, once validly consummated, is not to be nullified except by death. The re-marriage of divorcees while the other parties live is consecutive polygamy, and its degrading effects upon society cannot be prevented or remedied by civil sanction of it. Public scandal may indeed be lessened by such sanction, but at the cost of defiling the social conscience, and of opening gateways to legalized lust. The evidence for such a conclusion is very abundant.

Divorce *a mensa et toro* in exceptional instances is indeed a necessary means of protecting Marriage itself from hopeless degradation and one or other of its participants from unendurable conditions; but to legalize re-marriage in such cases, while both parties live, is to intensify instead of remedying the defilement of Marriage. The plea that the innocent party ought not to be punished by being debarred from what in many instances appears to be the necessary means of subsequent well-being is specious but morally indefensible. The innocence of the injured party does not, and cannot, change the fundamentals of social morality; and misfortune, however serious and enduring, cannot righteously be remedied by unrighteousness. The innocent party may be a proper subject of sympathy and of charitable provision, but cannot be exempted from moral law *ad rem* without disastrous results to the society which legalizes the exemption. The moral order works slowly, no doubt, but its laws sooner or later assert their authority by ruining any society that defies them. In all its forms polygamy, whether coincident or consecutive, either prevents or upsets any high moral development of the nation which allows it. In plainer terms, the privilege of carnal intercourse with more than one living person cannot be granted either coincidently or consecutively without hopelessly perverting the divinely instituted purpose of Marriage.

But the immediate moral aspects above referred to do not stand alone. The children have an indefeasible right to enjoy the advantages of uninterrupted home life and of parental care, both secular and religious; and the consequences of divorce and re-marriage are fatal to the enjoyment of such right. Other members of society who retain a righteous conception of social relations are entitled to protection from the grave social embarrassments which the re-marriage of divorcees engenders. The Church, in particular, is pledged faithfully to advertise and promote both the natural and the supernatural ends of Marriage, as God has revealed them. For it to sanction the re-marriage of divorcees while the other parties live is to be unfaithful to trust.

Very difficult questions of ecclesiastical discipline arise from the fact that the Church has often to deal with practically irreparable situations, created by previously accomplished divorce and re-marriage and frequently complicated by the existence of subsequent offspring. In such cases, individual souls have to be considered — their sin being in many instances one of ignorance. Hasty and arbitrary judgment and action is liable to convert a sin of ignorance into formal defiance of God's law and thus to have spiritually fatal results. Accordingly there is sometimes need that the clergy observe an attitude of official non-cognizance of accomplished facts and situations. The bishop's counsel should be sought in such matters.[1] But the limiting principle remains, that no priest can rightly solemnize the re-marriage of divorcees or commit himself to a sanction or approval of such re-marriages, while the other parties live. In dealing patiently with accomplished facts and conditions among those whose errors have been committed in a lower and not adequately Christian state of knowledge, the priest has God's example in the old covenant to follow; but he cannot lawfully sanction as Christian what he thus

---

[1] This is required by the American Canon 42, § IV, Digest of 1919.

ignores for the sake of not hopelessly repelling those for whom Christ died.

One alleged exception to our general contention has to be reckoned with — the case of those who are legally divorced from a non-sacramental Marriage, such Marriage not possessing the absolute indissolubility of sacramental unions. We have to acknowledge, of course, that non-sacramental unions have not the *intrinsic* indissolubility of sacramental Holy Matrimony; and if we reject the right of Christians to re-marry after purely civil Marriage and divorce, we have to do so on other than sacramental grounds. The writer maintains that Christians are under the primal law of God, which Christ reënacted for them, and that, quite apart from sacramental considerations, this primal law forbids re-marriage under any circumstances until the death of one of the original parties. A Christian is not morally free, therefore, to re-marry, after divorce from a non-sacramental union, until the other party dies; nor is a priest free to solemnize such re-marriage.

St. Paul is often quoted in support of the contrary opinion, but his language is not explicitly pertinent.[1] He says of the Christian convert whose heathen partner has departed from him or her, that he or she is not bound in such case. He does not specify in what respect or degree the binding is annulled. He may refer simply to cohabitation, having in mind what is called divorce *a mensa et toro*, for he does not say that

[1] 1 Cor. vii. 12-16.

the Christian party involved is free to re-marry; and the failure to say so is the more significant because when, in the same chapter,[1] he speaks of the different kind of unbinding accomplished for a wife by the death of her husband, he is careful to specify that she is free to re-marry. In this, as in other scriptural exegesis, the meaning of an obscure passage must be ascertained in the light of other pertinent passages that are free from ambiguity; and St. Paul is clearly committed to our Lord's teaching, that according to the primal law of God for mankind, binding upon Christians, death alone licenses those who have once been married to marry again.[2]

[1] In verse 39.
[2] On the so-called Pauline privilege, see T. A. Lacey, pp. 21-22. The usual opinion of ecclesiastical writers is contrary to the view here adopted, as is proved by F. W. Puller, in No. 8 of the first series of *Occasional Papers on Missionary Subjects*, Oxford Mission, Calcutta. The writer believes that this is largely due to the unreflecting assumption that divorce from nonsacramental unions leaves the parties *morally free* to re-marry, in spite of the contrary primal law of God to which Christ appealed. Cf., however, O. D. Watkins, pp. 441-448.

CHAPTER X

UNCTION OF THE SICK [1]

I. *Introductory*

§ 1. There can be no reasonable denial that Christ's work of healing the sick was intended to serve in some degree as an example for those to whom He finally delegated His earthly ministry. We say in some degree, for the obvious limitation has to be recognized that our Lord's miracles were signs intended to afford evidence of His mission and to illustrate symbolically His power to heal the disease of sin. This limiting aspect also attaches to apostolic miracles of the same kind. None the less, our Lord plainly treats physical and spiritual disease as mutually related; and He includes physical healing among the duties of those whom He commissions in unqualified terms which indicate that such work properly pertains to

[1] On which, see A. P. Forbes, *Thirty-Nine Arts.*, pp. 465–474; C. S. Grueber, *The Anointing of the Sick;* Robert C. L. Reade, *Spiritual Healing and the Anointing of the Sick;* F. W. Puller, *The Anointing of the Sick;* P. Dearmer, *Body and Soul, passim* (these two exclude the sacramental grace); F. G. Belton, *Manual for Confessors*, Pt. VI. ch. iv; Blunt, *Dic. of Theol.*, s.v. "Unction, Extreme"; St. Thomas, III. Suppl. xxix–xxxiii; Hastings, *Encyc. of Relig.*, and *Cath. Encyc.*, s.vv. "Extreme Unction."

their ministry.[1] We may reasonably infer that, after due allowance is made for the peculiar and passing demonstrations of power which were to be expected in connection with the initiation and firm establishment of the new dispensation, a permanent residuum of power to heal the sick was intended to be given to the Christian ministry.

Moreover, we find that when the Apostles went forth on their first missionary journeys, they adopted anointing with oil as the external method of healing.[2] Presumably they had some warrant for thinking that Christ authorized their doing so; although, in lack of direct evidence, we are not justified in asserting that He directly appointed this outward sign. But the presumption that their practice was divinely guided is confirmed by the evidence in St. James' Epistle of its being the prescribed method of healing in the apostolic Church.[3]

The conclusion deduced by catholic consent, and registered in prescribed rituals of the Catholic Church, is that anointing the sick for their saving is a divinely prescribed rite. That Christ expressly instituted it is not clear; but in school terminology He is rightly said to have instituted it *in genere*, that is, impliedly by giving power and commission to His ministers to heal the sick. The subsequent apostolic prescription of the

---

[1] He expressly gave them both authority and commission to heal: St. Matt. x. 1, 8.

[2] St. Mark vi. 13.

[3] St. James v. 14-15.

outward sign of anointing was undoubtedly given under the Spirit's guidance, and constitutes, therefore, the promulgation of Christ's will *ad rem*.[1]

There is some show of reason for not regarding St. James' charge, "And if he have committed sins, it shall be forgiven him," as intended by the sacred writer to define an effect of the anointing prescribed in the previous verse.[2] But such a conclusion does not at all determine whether there is any spiritual, as distinguished from physical, effect attached to Unction of the Sick. This is a distinct question, and one which can best be faced in a later section.[3] But the supposition that St. James would sanction the anointing of one who was neither previously in a state of acceptance with God nor brought into such state by the anointing is too incredible to be regarded seriously. That the subject of Unction is assumed to be at least a believing penitent, and that the effect of the rite, however to be defined, presupposes the forgiveness of sins, either previously to or coincidently with the anointing, can safely be taken for granted.[4] Every divinely appointed Christian minis-

---

[1] The Council of Trent says that the sacrament was *insinuatum* by St. Mark and *commendatum* by St. James: Sess. XIV, *De Sac. Extr. Unc.*, cap. i. On the divine institution, see C. S. Grueber, pp. 8–11; J. Pohle, *Sacraments*, vol. IV. pp. 5–15.

[2] F. W. Puller, pp. 21–41.

[3] In § 5. Cf. § 7.

[4] The *Rituale Romanum* requires that, if possible, the sacraments of Penance and the Eucharist shall first be administered, and both Roman and Eastern writers support this contention. See F. W. Puller, pp. 35–37.

tration must surely either postulate, or be the means of achieving, reconciliation of its beneficiary to God.

§ 2. The rite of Unction has a somewhat private nature; and this fact, along with absence of controversy on the subject, sufficiently explains the paucity of testimony in early centuries to its use and significance in the Catholic Church.[1] Origen quotes St. James' prescription of it, about 241 A.D., in a manner that implies its established use. Still earlier, 211 A.D., Tertullian speaks of the heathen Emperor Severus having been cured by a Christian anointing him with oil.[2] This case stands by itself as a special miracle, rather than a stated ministration of the Church; but it shows that anointing with oil was regarded as the proper procedure in such cases.

As the internal life of the ancient Church comes more into view, the evidences that healing the sick by anointing them with oil blessed by the bishops of the Church was an established rite, thought by all to be of apostolic origin and prescription, gradually increase in volume. In early ages laymen were permitted to take the blessed oil home, and to use it without calling in a presbyter;[3] but in the face of St. James' positive direction to call in the presbyters of the Church, this custom gradually disappeared.

[1] On its history, see F. W. Puller, chh. ii–vi; P. Dearmer, chh. xxii, xxv; *Cath. Encyc.*, vol. V. pp. 719–724; Hastings, *Encyc. of Relig.*, s.v. "Extreme Unction," 3.
[2] Origen, *Homil.* ii *in Levit.* § 4; Tertullian, *Ad Scap.*, ch. iv. Cf. F. W. Puller, pp. 42–45, 150–152.
[3] For instances, *idem*, ch. iv. *passim*.

Yet there is important support for the opinion that, when a priest cannot be had, the lay use of oil having proper consecration for the purpose is likely to be attended by divine blessing. The administration of the reserved sacrament by laymen affords a slight although imperfect analogy — imperfect because no sacramental conversion of the oil, properly speaking, is accomplished by its consecration.

The extant *formulæ* of prayer anciently employed in blessing the oil bear witness, on the one hand, that the primary purpose and effect of the rite was held to be physical healing, in which was thought to be embraced a healing of mind as well as of body. On the other hand, they also include spiritual healing, and in some cases specify remission, among the effects prayed for and looked for.[1] The supposition that the clauses referred to are of later interpolation has no real proof, but is based upon *a priori* considerations. The first synodical pronouncements on this subject occurred in the ninth century. The forty-eighth canon of the Council of Chalon-sur-Saône, after quoting St. James, says, "It follows that a medicine of this sort, which heals the sicknesses of soul and body, is not to be lightly esteemed." The Council of Pavia, 850 A.D., in its eighth canon, goes further and speaks of the restoration of bodily health by this

---

[1] Examples, *idem*, pp. 88–89 (Sacramentary of Serapion), 104–105 (Ethiopic Church Order), and 113–114 (*Testamentum Domini*) Father Puller's negative comments are more ingenious than convincing.

rite as a consequence of its effecting remission of sins.[1]

§ 3. From the age of Charlemagne the spiritual effects of Unction received an increasingly preponderant emphasis, partly perhaps because of the frequent cases in which physical recovery failed to follow. But this failure may have been an effect rather than a cause of the growing lack of attention to the physically curative purpose of the rite. Faith in its curative value is plainly a necessary condition of its physical benefit.

When the one-sided emphasis upon the spiritual benefits of Unction had finally removed from effective consideration its originally appointed physical benefit,[2] a further development naturally and quickly took place. Physical cure was no longer ordinarily expected, and therefore the rite came increasingly to be used only in the case of hopeless illness and impending death.[3] Whether the title *Extrema Unctio* originally meant unction *in extremis*, or simply designated its logical order in the whole series of unctions employed by the Church, in any case several centuries before the reformation the rite had come generally to be associated with the *viaticum;* and it was regarded almost exclusively as a means of cleansing

[1] *Idem*, pp. 72–78. We are indebted to Father Puller's book for numerous important data and references — not less so, because we feel compelled to dissent from some of his arguments.

[2] This benefit has never been denied by catholic writers. Cf. *Concil. Trid.*, Sess. XIV, *q.v.*, ch. ii.

[3] F. W. Puller, pp. 192–198.

and fortifying the soul in its conflict with the powers of darkness *in articulo mortis*.

The mediæval conception of Unction was crystallized in the thirteenth century by St. Thomas Aquinas. According to him, the primary end of the sacrament is to remedy spiritual debility, and this involves remission of sin. He acknowledges that bodily healing may also result, but treats this benefit as secondary, and as incidental to spiritual healing, which is declared to be the principal benefit.[1]

If we acknowledge, as we do, that this one-sided development and shifting of emphasis is a "corrupt following of the Apostles," we do not feel constrained to accept the equally one-sided view that physical healing is the only appointed benefit of Unction. That this rite is a true sacrament of grace will be maintained in due course.

§ 4. The first Prayer Book of Edward VI, 1549 A.D., provided a form at the end of the Order for the Visitation of the Sick, introduced by the following rubric: "If the sick person desires to be anointed, then shall the Priest anoint him upon the forehead or breast only, making the sign of the cross, saying thus:"

The form reads, "As with this visible oil thy body outwardly is anointed; so our heavenly Father, Almighty God, grant of His infinite goodness, that thy soul inwardly may be anointed with the Holy Ghost, who is the Spirit of all strength, comfort, relief and gladness: and vouchsafe for His great

[1] St. Thomas, III. Suppl. xxx.

mercy (if it be His blessed will) to restore unto Thee thy bodily health and strength, to serve Him; and send thee release of all thy pains, troubles and diseases both in body and mind. And howsoever His goodness (by His divine and unsearchable providence) shall dispose of thee: we His unworthy ministers and servants, humbly beseech the eternal Majesty to do with thee according to the multitude of His innumerable mercies, and to pardon thee all thy sins and offences, committed by all thy bodily senses, passions and carnal affections: who also vouchsafe mercifully to grant unto thee ghostly strength, by His Holy Spirit, to withstand and overcome all temptations and assaults of thine adversary, that in no wise he prevail against thee, but that thou mayest have perfect victory and triumph against the devil, sin and death, through Christ our Lord: who by His death hath overcome the prince of death, and with the Father and the Holy Ghost evermore liveth and reigneth God, world without end. AMEN."

This form officially declares the mind of the English Church in 1549 A.D. to be that Unction is for the healing of those who are physically ill; that this healing is obtained by the soul being inwardly anointed with the Holy Ghost; that the intended effect is mental as well as bodily healing; and that in connection therewith pardon for sin is to be besought, along with ghostly strength against the temptations which illness occasions and against their satanic author, sin and death. Granting for argument's sake only that the prayer for pardon and ghostly strength in the perils of sickness and death is a "sacramental" — a suitable accompanying prayer, rather than a signification of appointed effects of Unction *in se*, the fact cannot reasonably be denied that the anointing of the soul with the Holy Ghost is intended to be effected by the outward sign. That is, the rite is administered as being a sacrament of grace from the Holy Spirit, as well as an instrument of physical healing.

The rite of Unction was dropped from the English Prayer Book by the revision of 1552, and has never been restored. The American Prayer Book also perpetuates this unhappy omission.[1] But omission is not itself prohibition, unless what is omitted cannot be used consistently with the subsequent ritual and Canon Law. Obviously the use of Unction in the privacy of a sick-room cannot disturb either the proportions, the force or the meaning of any Prayer Book Office or prescription; and no canonical prohibition of its use exists. Furthermore, its omission cannot be shown historically to constitute a repudiation of the doctrine contained in the omitted rite. The Act ordering the second Prayer Book, in which the omission took place, expressly denies that the

[1] An amendment has been recommended to the American General Convention remedying this omission. The proposed form reads, "I anoint thee with oil [lay my hand upon thee], in the Name of the Father, and of the Son, and of the Holy Ghost, beseeching the mercy of our Lord Jesus Christ, that all thy pain and sickness of body being put to flight, the blessing of health may be restored to thee." The preceding prayer includes spiritual benefits.

first Prayer Book contains ungodly and superstitious matter.[1] Whatever may have been the personal views of those who produced the second Prayer Book, divine providence put them on official record as governed by expediency, and not by the purpose of making any doctrinal change. Therefore the official Anglican doctrine of 1549 continued to be such after the Prayer Book of that date had been revised.

The fact is that the omission of this rite from the Prayer Book, in proper official effect, is a branch of the wider eirenic policy which explains the strange combination of protestant phrases with subtle avoidance of any real repudiation of catholic doctrine in the *Articles of Religion*. This policy had serious dangers, and was attended by some unhappy consequences; but, the official language adopted being witness, the overruling Spirit saved the Anglican Communion from having her catholic position nullified through the more or less protestant aims and efforts of its reforming prelates.[2]

In so far as the Anglican Communion claims to be part of the Catholic Church of Christian history, it must be understood, in the undeniable absence of demonstrative evidence to the contrary, to retain after its reformation whatever had previously been everywhere taught in that Church to be an integral and necessary part of apostolic faith and precept. Theo-

---

[1] It calls the first Book a "very godly order, agreeable to the word of God and the primitive Church."

[2] Cf. *Introduction*, pp. 183-189.

logical opinions and pious practices may indeed vary in the Church, and may need reformation. But no Church which appeals to catholic authority is entitled to repudiate altogether any doctrine or rite which has been taught by such authority to be an essential element of catholic faith and order. The Anglican Communion, therefore, by virtue of its catholic claim, is to be understood as accepting the catholic rite of Unction in its catholic meaning. Its failure to provide for the use of Unction no doubt weakens its witness, but to regard this failure as equivalent to repudiation is not rationally justifiable.

Accordingly, when our *Articles of Religion* mention Extreme Unction among "commonly called sacraments" that "have grown partly of the corrupt following of the Apostles," "the corrupt following" must be understood of accretions that have disturbed the proportions of use and meaning of the apostolic ordinance, and not at all of that ordinance itself or of the New Testament and catholic doctrine concerning it. Anglicans are therefore committed to this doctrine concerning it, and, subject to lawful regulation, are free to use it.

II. *Expository*

§ 5. A sacrament, in the sense adopted in catholic theology, has for its distinctive mark the fact that it is an appointed outward instrument of sanctifying grace. But the phrase "sanctifying grace" must not be too narrowly taken. In particular, it may not be regarded as applying only to such operations of the Spirit as include remission of sins in the formal meaning of that phrase. It is true that every operation of the Spirit in human souls either presupposes or looks to the remedy of sin; and therefore it is not erroneous to associate remission with any bestowal of grace. Furthermore, it is inevitable and justifiable that we should regard every form of sanctifying grace as removing, indirectly at least, whatever needs to be removed of the stains which even the most faithful daily incur. But in formal description a rite may be sanctifying without having remission of sins as its specific or defined purpose.

Any divinely appointed means of supernatural benefit for men is sanctifying in so far as it is instituted in relation to the Christian covenant, and for furthering its purposes; for such relation or purpose includes it among the outward signs and instruments of a dispensation the all-controlling purpose of which is sanctification.

Furthermore, whether in St. James' phrase, "the prayer of faith shall save him that is sick," the word "save" ($\sigma\omega\sigma\epsilon\iota$) can be proved to have had a spiritual as well as a physical meaning or not, it certainly suggests a lack of clear separation in the sacred writer's mind between the physical and spiritual benefits of divine healing.[1] To separate them wholly is indeed

[1] This verb is used elsewhere in such expressions as, "Thy faith hath made thee whole" ($\sigma\epsilon\sigma\omega\kappa\epsilon$ $\sigma\epsilon$), St. Mark v. 34. Cf. other examples in St. Matt. ix. 21–22; St. Mark x. 52; etc.

rash. Divine healing always has a spiritual end in view, pertaining somehow to sanctification, and to regard its appointed instrument as extraneous in effect to the actual working of sanctifying grace is to hypothecate a sharper division in God's merciful dispensations than Christian experience permits to be acknowledged. The philosophy which thus divorces temporal and spiritual benefits is that of secular Utilitarianism rather than of Christianity. The parable of the Good Samaritan [1] certainly appears to unite in one conception the physical and spiritual healing of wounded humanity.

Still further, the healing of Unction is a benefit that is spiritually conditioned by faith, a condition exactly corresponding to that of beneficial reception of any species of sacramental grace. "The prayer of faith shall save him that is sick"; and such is the condition which is everywhere stipulated for the additional benefit, if it really is additional, "And if he have committed sins, it shall be forgiven him." It seems an incredible supposition that God will use a sacramental *modus operandi* for conferring a supernatural benefit, upon such spiritual conditions, without including any sanctifying grace in the benefit.

Finally we have an undeniable example of the fact that God does bestow sanctifying grace by an outward sign which is not in every case a means of remission. The Blessed Sacrament is to a degree remissive, when remission is necessary; but if the communicant

[1] St. Luke x. 30–35.

has already been absolved, and has not since fallen into sin, there is no place for remission in the strict sense of that word. Surely no catholic believer will say that for this reason no sanctifying grace is conferred.

Enough has been said to prove that, while the immediate divine purpose of Unction is physical healing, this does not preclude its also being an instrument of sanctifying grace. Catholic doctrine declares it to be such an instrument, and its being this is all that is meant by maintaining, as we do, that it is a true sacrament in the theological sense of that description.[1]

§ 6. The ultimate and controlling purpose of every divine instrument in the Christian covenant is the sanctification and entire salvation of men from sin. In this sense it might be said that the primary benefit of Unction is its sanctifying grace. But this is quite consistent with saying that the immediate and distinctive benefit for which Unction has been instituted is physical; although the fact that such healing is certainly designed to minister to salvation affords confirmation of belief that the rite in question is likely to be sanctifying as well as physically helpful in its working. We are now concerned with its physical benefit.

The term "physical" refers to both body and mind,

[1] *The Church*, pp. 298–299; C. S. Grueber, pp. 10–16; A. P. Forbes, *op. cit.*, pp. 465–474; T. A. Lacey, *Elements of Christ. Doctrine*, p. 261. The Eastern Church doctrine is given in *Orthodox Confession*, Qq. 117–119; and Macarius, *Théologie Orthodoxe*, as transl. in *Church Eclectic*, June, 1895, pp. 205–216.

for it is the union of these two that constitutes a human being in the physical sense. Moreover, the two are so intimately related and connected in human functioning that disease, or the upsetting of such functioning, cannot affect the body without disturbing the mind and *vice versa*.[1] When a man is sick, he is sick both in body and in mind; although a particular illness may seem more directly and observably to affect one or the other, and we customarily distinguish between bodily and mental diseases. It is through mental disturbance, for example, that we actually *experience* feeling ill, even when the illness pertains immediately to the body. Similarly, a mental disease, when carefully examined, is found either to have its source in bodily disorder or to induce such disorder. So it is that the cure of human sickness cannot be exclusively either bodily or mental, but whether directly or remotely, will affect both for the better, each in vital reaction upon the other.[2]

But there are two species of curative treatment of disease, one bodily and the other mental. The latter has been seriously studied only in recent days.[3] Its effect in bodily disease is based upon a certain very real although limited power which the mind has over

[1] *Creation and Man*, pp. 190–194; *The Church*, pp. 282–283.

[2] P. Dearmer, chh. iii–xi; D. H. Tuke, *Illustrations of the Influence of the Mind on the Body*; J. H. Hyslop, *Borderland of Psychical Research*, pp. 319–332.

[3] On mental healing, see P. Dearmer, *passim*; W. F. Cobb, *Spiritual Healing*; Hugo Münsterberg, *Psychotherapy*; E. E. Weaver, *Mind and Health*; Loring W. Batten, *The Relief of Pain by Mental Suggestion*; Robert C. L. Reade, Pt. I. chh. ii–iii.

bodily disorders to reduce their virulence and even to cure them. Mental treatment in all its forms rallies the native powers of the mind and directs them to the curative end in view. Surprising results are sometimes achieved, but they are usually confined to non-organic diseases.[1] Nervous illnesses are especially amenable to mental treatment. All this bears very directly upon what is perhaps the *modus operandi* of divine healing in Unction of the Sick, and upon the observed curative limitations of Unction.

The healing operation of Unction may be a reënforcing of the above described natural power of the mind over bodily conditions by supernatural and assisting grace. If so, the cures thus achieved are not miraculous strictly speaking, although sometimes phenomenal. Rather they are normal demonstrations of Christian grace, mediated through ordinary sacramental ministrations; and are not in the same category with the specifically miraculous cures performed by laymen as well as by ministers who have received extraordinary gifts of the Spirit.[2]

But cures by Unction differ not less from modern methods of mental healing than from miraculous cures. The difference appears to be that, whereas modern mental healing is due to a perfectly natural rallying of the sick man's native mental powers for the purpose of overcoming disease, the sacrament of

---

[1] P. Dearmer, pp. 90–92 and ch. xi.
[2] *Idem*, pp. 202–205; J. M. Hickson, *The Healing of Christ in His Church*.

Unction affords supernatural assistance to the sick man's mind, and enables him to triumph over his illness with a success that no rallying of his native powers alone could make possible. In brief, while cures by Unction are probably mental, they are also distinctly supernatural — the effect of sacramental grace.[1]

The normal operations of God, even in the sphere of supernatural grace, do not disturb the working of natural forces, apparently because this would upset the stability of the natural order, upon the ordinary maintenance of which depends a successful fulfilment of nature's assigned part in the divine drama. Grace, therefore, does not counteract natural law, but merely enhances moral and spiritual power in the use of it. The power of healing grace in Unction is therefore limited; and, unless exceptional miraculous gifts are concurrently exercised in its ministration, it fails to cure diseases which can be remedied only by miraculous power. This leaves room, however, for remarkable cures, as the history of Unction abundantly proves.[2]

But there is another and subjective limitation, and one which, as has already been suggested, accounts for the reduced frequency in modern days of cure by Unction. If Unction heals by enhancing the power of the sick man's mind and will over physical disorders, this result is obviously conditioned by the

---
[1] *Idem*, pp. 121-134 (to be read with discrimination).
[2] Instances are given by F. W. Puller, pp. 153-190.

sick person's mental response to the challenging aid thus afforded. Translated into New Testament terms, it is the prayer of faith upon which a successful reception and use of the grace of healing depends — faith of the recipient of Unction, as well as serious intention of the minister to do what the Church intends shall be done by means of Unction.

It is an evil consequence of the somewhat exclusive attention paid since mediæval days to the spiritual benefits of Unction that adequate faith in its physical results is not ordinarily possessed by the sick. Accordingly cures are less common than in early ages, because the subjective conditions of their working are not afforded — are indeed effectually suppressed by the ordinary association of the rite with expected death. One of the urgent needs of our time is a revived emphasis upon, and faith in, the divinely intended physical benefit of Unction of the Sick.

§ 7. Reasons have been given for believing, none the less, that divine healing cannot rightly be regarded as attended by no spiritual benefit.[1] What, then, is the spiritual benefit for which we can rightly look in the sacrament of Unction? It cannot be defined in terms susceptible of formal demonstration by means of proof-texts. We have to appeal to the intimate connection between every supernatural work of

---

[1] In § 5, above. On spiritual benefits, see C. S. Grueber, pp. 12–25; C. C. Grafton, in *The Church's Ministry of Grace* (N. Y. Church Club Lecs. of 1892), pp. 215–220; A. J. Mason, *Faith of the Gospel*, pp. 319–320; Jos. Pohle, *The Sacraments*, vol. IV. pp. 24–32.

mercy and spiritual blessings which is writ large in the New Testament, and confirmed by the experience of those who have devoutly received the anointing in question. Moreover we come to the consideration of the subject with the help of catholic theology, which is not likely to have gone radically astray in a matter so vitally connected with the doctrine of grace.

Thus prepared we discern in the "saving" of the sick a benefit pertaining to salvation of the soul, and to call this sanctifying grace seems to be no wresting of words. We cannot show that St. James intended to teach that forgiveness of sins is a formally appointed effect of Unction itself. But we find ourselves quite unable wholly to exclude from the benefit of an instrument of divine mercy like this the removal of such sins and moral stains as still require remedy. We of course assume, as we must even for any physical benefit of Unction, that the patient is penitent and believing. This is not to impugn the claim of Penance, for the benefit of remission is not in New Testament or catholic doctrine confined to that sacrament. The cleansing effects of Christ's grace are wrought manifoldly in the Church and through numerous channels — not merely by means of the sacraments which have remission for their specific end.

We have adversely criticized the somewhat exclusive emphasis which in later centuries has been placed upon the spiritual benefits of Unction, and the consequent widespread practice of postponing any use of the rite until the patient is *in extremis*. But the traditional conceptions concerning the reality and sanctifying nature of these spiritual benefits are supported by practically inevitable inferences from the revealed purpose of Unction, which is to save the sick, and from the observed distinctive spiritual needs of the sick — not at all likely to be left unprovided for by the merciful God in the only beneficent instrument which He has appointed especially for their help. We hope that we have said enough to justify the conviction that the following spiritual benefits may be expected from Unction of the Sick, when it is received with contrite faith.

(*a*) The soul is anointed with the Holy Spirit for the specific ends of the sacrament.[1] Such anointing is inevitably sanctifying.

(*b*) Both because the stain of sin, if any such remains in the sick man's soul, must necessarily give way to such anointing, and because the removal of sin and its internal effects is necessarily and always the first determinative work of divine mercy, remission of the sick person's sins and of their effects is accomplished, so far as this is necessary.

(*c*) For the purpose of physical recovery, the spiritual powers, debilitated by sickness, are fortified for their part in overcoming illness, if God so will.

(*d*) If physical recovery is not granted, this fortifying of the patient's spiritual faculties serves, none the

[1] Cf. opening sentence of the Form in the first Prayer Book, quoted p. 313, above.

less, for overcoming the peculiar temptations of the sick-bed and of the sick person's last agony, during which the powers of darkness are especially active. So it is that, except for the excessive and exclusive emphasis criticized above, Unction of the Sick is rightly said to be beneficial and desirable *in extremis*.

(e) If cure is vouchsafed, the fact that this is accomplished by the supernatural aid of God in Christ, through His Holy Spirit, makes the cure a kind of renewed consecration and sanctification of the sick person's rehabilitated powers for his holy Christian vocation.

§ 8. The language of St. James seems to imply that Unction is to be used in any illness which is serious enough to call for special ministrations of the Church; and the sick, or their families, are far more apt to err by neglect of priestly ministrations than by excessive use of them. A kind of superstitious fear that the coming of a priest into the sick-room is an ill omen, a harbinger of death, often hinders people from sending for him until death is indeed impending. And the undue stress upon the *viaticum* use of Unction, above discussed, probably explains this superstition in large part.

No doubt it is a proper sentiment that hesitates to make use of so serious a provision as Unction without really serious reason;[1] and its administration ought

---

[1] On the occasions and frequency of its use, see St. Thomas, III. Suppl. xxxii, 1-4; C. S. Grueber, pp. 33-35; Jos. Pohle, *op. cit.*, pp. 44-48.

not to be asked for in trifling indispositions. But in every case of really grave illness there are sufficient spiritual as well as physical reasons for resort to it. Unless what has been said above concerning the spiritual dangers of the sick-bed, and the spiritual benefits of Unction, is radically astray — a supposition contrary to ages of catholic experience — those who are suffering greatly, especially if passing through a crisis, ought not to hesitate to ask for this sacrament. *In extremis* it ought also to be used, of course.

There can be no determinate rule as to repeating its administration during the same illness. That it may be repeated seems clear, especially when the sickness is greatly prolonged, for in such case the patient will be in need of renewals of the fortifying grace which it is calculated to afford. But catholic opinion dictates that it should not ordinarily be repeated except in some new crisis of the disease.[1] It belongs to the category of major remedies, of extraordinary ministrations.

One frequent obstacle to its use is the conviction of many physicians that priestly ministrations are likely to hinder rather than promote recovery. So far as this conviction is not due to an alien standpoint and an inadequate idea of what spiritual ministrations, properly given, can accomplish in fortifying the rallying powers of the sick, it arises from the crassly stupid methods of some ministers in dealing with

[1] The Council of Trent, Sess. XIV, *q.v.*, ch. iii, limits repetition to "when they fall into another like danger of death."

the sick. Every unnecessary cause of excitement should be avoided. Calm, encouraging and comforting words should be used; and admonitions, if the higher requirements of the patient's salvation require them, should be given prudently and quietly, although seriously. When this rule is observed, the effect will often resemble that of a successful operation, because constituting a needed turning point in the patient's recuperative efforts. In any case, loud utterance, and artificial and emotional methods are deplorably inept, and may have fatal results. Every element of strenuous bustle and hurry should be wholly banished. The watch, for example, should not be consulted within the patient's range of vision.[1]

§ 9. The reason for mentioning these practical requirements, which belong to Pastoral rather than to Dogmatic Theology, is their bearing on success in reviving the use of Unction,[2] and of administration of the Blessed Sacrament to the sick as well.

The sacramental ministrations of the Church in sick-rooms have been widely neglected in modern days, especially since the notable decay of sacramental practice at large in the eighteenth century. And the later catholic revival has not been as effective in this direction as in others. The result has been not less inevitable than deplorable. The sick feel a

[1] Cf. V. Raymond, *Spiritual Director and Physician*.
[2] On the need of such revival, see A. P. Forbes, p. 474; F. W. Puller, ch. ix; P. Dearmer, pp. 293–298. A halting sanction appears in resolution 36 of the Lambeth Conference of 1908.

natural craving, even when blind to its significance, for higher aid than the physician's treatment can afford. If they are not given this aid by the Church, they will look for it elsewhere, and become easy victims of the specious substitutes for sacramental aid which the various cults of mental healing afford. That these systems do afford notable cures is undeniable; and although they cannot do what Unction does for the sick, they do supply them with subjectively comforting and encouraging thoughts which the sick are readily persuaded to be truly spiritual, although usually pantheistic [1] and always destructive of true religion. Thus many are led astray and wholly lost to the Church.

In ancient days the name "villager" was equivalent to a heathen, *paganus;* and true Christianity is still comparatively weak in rural districts. But we are now confronted by a new danger, that the sick and ailing will become pantheistically pagan from the same cause, the Church's failure to minister adequately and faithfully to them. The evil cannot be remedied suddenly. There is needed a long-continued propaganda of those aspects of Christian doctrine and practice which are of special application to the sick, and a revival of habitual administration of the means of help which God has provided for them in His

---

[1] Christian Science, so called, affords a notable example; on which, see Georgine Milmine, *The Life of Mary Baker G. Eddy and the Hist. of Christ. Science;* Alice Fielding, *Faith-Healing and Christ. Science;* W. F. Cobb, *Spiritual Healing*, ch. vi.

Church. We sorely need a full restoration of Unction of the sick.

Nothing hinders such revival except ignorance, indifference and inertia, which we surely ought to overcome. The rite has not been forbidden and is entirely lawful in the Anglican Communion.[1] Many bishops are willing to bless the oil, and the emergency would seem to justify following the Eastern usage of priestly blessing when a bishop's blessing is not available. The positive warrant for such revival is the divinely inspired apostolic rubric, which no provincial Church is competent to nullify, "Is any among you sick, let him call for the presbyters of the Church; and let them pray over him, anointing him with oil in the name of the Lord." It is a clear case of obedience to the divine Word, to which important blessings are surely pledged.

[1] Cf. pp. 315-317, above.

Made in the USA
San Bernardino, CA
15 September 2013